Langsdorff of the Graf Spee
Prince of Honor

Joseph Gilbey

The commandant of the *Graf Spee* fought and died as a Gentleman

---

Canadian Cataloguing in Publication Data

Gilbey, Joseph, 1928-
Langsdorff of the Graf Spee : prince of honor

Includes bibiliogaphical references and index.
ISBN 0-9685994-0-0

1. Langsdorff, Hans 2. Admiral Graf Spee (Battleship)
3. Rio de la Plata, Battle of the, 1939. I. Title.

D772.G7G54 1999 940.54'29 C99-901233-9

Joseph Gilbey
P.O. Box 518
Hillsburgh, Ontario, Canada N0B 1Z0
(519) 855-6126

www.grafspee.com

Contents

Author's Notes

Theme: *Langsdorff of the Graf Spee, Prince of Honor* is a true story. Every effort has been made to ensure accuracy in all historical detail. Dialogue, by necessity, employs some poetic licence.

Time: In the Battle of the River Plate the British and German ships used 'zone plus 2' naval time. Any naval times quoted in this book, using the 24-hour clock, comply with this formula. Other times stated, using the 12-hour clock, refer to local geographical times.

Distance: All sea distances stated in this book are nautical miles (2,014/2,035yds).

Rank: German naval ranks are translated into United States naval equivalents.

Joseph Gilbey

Acknowledgements

CAPTAIN KURT DIGGINS.
Adjutant to Captain Langsdorff on *Graf Spee.*

Captain Hans Dietrich
Successor to Diggins in Buenos Aires.

Sr. OMAR MEDINA.
Owner-Director, Malvin Maritime Museum, Montevideo.

Dr. INGE NEDDEN (Langsdorff).
Daughter of Captain Langsdorff.

Dr. RÜDIGER NEDDEN.
Husband of Inge Langsdorff.

CAPTAIN F.W. RASENACK.
Chief Gunnery Artificer on *Graf Spee.*

Sra. DORETEA SÖRENSEN.
Wife of *Graf Spee* merchant Officer, Lieutenant Paul Sörensen.

I extend sincere thanks to the above mentioned for their help and encouragement in creating this book. Many others also contributed to the project. I recognize and thank them all.

Joseph Gilbey

Foreword

by

Captain F.W.Rasenack

(Senior Gunnery Artificer Graf Spee, 1939).

On December 20, 1939, I was shocked when I heard Captain Langsdorff had committed suicide, following the scuttling of his ship, to preserve the honor of the flag and his crew. I felt like I had lost my father and I think all of the ship's crew felt the same. We trusted Captain Langsdorff like our own father and knew he would always decide in our best interests in any situation.

Since sixty years, many books have appeared writing about the pocket battleship *Admiral Graf Spee,* and the Battle of the River Plate, but none have been written about the noble character of Captain Langsdorff. Our Captain commanded his ship in a very honorable way: Nine merchant ships were captured but no one lost their lives – a very rare example in the Second World War.

Joseph Gilbey has now written about the life and career of Captain Langsdorff. In *Prince of Honor* Mr.Gilbey expresses the noble, gentle-manly personality of Captain Langsdorff and the high esteem and admiration held by *Graf Spee's* crew for their captain.

Captain F.W.Rasenack
La Falda, Argentina(1999)

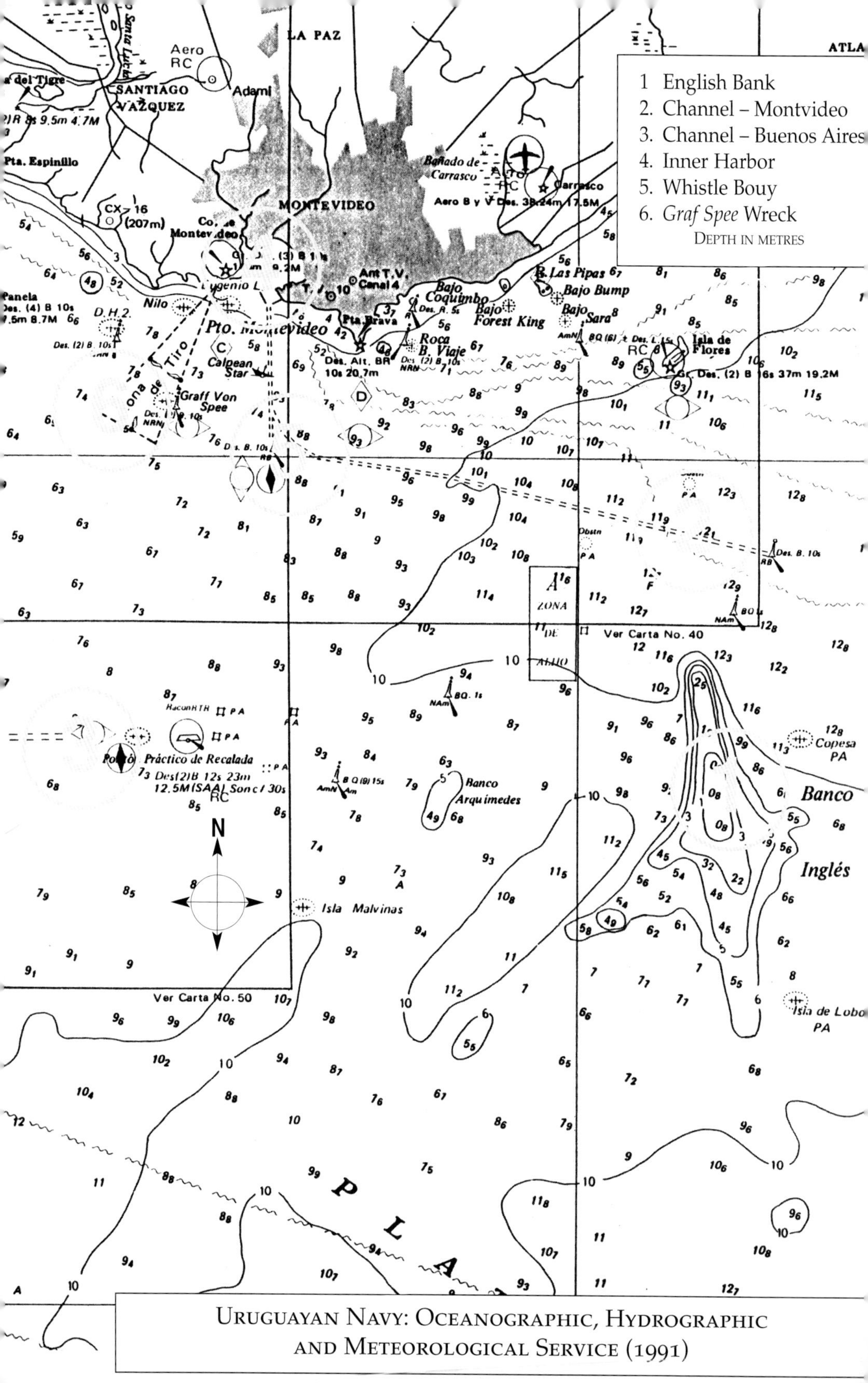

Uruguayan Navy: Oceanographic, Hydrographic and Meteorological Service (1991)

Introduction

In the Second World War mankind sank to abysmal levels of inhumanity. But, in the first months of the war, Captain Hans Langsdorff gave the World a matchless example of courage, personal integrity and human compassion.

On December 13, 1939, a great sea-battle in the South Atlantic captured international news headlines. One of Germany's fabled pocket battleships, *Panzerschiff Admiral Graf Spee,* had engaged three British cruisers in the South Atlantic, off Uruguay.

Six decades after the Battle of the River Plate significant details remain obscure. Captain Langsdorff's major role is misunderstood and unexplained. History recognizes his impeccable compliance with the Hague conventions but casts doubt on his martial qualities. Today, an objective analysis of the facts shows clearly that Langsdorff's military decisions were justified.

This exceptional officer gave his life in an honorable way but suffered discredit. For the first time his story is revealed in detail. He deserves his day in court.

Joseph Gilbey

PANZERSCHIFF ADMIRAL GRAF SPEE

Built: Keel laid down Wilhelmshaven, 1 October 1932, launched 30 June, 1934, commissioned 6 January, 1936.

Displacement: 12,100 tons

Armament: 6 x 11-inch, 8 x 5.9-inch, 6 x 4.1-inch, 8 x 37mm, 8 x 21-inch torpedo tubes, 2 x Arado 196 aircraft (1 knocked down)

Power: 8 Mann Diesel Engines - 54,000shp

Speed: 26 knots

Dimensions: 187.9 x 21.6 x 7.4 m

Protection: sides 80mm, longitudinal torpedo bulkhead 45mm, transverse bulkhead 50mm, deck 45mm, turrets 140mm, barbettes 100mm

Chapter 1

Honor Bound

The Second World War began on September 3, 1939, when Great Britain and France declared war an Nazi Germany. On September 10, the Dominion of Canada joined the Allied side. Meanwhile, the United States and the rest of Continental America remained neutral. In this early stage, the European conflict seemed remote: a happening thousands of sea-miles away.

At 10am on December 18, 1939, two Argentinean tugs, *Coloso* and *Gigante* (with the barge *Chiriguano* in tow) approached Buenos Aires. One thousand German sailors crowded every corner of the three ships. They overflowed the gunwales and clung to the rigging, trying to find breathing space. Exhausted and hungry, their white uniforms sweaty and crumpled, the sailors had just escaped disaster. On the black headbands of their hats, printed in Gothic gold letters, blazed the name *Panzerschiff Admiral Graf Spee.*

Graf Spee, a magnificent pocket battleship, now lay a smoldering wreck, settling slowly into a shallow mud-flat near Montevideo. Only

18 December 1939: Argentinean tug Gigante *arrives in Buenos Aires.*
– Diego M. Lascano - Enrique Moneda Collection

Graf Spee *scuttled off Montevideo.* — MALVIN MARITIME MUSEUM

the upper parts of the warship's control tower and superstructure remained above the greasy waters. Captain Hans Langsdorff had scuttled his ship, causing a funereal end to a beautiful ship and a successful raider mission.

Since September 30, *Graf Spee* had sunk nine British merchant ships in the South Atlantic: a loss of 50,000 tons. The British Admiralty had organized four groups of capital warships to seek and destroy the ghost raider. The hunt became an exciting 'cat and mouse' game, with many dangerous moments. Captain Langsdorff's uncanny ability to avoid the hunters raised confidence in the warship's crew. They dreamed of completing a successful mission and a triumphant return to the Fatherland.

The raider's success rose to an exceptional level because her commander religiously followed the Hague Conventions in his operations. He pursued the honorable traditions of her namesake, Graf von Spee. This World War I hero, a staunch Catholic, had perceived a mystical bond with Providence in the ever changing moods of the oceans. He had seen God's hand in the risks of a seaman's life.

Young Langsdorff had grown up in Düsseldorf, near the Count's family estates. Although he was not a Catholic he shared much of the same spiritual essence as Graf von Spee. As a young naval officer, Langsdorff had deemed the honorable count his mentor. As commander of the *Graf Spee,* he had resolved his ship would preserve the noble name of von Spee and the honor of the German navy.

Turret Anton: 11-inch firepower.

– Gilbey Collection

Panzerschiff Admiral Graf Spee, was the third of three special warships designed to raid commerce. Built under the weight restrictions of the 1919 Versailles Treaty, they were 12,000-ton armored ships with 11-inch armament. About one-third the weight of regular battle cruisers, they looked like small battleships. Hence the nickname – pocket battleship. The distinctive warships incorporated many ingenious innovations. With welded hulls, electronic controls, radar, high-tech communications and diesel engines they were ahead of their time.

A top-secret gun-sight system controlled their 11-inch armament. One electronic component – *krängungsgerät* – compensated for the roll and pitch of the warship. Another electronic masterpiece – *seitenvorzündverk* – automatically fired the main guns in heavy seas. The system, aided by electronic devices that measured range and allowed for atmospheric conditions, was extremely effective.

Aboard *Graf Spee,* Lieutenant F. W. Rasenack was responsible for maintaining the high-tech system. He had tended and nursed the equipment since joining *Graf Spee* in 1936.

Early in the morning of December 17, in Montevideo, Rasenack could hardly believe instructions he received to destroy the gun-sight controls. But orders from Berlin had been clear. If the Captain decided to scuttle his ship, he must destroy all secret technology. Rasenack and his men had ruined many small instruments with hammers or grenades before massive explosions scuttled the ship and wrecked everything else of import.

Graf Spee had broken in half and recurring explosions convulsed the stricken warship. Although the forward turret did not explode in the blast, diesel fuel and other combustibles caused a furnace-like fire that ravaged the ship.

Rasenack last sighted the burning ship from the tug *Coloso.* With fourteen fellow officers he crowded into the tug's wheelhouse on its way to Argentina. In Buenos Aires, they hoped to land as shipwrecked seamen and perhaps go free.

When the overloaded tugs arrived in Buenos Aires roads, word quickly spread throughout the city. Dozens of small boats greeted the weary sailors. German immigrants, living in Buenos Aires, quickly provided practical support for their compatriots. They passed food, fruit and fresh milk to the men who had not eaten in twenty-four hours. This nourishment helped them endure the scorching heat of midday.

While the tired seamen waited for instructions, Captain Langsdorff persuasively argued for their acceptance as refugees from a shipwreck. Argentine government officials pondered the German commander's argument for several hours but ruled that deliberate destruction of a warship fell short of shipwreck. Argentina would intern the Germans, applying the Hague rules of a neutral country in wartime.

In the afternoon the seamen landed in Buenos Aires. Most of them marched with an escort to the main hall of the Immigrants Hotel to be enumerated and billeted. *Graf Spee's* officers were accommodated in the Naval Arsenal, an adjoining building on the North Dock.

Finally, the exhausted men showered, ate some food and thankfully went to bed. *Admiral Graf Spee* had sailed from Wilhelmshaven on August 21, thirteen days before the declaration of war. Four months at sea fostered an appreciation of dry land.

Next evening, December 19, two Argentinean marines stood on guard at the main entrance of the Arsenal. Front windows of the three-story building were dimly lit. People moving inside the rooms showed against the faded curtains. As the hours crept past, the windows progressively darkened when the men went to bed.

Shortly before midnight, in an exterior room on the ground floor of the Arsenal, Captain Langsdorff carefully wrote a letter. Huddled over a small wooden desk in the yellow light of a table lamp, he struggled to find the right words. There was so much to say and scarce time to say it. In one week the life of Captain Hans Langsdorff had crashed from triumph to tragedy.

From the end of September until December 12, good luck had sided with good judgment. He had sunk nine enemy freighters without loss of life. *Graf Spee's* commander, with two senior officers, and one hundred crewmen had received Iron Cross decorations for a brilliant raider cruise.

An armada of powerful enemy warships was organized to protect their shipping lanes. *Graf Spee* successfully evaded contact with them but four months at sea had caused havoc with the ship's engines: She needed urgent dock repairs.

On December 13 Langsdorff engaged three British cruisers in a fierce sea battle. Thirty-six of his young crew lost their lives and his critically damaged ship forced to seek sanctuary: British shells had wrecked an essential fuel cleaning system.

Germany had no friendly port in South America. Information overheard in radio intercepts, suggested that British warships used the neutral port of Montevideo. Langsdorff remembered a World War 1 incident when a battle-damaged British cruiser had been dry-docked for a week in neutral Brazil; the Hague Conventions allowed such sanctuary. He decided to take his ship into Montevideo and perhaps arrange something similar.

This choice, although verified with High Command, proved disastrous for a German warship seeking refuge. Neutral Uruguay held robust British and French political sympathies. Mr. Eugen Millington-Drake, the British envoy, had promoted pro-British tenets in Uruguay for many years.

Graf Spee received a seventy-two-hour deadline to make repairs and leave Uruguayan waters. If she refused, Uruguay would intern the ship and her crew. A strong British cruiser squadron waited in the estuary, ready to engage *Graf Spee* when she left neutral waters. In the previous battle the ship had shown that she could not absorb punishment from 8-inch or 6-inch shells; her side armor was barely 3-inches thick. To reach open water meant passing a gauntlet of cruisers through 27-miles of shallow water. Odds were overwhelmingly high the ship would be grounded and helpless to prevent capture.

In Langsdorff's assessment he must fight a hopeless battle or scuttle the ship. Signals from Berlin had left the decision in his hands. In any case, the ship must not be captured salvageable. Langsdorff had chosen to destroy his ship. He believed this fullfilled his military obligations and his moral responsibilities to his young crew.

Some of his officers opposed this action. Lofty traditions of the German Navy demanded they fight to the finish. Langsdorff, himself a firm traditionalist, had often argued that a captain should go down with his ship. Discussion grew heated and the fiery officers cited the case history of courage and valor shown by German warships in the 1914 Battle of the Falklands.

In that famous sea-battle, hopelessly outclassed German warships had fought to the final moment. They had shown derision to the British victors even while their ships were going down. Graf von Spee, with his two sons and his heroic men had lost their lives but achieved a prominent place in history.

Captain Langsdorff could not dismiss or avoid his commitment to protect the honor of his flag and his men. He decided to write a final letter addressed to Baron von Thermann, German Ambassador Buenos Aires, dated December 19, 1939:

> *Your Excellency,*
>
> *After a long inward struggle I reached the grave decision to scuttle the pocket battleship Graf Spee in order to prevent that it should fall into the hands of the enemy. I am convinced that under the circumstances this decision was the only one that I could take after I had taken my ship into the trap of Montevideo.*[1]

Langsdorff laid down his pen and read the paragraph several times. Montevideo had become a trap, an open cage that held him in check. Langsdorff had misgivings when he entered Montevideo but he had few choices.[2] *Graf Spee* had a serious fuel problem that needed shore help to fix. In addition, severe deterioration of the auxiliary and main engines required dock repairs.

In hindsight, his decision to seek sanctuary in Montevideo revealed a flaw in Naval planning. The German Navy had overlooked the political muscle of the enemy in South America. *Graf Spee's* experience had shown that ships in distress needed political assistance to get help in neutral ports. Germany had stationed only one Naval Attaché in all of South America.

Cohesion between the Navy and the Foreign Service needed improvement. Captain Langsdorff had no prior knowledge that

Uruguay carried the British flag close to her breast.[3] Naval High Command, who had affirmed his signal to enter the Uruguayan port, evidently shared the captain's ignorance of the political implications.

Elbows on the desk, his head between his hands, Langsdorff gently rubbed the corners of his eyes with the tips of his forefingers. After turning the words over in his mind he picked up his pen and resumed writing.

> *With the ammunition remaining, any attempt to break out to open and deep water was bound to fail. And yet only in deep water could I have scuttled the ship after having used the remaining ammunition, so preventing her falling into the hands of the enemy. Rather than expose my ship to the danger, after her fight, of falling partly or completely into enemy hands, I have decided not to fight but to destroy the equipment and sink the ship.*[1]

Again, he paused to revisit his thoughts. Clearly, the situation guaranteed that *Graf Spee* would take hits in an attempted breakout. The maximum water depth within twenty miles of Montevideo was 25ft. *Graf Spee* drew 21ft. Any loss of draft in the shallow waters would ground the ship. In this scenario, every shell used in action would have depleted the explosives needed to destroy the vessel. Wearily, he continued his letter, writing in old German script.

> *It was clear to me that this decision might be misinterpreted whether intentionally or unwittingly by persons ignorant of my motives as being attributable partly or entirely to personal considerations. Therefore, I decided from the beginning to bear the consequences involved in this decision. For a Captain with a sense of honor cannot separate his own fate from that of his ship.*[1]

At this point, Captain Langsdorff placed his pen on top of the paper and reached for his pipe. Slowly he filled the bowl and lit the tobacco. Leaning back in his chair he puffed until a cloud of blue smoke billowed over his head. Totally relaxed and calm he lapsed into his thoughts.

Hans Langsdorff had very few personal considerations. Love of the sea had drawn him into the Navy. Admiration of the persona and lifestyle of Graf von Spee had motivated him to achieve the highest rank possible in his profession. Service to the German nation was inherited from long family tradition.

Circa 1911: Judge Ludwig Langsdorff and Wife Elizabeth. – LANGSDORFF FAMILY

The Langsdorffs had served as court officials for generations. His father had been a High Court judge and most of his mother's family had been parsons. Personal integrity and National pride combined to fire Langsdorff's character. Any stain on one automatically blemished the other. Responsibility rested easily on his shoulders when the parameters of a decision remained in his hands. His duty required he carry out distasteful orders in the National interest. But they must fall within the strict confines of his Christian conscience.

No-one could ever know his internal conflict when faced with a pointless battle to appease tradition. Duty and tradition wrestled with his compassion for human life. Loss of life in any circumstance was a tragedy. Useless loss of life was a sacrilege. However, tradition must prevail. Langsdorff's conscience directed him to trade his own blood rather than spill the blood of his young men. Keeping the pipe clasped in his teeth, he rearranged the paper and picked up the pen.

> *I postponed my intention as long as I was still responsible for the welfare of the crew under my command. After today's decision of the Argentine Government, I can do no more for my ship's company. Neither will I be able to take an active part in the present conflict of my country. Now I can only prove by my death that the fighting services of the Reich are ready to die for the honor of their flag.* [1]

Langsdorff stopped writing and gazed absently at the sheet. Automatically, he tamped the partially burned residue in his pipe and relit the briar. Enjoying the familiar taste, he rose from his chair and began slowly pacing the room, deep in thought.

In these initial days of the war the Third Reich was perched like a large snowball on top of a mountain. Balanced delicately, the Nation and the world awaited the outcome of the bloodletting in Poland. If appeasement failed, the snowball would topple and start an avalanche accumulating everything in its path. Where would it end? Langsdorff's father, before his death in 1934, had warned of the dangers of an unchecked dictatorship:

Circa 1932: Judge Ludwig Langsdorff.
– Langsdorff Family

'If Hitler does not soften his rampant nationalism in a spirit of compromise, war will again arise. A more terrible war than any before. New technology will reshape the nature of war. Submarines, bombers and tanks, guided by new communications systems, will deliver ever advancing levels of destruction. Civilian intimidation on a grand scale will equal military targets as a priority. The pursuit of victory will bye-pass any Hague guideline that becomes inconvenient'.

As Langsdorff slowly paced the room his eye caught the bright color of folded cloth lying on a small table beside his bed. Still neatly folded, the battle flag of *Admiral Graf Spee* comforted him in his reflections.

Captain Langsdorff's patriotism focused on his love for the Navy. This flag represented everything he believed in regarding the Navy and the Nation. In theory the Navy remained apolitical but current policy required an oath of allegiance to Adolf Hitler, the supreme commander of the armed forces. The Führer now held the future of the Nation, in every dimension, in his hands. Providence must steer him on the right course.

Returning to his desk, Langsdorff put down the pipe and quickly finished the letter:

I alone bear the responsibility for scuttling the pocket-battleship Admiral Graf Spee. I am happy to pay with my life to prevent any possible reflection on the honor of the flag. I shall meet my fate with firm faith in the cause and future of the nation and of my Führer. I am writing this letter to Your Excellency in the quiet of the evening, after calm reflection, in order that you may be able to inform my superior officers, and to counter any public rumors if this should become necessary.[1]

(signed) Langsdorff, Captain
Commanding officer of the sunk pocket-battleship
Admiral Graf Spee.

His task completed, Langsdorff addressed a large envelope, folded the letter carefully, and sealed it firmly inside. He placed the envelope beside another one lying on his desk – his last letter to his wife Ruth, bringing her his final thoughts.

Chapter 2

Langsdorff's Mission

Some men are born with an irresistible call to the sea in their bones and a spirit of adventure in their souls.

At the beginning of the Second World War many senior officers in the opposing navies were World War 1 veterans. In the Battle of the River Plate Commodore Henry Harwood with Captains Woodhouse *(Ajax)*, Bell (*Exeter)* and Parry *(Achilles*) represented the best traditions of the British Royal Navy. All were tough professionals who carried the honor of their country and their flag like a precious jewel. This engagement of three British cruisers against a German pocket battleship marked the end of traditional sea-battles. Swiftly advancing aircraft technology changed the previous reliance on powerful surface warships.

Captain Hans Langsdorff, who commanded *Admiral Graf Spee*, came from the same mold as his British foes. In 1939, he was a decorated veteran with twenty-seven years service in the German navy. However, despite long years of martial training, Langsdorff retained an uncommon degree of compassion for his fellow man. While faithfully fighting to preserve the honor of his nation and his flag, Langsdorff placed high value on human life. Honor and self esteem were shining facets in the life of this unusual man.

Hans Wilhelm Langsdorff was born in Bergen auf Rügen April 20, 1894. His brother Reinhard arrived a year later. In 1898 the young family moved to Düsseldorf where their lawyer father, Ludwig Langsdorff, became a High Court Judge.

A passionate spiritual faith drove the matriarch of the family. Elizabeth Langsdorff, nee Steinmetz, had grown up in a parsonage. In the previous generation both her grandfathers had been Lutheran parsons. Elizabeth raised her family strictly, with solid Christian tenets.

In 1901, a daughter, Anneliese, enlarged and completed the family. As the children matured, Elizabeth prayed that one of her boys, perhaps Hans, would become a pastor in the family tradition.

Circa 1911: Elizabeth Langsdorff with Hans and Anneliese
– Langsdorff Family

At the turn of the century Düsseldorf offered every amenity available in larger centers. Reichgraf Maximilian von Spee's castle and estates stood nearby and members of the aristocratic family frequently visited the city. The Count held vice-Admiral rank in the Kaiser's Imperial Navy. He had joined the Navy in 1878 at the age of eighteen. Von Spee's elder son Otto followed his father's example and joined the Navy at eighteen. Heinrich, the Count's second son, about the same age as Langsdorff, also joined the Navy when eligible. As a youth, Hans often saw von Spee's family walking in the park near the Langsdorff s home. He yearned to join this elite company in the Imperial Navy.

On April 1, 1912, Hans' dreams came true when he reported to Kiel for induction. Officer Cadet Langsdorff and the other course entrants joined the training ship *Hertha.* Designated 'the crew of 12', members of the class would retain this title during their naval careers. All the cadets would be rigorously trained as officers and gentlemen.

○ ○ ○

World War 1 began August 4, 1914, and Langsdorff joined his first ship. *Medusa,* a small cruiser, lying out of service at Danzig, was hastily fitted and assigned to Cuxhaven. Based in this important port, *Medusa* helped protect the mouth of the River Elbe against submarine attacks. Ensign Langsdorff manned a searchlight and a machine-gun.

On March 22, 1915, Langsdorff received promotion to Lieutenant. Six months later, September 20, Lieutenant Langsdorff joined *Grosser*

Kurfürst, a battleship in the High Seas Fleet based at Wilhelmshaven.

At 0330hrs, 31 May 1916, Admiral Scheer went to sea with the German High Seas Fleet. Close to one hundred ships, they steamed purposefully north. Britain's gigantic armada, stationed in Scapa Flow, had threatened the entire German Navy since the outbreak of war. Scheer hoped to break the 'fleet in being' stalemate that had penned his fleet in home harbors. The battleship *König* led Scheer's powerful battle line. Second in line steamed *Grosser Kurfürst* with Lieutenant Langsdorff as flag lieutenant.

Circa 1914: Ensign Hans Langsdorff.
– Langsdorff Family

Scheer's original plan, to lure a small squadron of British warships into battle, backfired. Consequently, the entire British Grand Fleet engaged Scheer's High Seas Fleet in the Battle of Jutland.

Total material losses in the Battle were high. Britain lost six heavy ships and eight destroyers while Germany lost six capital ships plus five destroyers. Counting both sides, 8,648 courageous seamen lost their lives. British fatalities were higher than the Germans because three battle cruisers, HMS*Queen Mary,* HMS*Indefatigable* and HMS*Invincible,* blew up when hit: Cordite flashes infiltrated the powder magazines and caused gigantic explosions.

Courageous deeds and actions on both sides were rewarded with praise, promotions and medals. *Grosser Kurfürst* sailed to Hamburg for major repairs and Lieutenant Hans Langsdorff went home on leave to Düsseldorf. On his breast he proudly wore an Iron Cross. In his heart he carried troublesome memories of the tragic loss of life.

Langsdorff spent the remainder of World War 1 in mine-sweeping activities that continued into the postwar years. His rank rose progressively. On April 1, 1922, he reached Lieut-Captain.

Circa 1932: Hans with wife Ruth, Kläuschen and Jochen.

– Langsdorff Family

In 1923, he met Ruth Hager in Dresden. The twenty-three-year old daughter of a career military officer worked in the offices of the Reichswehr. They were married March 29, 1924, and Jochen, a robust baby boy, was born December 14, in the same year. On October 1, 1925, Langsdorff was posted to Berlin.

Buoyant and happy, the young family quickly settled into a small apartment in Lichtenrade, 15 kilometers south of the city center. Hans' move to Berlin promised a second honeymoon and a lifestyle change in his first land posting.

Langsdorff enjoyed working as a liaison officer between the navy and the Reichswehr. In 1927 he was selected for a leadership course. This important step in his career led to command of a half-flotilla of torpedo boats – four ships. On April 1, 1930, he was promoted to Lieut-Commander.

In the fall, 1931, he was again posted to Berlin. On September 25, he began a semi-political career in the Department of National Defense. Langsdorff had excellent administrative skills and soon became an adjutant in General Schleicher's Ministry. This was a new opportunity and he accepted it with enthusiasm.

But when Hitler came to power in 1933, Langsdorff began to lose interest in the messy political scene. Nazi politicians were infiltrating and taking over the old established ministries.[1] He requested a return to sea duty and on February 1, 1934, moved into department 'J' of Wilhelm Frick's Ministry of the Interior.

Later that year, June 30, his previous boss General Schleicher lost his life in the murderous Röhm purge. Coincidentally on the same day, June 30, 1934, Countess Huberta von Spee launched *Admiral Graf Spee* in

Circa 1937: Graf Spee *in Kiel Canal.* – GILBEY COLLECTION.

Wilhelmshaven. Langsdorff returned to sea duty on August 10, 1935 after spending four years in Berlin.

September 1, 1935, Langsdorff received a promotion to Commander. Next year, on December 10, 1936, he was assigned staff officer to Admiral Böehme, commander of the prestigious pocket battleships.

Conceived in the late twenties as armored ships these high-tech warships commanded respect. Although the Versailles Treaty had restricted new German warships to 10,000-tons, three *Deutschland* class warships emerged with 11-inch main armament and prototype diesel engines. The innovative diesels gave enormous range without refueling and a cruising speed of 14-knots could change to 26-knots with the turn of a switch.

Configured like small battleships, *Deutschland, Admiral Scheer* and *Graf Spee* were dubbed pocket-battleships. This proved to be a misnomer. Apart from the main turrets and command tower, the ships lacked adequate protective armor.[2] Three-inch armored sides and skimpy decks belied any claim to battleship status. Designed specifically to raid commerce, this was their forte.

On January 1, 1937, Commander Langsdorff was promoted to Captain. Later that year, in May, *Admiral Graf Spee,* the flagship of the German fleet, sparkled in the International Naval Review at Spitshead.

In October 1937 Captain Warzecha replaced Captain Patzig as commander of *Graf Spee* and the following year, on October 29, 1938, Captain Langsdorff replaced Captain Warzecha. Meanwhile Admiral Böehme had transferred his flag to *Scharnhorst,* a new battle-cruiser.

○ ○ ○

In August 1939, German troops were poised to march into Poland on any pretext. Neville Chamberlain, Prime Minister of Britain, clutching a rolled umbrella in his hand and hopes for peace in his heart had negotiated in good faith. Britain, France and many countries in Europe, including Germany, still suffered the psychological pain of World War 1. Everyone fervently prayed that a new war would be averted.

Hitler ruthlessly exploited the popular distaste for war and increasingly pushed his demands beyond acceptable levels. Sensing the coming conflict, the German Naval War Staff had prepared a plan for wartime action against commercial shipping. Two pocket battleships, specifically designed for such action, would feature prominently in this.

The commanders of these ships, Captain Hans Langsdorff (*Admiral Graf Spee*) and Captain Paul Wenneker (*Deutschland),* received instructions to govern their roles in a war on commercial shipping. *Graf Spee* with her supply ship *Altmark* would operate in the South Atlantic and Indian Oceans, and *Deutschland* with her mother ship *Westerwald* would strike in the North Atlantic. Germany's third pocket battleship, *Admiral Scheer* was excluded from the initial operation as she needed a major overhaul.

In case of war with Britain, the ships' orders read in part:

> Disrupt and destroy enemy shipping by all possible means. Enemy naval forces, even if inferior in strength, are to be engaged only if it furthers the principal task of commerce raiding. Frequent changes of position in the specified operational area will create uncertainty that will restrict enemy shipping. A submarine fleet will also operate in the North Atlantic and general control will remain in the hands of the High Command. All commanders, by necessity, will operate with relative freedom of action.

A political assessment given to the captains stated that Britain and

France would probably intervene in a German war against Poland. Italy would likely join with Germany. The Soviet Union, tentatively, would remain neutral at the beginning of any war against Poland.

August 17, 1939, *Graf Spee*, involved in torpedo firing exercises, was recalled to Wilhelmshaven and ordered to prepare for war duty. In three days of nonstop hustle, Commander Walter Kay, the executive officer, Lieut-Commander Karl Klepp, chief engineer, and Lieut-Commander Paul Ascher, gunnery officer, under the watchful eye of Captain Hans Langsdorff prepared the pocket battleship for a long voyage.

Commander Kay released excess numbers of the young reservist crew and reorganized accommodations to handle a wartime complement. Busy crewmen stored adequate war provisions and supplies aboard.

Graf Spee's primary design included two Heinkel 60 spotter aircraft. Testing, now under way, planned to replace the Heinkel model with an Arado. Two Arado prototypes were under review. The first plane had a center float installed between two outboard floats and the other – Arado 196 – had two outboard floats.

Time restrictions decreed this model remain aboard when *Graf Spee* was mobilized. Various teething problems had caused some anxiety but time had run out. Unresolved problems experienced with the new spotter plane must be left for correction at sea. One Arado 196, ready for action, remained in her catapult and a 'knocked down' second unit stowed aboard. On August 20, Captain Langsdorff declared *Admiral Graf Spee* ready to sail.

In late afternoon August 21, five merchant marine officers boarded *Graf Spee*. They had sailed the world's oceans in commercial ships. Their contribution to the mission would be invaluable as prize-crew officers and advisors of commercial traffic.

At 2000hrs, August 21, *Graf Spee* quietly slipped out of Wilhelmshaven. She had orders to avoid all contact with other ships and take position in the South Atlantic. On the bridge, Captain Langsdorff, in a deeply pensive mood, mentally reviewed his mission:

In 1939, German Naval strength comprised two new 26,000-ton battle cruisers, *Scharnhorst* and *Gneisenau*, and three pocket battleships. Twenty-seven U-boats plus various light cruisers, destroyers and torpedo boats completed the fleet.

Schleswig-Holstein, an ancient battleship, and other remnants of

Germany's World War 1 fleet were bordering on obsolescence. Two new heavy cruisers, *Hipper* class, were almost ready for service and two new battleships were in the stocks. But by any measure, the German Fleet was a smidgen compared to the size of the combined Royal Navy and French Fleets. Despite this imbalance, Captain Hans Langsdorff felt privileged to command a premier warship of the German Navy.

Assigned to commercial raiding duties in the South Atlantic, *Graf Spee* was perfectly suited to the task. New diesel engine technology gave her enormous range and great flexibility of speed. Coupled with 11-inch guns she made a fearsome merchant raider.

Hans Langsdorff knew the perilous odds against a solo raider avoiding eventual calamity but he had immense confidence in his ship and crew. Some of his reservist crew, enthusiastic teenagers, were short in age and experience but all were dedicated to the cause.

Through the dark night, maintaining radio silence, *Graf Spee* cruised off the Norwegian coast. A single light on her foretop conveyed the image of a freighter to any casual viewer. She followed a course used successfully in recent days by submarines heading toward the Atlantic. Gloomy weather helped the warship in her secret passage.

In the morning, August 22, Captain Langsdorff assembled his crew on the rear deck and briefly explained their mission. *Graf Spee* had orders to take position in the South Atlantic and await developments in Europe. If war began, they would attack commercial shipping to disrupt enemy supply lines.

Two days later, August 24, radio signals broadcast the news that Germany and The Soviet Union had signed a non-aggression pact. Discussion raged throughout the ship regarding the significance of this Pact. Lieut-Commander Hans Fuchs, expressed approval and drew furious argument from some of his peers. It was unbelievable that Hitler would join with the Communists, previously labeled bitter foes.

However, the military implications of the Pact reduced expectations that Britain would support Poland in case of war. Supplies from The Soviet Union would belittle a naval blockade. Why would Great Britain fight a deadly war against Germany? She had nothing to gain and much to lose.

However, Britain remained firm. The following day, August 25, she ratified her guarantee of support for Poland. *Graf Spee's* crew debated the issues of the developing crisis and an element of uncertainty settled on the mission.

Next day, August 26, foul weather came down with fervor. A full scale hurricane blew the 12000-ton ship around like a cork in a rain-barrel. Petty-officer Herbert Matzker was swept overboard and raucous klaxons signaled an alarm.

Immediately, the ship reduced way to try to recover the unfortunate seaman. For two hours the difficult search went on but found nothing. Sadness filled the crew. In war and peace the unrelenting sea will claim her victims.

In the North Atlantic, heading southward toward her point of operation, *Graf Spee* listened to British wireless transmissions. The pocket battleship carried a device that monitored transmissions 'round the clock' and reported their occurrence. Included in her crew, a specialized staff of code experts could decipher most codes. Any code beyond their capability, when relayed to Berlin, was usually broken within twenty minutes. Besides regular wireless traffic from High Command, *Graf Spee* could intercept radio signals from every source in a wide area.

Captain Langsdorff knew that Allied ships were notifying the British Admiralty the position of any German warships they sighted. The Admiralty had instructed all British ships to sail without lights, outside the normal shipping lanes, and use wireless sparingly.

On August 28, Langsdorff's operators listened to ships signaling their positions to *Beothik,* a British flying-boat. Canny plotting of the merchant ships' positions allowed Lieut-Commander Jürgen Wattenberg, *Graf Spee's* chief navigator, to chart a course through vacant waters. *Graf Spee* sailed on unseen.

Captain Langsdorff and his chief in Berlin, Admiral Erich Raeder, had seen active service in World War 1. Both had won iron crosses at Jutland. British 15-inch shells had pounded Langsdorff's battleship *Grosser Kurfürst* leaving her seriously damaged. Meanwhile, Raeder had experienced incredible front-line action while on board the battle cruiser *Lutzow.*

World War 1 experience had frequently proved the uncanny ability of the British Admiralty to intercept and decode wireless transmissions. Langsdorff must exercise caution when using wireless, even with coded messages. *Graf Spee* had thus far maintained radio silence but must now verify meeting her supply ship, *Altmark.*

High Command had prearranged a date, time and place for the meeting. Langsdorff transmitted confirmation of the rendezvous but deliberately quoted false coordinates. Enemy eavesdroppers would expect the meeting to take place hundreds of miles north of the actual rendezvous.

Moving south, past the Azores, tropical weather baked the steel-clad warship. Officers and crew switched from midnight blue serge to white cotton uniforms. Daytime on deck under blue sunlit skies was enjoyable but nights in blacked-out cabins felt clammily humid and hot.

Radio news said the Government had imposed partial food rationing in Germany. In the interests of morale, Captain Langsdorff ordered the food ration on board equalized. Officers and men would receive the same rations. Previously, officers ate a little extra cold meats and steak but all accepted the Captain's orders with good grace.

Graf Spee continued at leisurely speed through the vast open space of the South Atlantic. Daily exercises simulating action included the Arado aircraft. She acted well in catapulting from the ship and in target practice with small bombs and machine guns. However, in moderate seas the plane could not reduce landing speed enough to avoid splashing the engine block with sea-spray. Also, bringing the plane aboard *Spee* gave the crews of the ship and the plane troubles. A specially designed landing sail, installed on the port side of the warship, proved unwieldy. Difficulties in coordinating the speed of the ship and the approaching plane, bobbing around in the Atlantic swell, made the sail ineffective. Langsdorff ordered it dismantled and eventually discarded.

To ease the plane's landing hazards the ship created an artificial 'duck-pond'. The helmsmen steered *Graf Spee* in a tight circular course to create a calmer central landing space. Still, even with reduced sea action, the plane's high landing speed sent showers of cold sea-spray over the engine cowling. This seriously affected the air-cooled engine block.

Without question, the Arado spotter plane outpaced the older Heinkel model but considering the inherent difficulties, speed became a dubious benefit. In practice sessions, Lieutenant Dietlef Spiering and his pilot, Petty-officer Heinrich Bongardts, handled the machine very well despite the hazards.

August 31, Captain Langsdorff assembled all hands on the after-deck. Standing before the hushed crew, Langsdorff summarized instructions from the High Command:

At dawn tomorrow, September 1, German storm troops will cross the Polish frontier. In the morning *Graf Spee* will meet her supply ship, *Altmark,* and wait for further orders. We are instructed to open fire only if attacked.

Fate had chosen Captain Hans Langsdorff to uphold the honorable name of his mentor, Graf von Spee, and the high traditions of the German Navy. As a young officer, he had strived to emulate the Count in an honorable naval career. In 1914, when Graf von Spee and both his

Arado 196 landing in "duck-pond".

– Gilbey Collection

Captain Langsdorff addresses crew on after-deck. – Gilbey Collection

sons lost their lives at the Battle of the Falklands, Langsdorff's resolve deepened.

During World War 1 he had proudly read the honorable stories of the sea-raiders *Emden, Möwe* and *Seeadler*. Captains von Müller, Dohna-Schlodien and von Luckner had earned the respect of the World. They accomplished remarkable martial success as commerce raiders while following the humanitarian principles of the Hague Conventions. A credit to their ships and their nation, each captain received international acclaim for courage and chivalry.

Captain Langsdorff now commanded a ship that could surpass the feats of those heroes. *Graf Spee* was perfectly suited to raid commerce on the high seas. Shaped like a small battleship and bristling with firepower her presence would intimidate any merchant ship to obey orders. Langsdorff firmly believed his ship could outrun any battleship matching his 11-inch armament and outgun any cruiser running faster than *Graf Spee.*

Still, mixed emotions filled his thoughts. He passionately loved his nation, his flag and his vessel yet found a twinge of conscience at the prospect of attacking unarmed merchant ships. Truly, Captain Langsdorff abhorred his assigned task. He considered merchant seamen as civilians doing a time-honored job on the high seas. It created a bizarre paradox that his duty made them his target.

However, responsibility for his ship and his men must take first place in the fulfillment of his duty. Langsdorff found his task distasteful, but believed he was a principal standard bearer for the German Navy and the Nation in these difficult times: Political negotiation may yet achieve a compromise to avoid full-scale war.

He pledged to follow the path of the World War 1 raiders and fulfill his duty with courage and honor. Langsdorff prayed he would accomplish his task with valor and minimum bloodshed.

CHAPTER 3

Commence Hostilities

September 1, in a remote section of the South Atlantic (25°52'N/35°49'W), *Graf Spee* met *Altmark.* Lieut-Commanders Wattenberg and Höpfner, responsible for navigating the pinpoint location, accepted congratulations from their peers.

At 0730hrs on a balmy tropical morning, *Altmark* looked magnificent. Flying a Norwegian flag and boldly displaying the false name *Sogne,* the 7,000-ton tanker gave comforting companionship to *Graf Spee.* Captain Heinrich Dau, a gruff rough-hewn seaman of the old school, commanded the supply ship. Dau, a tall angular man with a gray goatee, came aboard *Graf Spee* with some senior officers to meet Captain Langsdorff.

After the short visit, both ships set a course southward with *Altmark* in the lead. *Graf Spee* refueled astern while under way. An ingenious arrangement of hoses, supported by floats, connected the ships as *Spee* trailed in *Altmark's* wash. The system left a tricky chore for *Graf Spee* helmsmen but refueling took place without incident.

Graf Spee's *supply ship* Altmark. – GILBEY COLLECTION

Graf Spee *refuels under way.*
– Gilbey Collection

Radio reports from Berlin gave highlights of the blitzkrieg attack on Poland. Field Marshall Göring's air-force had pummeled Polish airports and destroyed many airplanes on the ground. Naval news reported *Schleswig-Holstein,* an ancient battleship, had heavily bombarded the shipyard district near Danzig. German panzers and ground troops were crashing through Poland with devastating speed.

Far removed from the sickening realities of war, *Graf Spee's* crew greeted the news from the front with mixed feelings. Britain and France must surely declare war on the Fatherland but a becalmed silence hung over the West. Britain's Prime Minister, Mr. Chamberlain, had postponed the House of Parliament sitting on September 2, that should have debated the issue. Mussolini, the Führer's cautious friend, had declared Italy neutral. Would the war remain confined to Poland as the Führer had guessed? A feeling of apprehension unsettled *Graf Spee's* crew.

Radio news on September 3 broke the pre-storm restlessness. *Graf Spee* wireless operators intercepted a British transmission from Rugby, England:

'1100HRS: COMMENCE HOSTILITIES AT ONCE AGAINST GERMAN SHIPPING.'

Within forty-five minutes *Graf Spee* received a signal from Berlin:

'COMMENCE HOSTILITIES WITH ENGLAND IMMEDIATELY.'

Later bulletins reported Britain had refused to negotiate peace unless German troops left Poland. War was under way!

Graf Spee and *Altmark* promptly set course for a designated area (within 5°/10°N and 25°/35°W) to begin operations. In the afternoon,

Graf Spee received a news update. Effective 1700hrs September 3, France had also declared war on Germany.

Paradoxically, the High Command in Berlin ordered Langsdorff to refrain from attacking Allied ships. Hitler hoped to dissuade the Western Powers from going to full scale war. The Führer held high expectations that Britain and France, having fulfilled their political commitment to Poland, would find a way to come to terms with Germany.

Captain Langsdorff reviewed his orders to avoid aggressive action. It posed great difficulty to remain in the shipping lanes *incognito.* Any enemy or neutral ship that sighted *Graf Spee* could report her position. After consulting with Wattenberg and Höpfner, he decided to lie low in an area west of Saint Helena and east of Trinidad Island. The navigators knew this position was removed from normal shipping lanes and they might remain unobserved.

Radio news continued to undulate between good and bad. Winston Churchill was named Lord of the British Admiralty – as in World War 1. Churchill's revival from political disfavor signaled a quick turnaround in British attitude. 'Peace at any price' had changed to 'war if necessary'. President Roosevelt had already declared the United States would remain neutral.

Meanwhile, the British lost no time in baring their fangs. Royal Air Force planes bombed the entrance to the Kiel Canal and HMS*Ajax* captured two German freighters off the Brazilian coast. *Ajax*, a light cruiser, took off the crews of *Olinda* and *Karl Fritzen* and sank the German merchants. The Royal Navy correctly followed the Hague Conventions.

However, civilian passengers aboard the British liner *Athenia* were not so lucky: They lost their lives when torpedoes sank the liner 200 miles off the Hebrides. *Athenia* was struck without warning September 4, while carrying 1,400 passengers from Liverpool to Montreal. One-hundred and twelve souls went down with *Athenia,* including twenty-eight Americans.

German propaganda claimed British responsibility, aimed to entice the United States into the war. Dr. Joseph Goebbels blatantly accused Winston Churchill of complicity in the sinking: Admiral Raeder had confidently assured Goebbels that German submarines were not involved. This advice later proved false when Lieutenant Lemp, commanding U-30, confessed he had mistaken the liner for an armed auxiliary. [After the war, Raeder claimed prior ignorance of Lemp's action.]

Aboard *Graf Spee*, great joy greeted news of the safe return of the German liner *Bremen* to Murmansk. Goebbels, the Nazi propaganda expert, published derisive headlines noting the ineptitude of the Royal Navy. Meanwhile in Britain, a submarine commander endured serious scolding for letting the passenger liner pass unmolested. This is the nature of war.

Days ticked past under the scorching sun. As they approached the equatorial line, extremely high water temperatures affected the engines' cooling system. It depended on sea-water drawn from the keel area that circulated through the system. Lieut-Commander Klepp, the chief engineer, reported his engines could deliver only 21-knots at maximum speed in the 27°C sea-water.

To help relieve monotony and the repressive heat, the crew engaged in some tomfoolery. When the ship crossed the equatorial date line, a dressed-up crew member represented the God Neptune in the traditional 'crossing the line' skit. Laughter and goodwill echoed around the ship.

Suddenly, *'action stations'* rang out. *'Smoke on the horizon'*. Crew members and officers ran automatically to their posts. Watertight doors clanged into locked position. In minutes the ship was battle-ready.

As quickly as it arose, the emergency dissipated. The thin column of smoke first sighted on the horizon, was a Brazilian neutral that *Graf Spee* easily evaded. Captain Langsdorff expressed his pleasure with the fast response to the alert. Commander Kay's daily drills were quickly molding his young crew into a fighting unit.

On September 10, *Graf Spee* and *Altmark* coasted in their hideout area, at 8°42'S/24°13'W.[1] Next day, the Arado on a routine reconnaissance flight spotted a warship at the limits of visibility. Lieutenant Spiering, in command of the plane, immediately returned to *Graf Spee*. Hastily, the pocket battleship and her supply ship made way and steered away from the danger.

Anxious moments passed as radio operators listened for increased wireless signals. Good luck helped the German warship. HMS*Cumberland* was zigzagging routinely while running toward the

River Plate. Following a preset pattern, the British heavy cruiser changed her course and barely missed *Graf Spee* and *Altmark*. It was a close call. Captain Langsdorff did not relish a military confrontation before his mission had begun.

In wartime, the most punishing, aggravating part of a mission is waiting for clear instructions. Two miserable, slow-moving weeks trickled past. Langsdorff kept *Graf Spee* in close contact with *Altmark* within their hideaway area and impatiently awaited orders.

Temperatures on board ranged from blistering tropic heat to bitter cold breezes. Heavy seas sometimes added variety to the day. Practice sessions with anti-aircraft weapons and calls to action stations honed the men and helped to pass the weary hours. Every inch of the ship was kept in top condition and her fuel tanks full.

Entertainment aboard *Spee* comprised, films, shuffleboard, choral singing, band-practice and war gossip. Wireless news from Europe was picked up and relayed daily to the men. On September 17, Soviet troops had swept into Poland along the entire length of the eastern frontier. Josef Stalin claimed he must protect the interest of Slavs and White Russians living in this region. Hitler and Stalin agreed on new boundaries for the partition of Poland on September 25. Despite brave but futile resistance the country had been overwhelmed in less than one month of fighting.

Mussolini, the Fascist Italian dictator, proposed a plan for peace. Hitler also offered to negotiate peace but refused to give up any of his gains. An appetizing peace carrot dangled temptingly before Great Britain and France but the Allies firmly demanded that Hitler withdraw from Poland before any peace talks began.

German naval war news, liberally coated with propaganda, was encouraging. Submarines had sunk a total 135,000 tons of Allied ships. U-29 had sunk the British aircraft carrier, HMS*Courageous*. Nevertheless, boredom and inaction continued to plague the waiting men of the *Graf Spee.*

A wireless broadcast on September 23 had mourned the death of General Freiherr Werner von Fritsch. The ex-commander-in-chief of the German Army had met his end on the Polish front near Warsaw. In the officer's mess, animated conversation recalled the scandal that had emerged around von Fritsch in January 1938.

Heinrich Himmler, the Nazi police chief, had charged von Fritsch with homosexual activity. Subsequently, the charge proved false. Himmler, jealous of von Fritsch's power, and Hermann Göring, seeking Germany's top military post, had organized a complicated frame-up. This faked scandal followed closely another scandal that caused the resignation of General von Blomberg, Chief of the General Staff.

Hitler had quickly used this opportune moment to totally reorganize Germany's Armed Services. On February 4, the Führer assumed personal command of all the Armed Forces. This new structure formed the all-powerful High Command of the Armed Forces under Field Marshall Wilhelm Keitel. Adolf Hitler personally asserted his place as Supreme Commander. General von Fritsch claimed ill health and resigned.

In March, following the annexation of Austria, a military court-martial cleared von Fritsch of Himmler's accusations. Rumors circulated that the proud Prussian nobleman had written a challenge to duel with Himmler but the stories remained unsubstantiated.

General von Fritsch was subsequently recalled to lead his old regiment in the Polish campaign. Despite anti-Nazi sentiments, which he had publicly declared, the General accepted declassification and served his nation gallantly to the end.

Some *Graf Spee* officers, who had joined the ship in 1936, compared von Fritsch with Captain Patzig, their first commander. Von Fritsch and Patzig had often publicly expressed strong anti-Nazi sentiments. Patzig had frequently addressed his crew criticizing the fanatical, immoral drive of the Nazi Party. In a navy supposed to be apolitical this was unusual conduct.

Captain Warzecha replaced Patzig at the end of his tour on October 1, 1937. One year later, on October 1, 1938, Captain Langsdorff took command of *Graf Spee* but kept his political thoughts to himself.

On the same day that Hitler and Stalin shared Poland, September 25, activities on *Graf Spee* picked up pace. Piquet boats transferred provisions of all kinds from *Altmark* to the warship. One sling containing several steel cylinders of compressed carbonic acid fell overboard. Commander Kay bawled out the unhappy crewmen involved. Under suffocating heat the work continued.

Next day, men selected for prize-crew duty practiced 'capturing' *Altmark*. From *Graf Spee* the prize-crews, led by a merchant officer, boarded a sea-boat. At full speed they crossed the rolling sea to *Altmark* and clambered aboard the freighter. Swiftly, with side arms drawn, they took possession of the bridge and engine room. First attempts were clumsy but soon, in a spirit of competition, each crew achieved proficiency. All hands sensed that *Graf Spee's* waiting period had expired.

On September 27, the British Prime Minister, declared a blockade on Germany. Mr. Chamberlain still showed hesitancy in adopting a more aggressive tactic. A ground-attack across the French frontier guaranteed heavy bloodshed. Meanwhile, Hitler took advantage of Britain's soft strategy to transfer troops from the Polish front to bolster his defenses on the west wall. On the same day, Naval High Command ordered Langsdorff to commence hostilities in the South Atlantic. The Captain immediately gathered his officers to plan operational strategy.

In the North Atlantic Germany's initial submarine campaign had concluded. Most submarines were withdrawn for maintenance and reassignment. Surface warships would operate in their place. *Scharnhorst* and *Gneisenau,* a pair of powerful battle-cruisers, would patrol in company. *Deutschland, Graf Spee's* sister ship, would operate as a solo raider, supported by *Westerwald. Graf Spee* and *Altmark* would operate in the South Atlantic.

Intelligence from High Command supplied Langsdorff with precise details of enemy sea forces. British capital ships, HMS*Hood*, HMS*Renown* and HMS*Repulse* were in home waters. Cruisers *Cumberland, Exeter, Ajax* and *Dispatch* with destroyers *Hotspur* and *Havoc* plus the submarine *Severn* were on the Atlantic Coast of South America. Three cruisers and one submarine were patrolling the West African coast.

At their daily meeting Langsdorff explained his orders to the officers. *Graf Spee* must engage in a hit-and-run campaign against merchant vessels. They would evade conflict with warships. The Captain stressed that their mission was a team effort and welcomed suggestions from officers or men to enhance the task. But he stressed that any decision or order must be concluded. All officers accepted their responsibilities and confidently affirmed his role as leader.

At 1700hrs, Langsdorff addressed all hands on the after-deck. A cheer greeted his news that *Graf Spee* would commence action. Their task was to cut off essential supplies going to Britain and add pressure on the Allies to negotiate peace. He explained the hit-and-run nature of the

S.S. Clement: 5,051 BRT. Captain C.F.P. Harris. – Gilbey Collection

operation. *Graf Spee* would become the object of a great hunt but the Atlantic provided thirty-four million square miles of hiding space. Langsdorff suggested that camouflage would help immensely in their success. They must try to confuse the enemy. *Graf Spee* would play a dual role and use *Admiral Scheer's* name and call-signal. Members of the prize-crews would get *Admiral Scheer* headbands to wear in operations. With luck and good work the mission to disrupt the shipping lanes would be successful.

Langsdorff closed his speech reminding the men that Britain desperately needed good propaganda. Therefore, any gain of prestige by the enemy was undesirable. *Admiral Graf Spee* represented the honorable name of Graf von Spee and the high traditions of the German Navy: 'Thus, in this pattern we will discharge our duty'.

○ ○ ○

At 1120hrs on September 30, a Booth Line steamer sailed through calm seas off Pernambuco, Brazil. On watch, 3rd Officer H.J.Gill scanned the seas ahead. Off the port bow he saw a man-o-war and called his captain on the voice tube.

Captain C.F.P. Harris, in command of SS *Clement*(5,051BRT), went immediately to the bridge. Harris, a World War 1 merchant veteran, remained unconcerned. The fast-moving warship closed him head-on

Clement crewmembers in sea-boat. – GILBEY COLLECTION

but he accepted her as *Ajax* or another friendly cruiser. Harris ordered Gill to fly the Red Ensign then went below to tidy up, anticipating a visit from the Royal Navy.

Conversely, on board *Graf Spee* five sharp bleeps sounded *'action stations'*. Smoke sighted at 35km had revealed a British steamer. Painted gray, the freighter stood out in the cloudless midday light. Approaching quickly to four miles from the merchant, *Graf Spee* hoisted her war flags and signaled the British ship:

'STOP, DON'T USE WIRELESS'.

Captain Harris' men reacted sharply when they saw *Graf Spee's* flags. *Clement's* radio officer sent an S.O.S. and Chief Officer Jones ordered the boats swung out. Captain Harris gathered his ship's papers and dropped them over the side in specially weighted bags.

Suddenly, an airplane roared overhead. The British seamen saw black German crosses on the underside of the Arado as she swung over their ship. Next time around, the Arado's machine guns rattled and bullets pinged off the bridge and wireless room. A Brazilian ship answered *Clement's* distress call and the radio operator immediately stopped transmitting. However, three or four more times, the Arado attacked the ship. *Clement's* Chief Officer Jones was hit twice in his right arm. Captain Harris ordered 'ABANDON SHIP' and all hands took to the boats.

Graf Spee's prize-crew, in the warship's launch, scudded toward the merchant ship. They picked up Captain Harris and Chief Engineer Bryant from a sea-boat and returned them to *Clement*.

Aboard the freighter they found that Harris had complied perfectly with Admiralty instructions. Engineers had wrecked *Clement's* engines and Harris had disposed of the ships' secret papers. Captain Langsdorff could not use the ship or her cargo of paraffin.

After searching the freighter, the prize-crew brought Captain Harris and Chief Bryant to the warship. On board *Graf Spee,* the Britishers saw the name *Admiral Scheer* emblazoned on the after quarters of the warship. Also, as intended, they saw the false headbands of the crew members. Both British officers met Captain Langsdorff who apologized for taking their ship. 'It is war,' he explained. 'We must sink her.'

Captain Harris and Chief Bryant watched while *Graf Spee* sank their ship. It turned out a sloppy effort. Two torpedoes missed *Clement* completely and twenty-five rounds of six-inch shells failed to put her down. Finally, five eleven-inch shells sent her to the bottom. At 1640hrs, she reared like a great whale and slid into her ocean grave. 'What a damned hard ship,' commented Captain Harris, with a mixture of pride and sadness.

While lacking joy at his conquest, Captain Langsdorff saw much room for improvement in his first active operation. *Graf Spee's* prize-crew had taken too much time to board *Clement* and he had used excessive ammunition to sink the freighter.

As *Graf Spee* made way southward, a whiff of smoke appeared on the horizon. It revealed a Brazilian ship responding to *Clement's* distress signal. Since they were only 50 miles from land Langsdorff had also sent an S.O.S. to the wireless station at Olinda, Pernambuco:

'PLEASE SAVE LIFEBOATS OF CLEMENT 09°04'S/34°04'W.'

He signed his signal with *Admiral Scheer's* code and the station replied:

'THANKS O.K. HASTA LUEGO.'

Now Langsdorff needed to quickly get out of the area.

○ ○ ○

During the action, the Captain had noticed the Arado attacking *Clement* after she had stopped using her wireless. Lieutenant Spiering, one of Herman Göring's haughty flyers, commanded the plane. His inclination to defy naval discipline had constantly annoyed *Spee's* Executive Officer; Spiering's surly attitude undermined Commander Kay's authority.

Immediately *Clement* was sunk, Kay on Langsdorff's orders, escorted the plane's crew in front of the Captain. In the past, Langsdorff had suggested that Kay sometimes acted too harshly in his expectations of the crew. On occasion the ship's captain, in the higher interests of morale, had avoided punishing offenders that Kay had reported. The Executive Officer knew Langsdorff deplored Spiering's conduct. He wondered how Langsdorff would handle this situation. Kay hoped Spiering's fall would be long and his landing heavy.

In the Captain's cabin, the two 'culprits' stood at attention before Captain Langsdorff with their heads uncovered. Commander Kay sat in a chair to the side of Langsdorff's desk and the escort stood behind the errant officers.

Langsdorff continued working on his papers for two deliberate minutes before he looked up at the men. They stood to attention with their caps tucked under the left arm. The Captain's blue eyes shone coldly. In a soft voice he said, 'Lieutenant Spiering, you will please explain to me why you fired your weapon on a defenseless cargo vessel.'

Spiering, at attention, looked straight ahead. 'I understood we were attacking an enemy, Sir,' he replied.

Langsdorff nodded his head. 'Yes, but the ship had stopped and her wireless was silent. Did you see *Graf Spee* firing at the ship?' he asked.

'No Sir,' replied Spiering, in a firm voice.

Langsdorff pressed his point, 'Why did you think our ship was not firing at the freighter?' he asked.

'Because she was stopped and under our orders,' answered the flyer.

Langsdorff looked into Spiering's face. Strict authority steeled the Captain's voice. 'Exactly lieutenant,' he said. 'She was under My orders, like you and everyone else on board this vessel.' Langsdorff paused, waiting for an argument. Spiering kept silent. 'You were not under attack but you fired your guns on innocent civilians. You should be thankful that no one was seriously hurt,' he added.

Spiering tried to defend his position. 'With full respect Sir, in the Air Force we strike at every opportunity against all factions of the enemy.'

Langsdorff controlled his rage with difficulty. 'You are under my orders Mr. Spiering and I will conduct this campaign to my standards. You will never, ever, fire your weapon on a merchant ship unless by my specific order, or, in case of defending yourself. Do you understand?'

Spiering did not wish to dig the hole any deeper. 'Yes Sir,' he replied.

Langsdorff addressed petty officer Bongardts. 'Do you understand that I consider unarmed merchant seamen as civilians?' The Captain did not wait for a response. 'We will not attack them without just cause,' he said softly.

The rigid petty officer looked straight ahead, 'Yes Sir,' he replied quickly.

Langsdorff glanced at Commander Kay. 'Very well,' he said. 'No one was seriously injured and this is the first time I have stressed this point. So, I am prepared to dismiss disciplinary action.' Turning toward Kay, he said, 'Commander, I believe these gentlemen have learned a lesson. Please suppress any official report of this talk.'

Kay was not enthusiastic. 'Yes Sir,' he glumly replied.

Graf Spee cruised southward. At 2000hrs she sighted smoke. An alarm rang out and the warship closed quickly on the Greek freighter *Papalemos,* headed for Saint Vincent. Langsdorff arranged to transfer Captain Harris and Chief Bryant to the merchant.

The Captain shook hands with the British officers when they left *Graf Spee.* He knew they would report their adventure to Naval authorities when they landed. It would help his mission if they reported that *Admiral Scheer* had sunk *Clement.* When the Greek vessel crossed the horizon *Graf Spee* altered course eastward and rang full speed.

Captain Harris and Chief Bryant landed in Saint Vincent nine days later. They reported that the pocket battleship *Admiral Scheer* had sunk *Clement.* Both men, in the tradition of the brotherhood of the sea, remarked on the decent conduct of the German Captain.

The British Admiralty already knew about a raider in the South Atlantic. Now they learned her identity. *Admiral Scheer* [sic], a pocket battleship was prowling the shipping lanes. Still, the British were unsure if one or two raiders menaced their merchant ships. Anyway, a task force of four groups of powerful warships now searched for a voracious wolf in a vast chicken range.

CHAPTER 4

A Gentleman Raider

Dawn's first light on October 1 found *Graf Spee* in mid-Atlantic speeding southeast. A mood of elation energized the crew. At last, the gloves were off. If there must be war they would contribute their part. However, Captain Langsdorff had scathingly criticized the lackluster performance in capturing and sinking *Clement.* To his credit the Captain assumed his share of the blame as commander of the operation.

Graf Spee had left too much time between challenging the British ship and landing a prize-crew on board. Wireless transmissions from a victim imperiled *Graf Spee* and the entire mission. In future, they must close within a mile of the target to apply the full threat of their firepower. Embarkation of the prize-crew must be swift and the enemy wireless facility secured immediately.

Lieut-Commander Ascher, the gunnery officer, apologized for a dismal show in sinking *Clement.* Ascher explained that the warship's gun systems operated at maximum efficiency with *Graf Spee* and her target under way. Ascher suggested they use explosive charges to sink future prizes.

While not a factor in the *Clement* fiasco, Ascher reported difficulty refrigerating the powder magazines. Already, they had used most of their carbonic acid, an essential coolant in the tropical heat. Ascher's information meant *Graf Spee* could not operate safely within 5° latitude of the equator until she obtained additional coolant.

Despite teething problems encountered on their first strike, Captain Langsdorff complimented the dedication and enthusiasm of his men. Playing hide and seek with the Royal Navy would be a challenging, deadly game. Langsdorff, joking, compared the ship to the mythical '*Flying Dutchman*'(here, there and everywhere).

The Captain readily approved a suggestion to paint the fighting top of *Graf Spee* to camouflage its unique shape. This high pyramid could be seen and recognized from a great distance. They decided to paint the center of the tower in a light color leaving the outside edges gray. From afar this would alter the battleship's silhouette.

Bearing eastward, about latitude 22°S, *Graf Spee* ploughed through the empty blue seas. Communications from the High Command had been extensive, explicitly detailing the strength and relative positions of enemy warships. On board *Graf Spee,* wireless operators listened to transmissions between merchant ships and shore stations. With reliable information and a little luck Langsdorff looked forward to evading powerful hunters and finding soft victims in the endless ocean spaces.

At 0630hrs, October 5, *Spee* lookouts sighted smoke on the horizon. Telegraphs rang full speed and *Graf Spee* surged toward the distant ship. A shrill whistle alerted the prize-crew under the command of Lieutenant Heinrich Schünemann. Moments later, *'action stations'* resounded through the ship. Watertight doors clanged shut and *Graf Spee* raced toward the gray painted steamer in full view ahead. SS*Newton Beech* (4,650BRT), carrying a cargo of maize, was puffing from Capetown to Freetown. At Freetown she would join a convoy for Britain.

Captain Langsdorff closed *Graf Spee* to 1,800 meters then swung broadside. He broke out his battle-flags and signaled:

'HEAVE TO, DO NOT USE WIRELESS.'

With 5.9-inch guns trained on his ship and a boarding party halfway across, there was little time for the British captain to react. His Radio Officer sent an S.O.S. but the weak signal stopped immediately Schünemann and his men arrived. Captain J. Robinson, a gaunt, thin-faced Englishman, greeted the Germans with wry humor. 'You are damned early, Gentlemen.'

Newton Beech officers on board Graf Spee.
– Gilbey Collection

Quickly, efficiently, the prize-crew took control of the freighter. They wrecked a small gun mounted on the after-deck and tossed the ammunition overboard. *Newton Beech* was taken undamaged and Langsdorff decided to keep her as a temporary holdall.

Within two hours they were under way with *Newton Beech* trailing behind *Graf Spee.* Puffing clouds of black smoke, the freighter rolled along at nine knots, almost bursting her boilers. In stark contrast, the sleek warship skimmed along effortlessly, operating four of her eight diesels. The two ships made an incongruous procession.

In the merchant's wireless room the prize-crew had found instructions and codes for British ships to use in case of attack. An RRR prefix, plus details, signaled a ship under attack by surface raider. SSS or AAA followed by a message meant submarine or aircraft attack. British warships would respond with a CT prefix. Langsdorff appreciated this valuable information.

Next day, October 6, wireless from Germany relayed Hitler's speech from the Reichstag to the world. His message called for peace. He spoke with eloquence and 'heart rending sincerity':

'Germany and Britain must come to an understanding . . . Germany and France must bury their ancient enmity . . .'

The Führer benevolently proposed a conference to settle the World's problems. He invited the Allies to accept his word, his unsavory gains in Czechoslovakia and his devastation of Poland. Without embarrassment at his renowned disregard for treaties, pacts and promises the Führer advanced his proposals. He made it clear in his speech that if the Allies insisted on continuing the war it would be a fight to the finish.

The men aboard *Graf Spee* reflected on Hitler's speech. Germany had accomplished much since 1933 but the idea of a long war presented a gloomy prospect. Perhaps a significant interruption of Allied inbound shipping would help bring them to the bargaining table. Presently cruising in the temperate tropics with a comfortable swell on the blue sea, the war seemed remote.

A distant droning sound announced the Arado's return to the ship. She had made a large sweeping search and found only the empty sea. As usual her landing caused sea-spray to splash over the engine but the retrieval party easily snagged and winched her aboard.

Shortly after breakfast next day, October 7, lookouts sighted a line of smoke to the south-west. Within minutes, the optical range finder on the foretop confirmed a probable target. *Graf Spee* switched to full speed and made her customary head-on charge toward SS*Ashlea*(4,200BRT) that was under the command of Captain C.Pottinger.

Watching the warship coming fast toward him, Pottinger thought she was a French battleship, perhaps *Dunkerque* or *Strasbourg*. When she closed to less than a mile, still head-on, he still could not see which flag she flew. *Graf Spee* then swung broadside, displayed her battle ensign and signaled. 'STOP, DON'T USE WIRELESS OR WE WILL FIRE.' A sea-boat was already scudding toward *Ashlea.*

Pottinger scooped up his ship's papers but felt nervous about dumping them overboard. Even in specially weighted bags the Germans might retrieve them before they sank. Captain Pottinger preferred to burn them in the engine room furnace. He ordered his First Officer to somehow delay the German boarding party and gain him some time.

While Pottinger hurried toward the distant engine room, his men hauled up the rope ladder dangling from *Ashlea's* leeward side. Taking as much time as possible, they slowly fastened it to the windward side of the ship. This forced the prize-crew to round *Ashlea's* hull to get aboard. Nevertheless, Pottinger barely had time to throw his papers into the furnace before the Germans seized control of his ship: Split into three groups the armed men took over the bridge, engine room and the wireless station without fuss.

Lieutenant Bruno Herzberg, in command of the boarding party, had worked with the Hamburg America Line for many years and spoke perfect English. He treated Captain Pottinger with respectful courtesy and told him he must clear his ship.

Herzberg allowed Pottinger and his men time to gather some belongings. A few Lascar crew members decided to wear their suits, one on top of the other. Sweating profusely they clambered into the boat waiting to take them to *Newton Beech*(*Spee's* prize lay nearby). Captain Pottinger, speaking for his men, thanked Herzberg for his considerate treatment and expressed the wish they may meet again in better circumstances.

A symbiotic fellowship bonds all seamen no matter their nationality. *Ashlea* reflected the pride and care of her Captain. She looked spic-and-span with her officers dressed in crisp whites but sadly the Germans must sink the ship.

Graf Spee's prize-crew confiscated two tons of *Ashlea's* sugar cargo and some potatoes then placed explosive charges on the freighter. When the British ship was cleared and the prize-crew returned to *Graf Spee* a

*S.S.*Ashlea*: 4,222 BRT. Captain C. Pottinger.* – Gilbey Collection

great explosion erupted. *Ashlea* rolled over onto her side and in six minutes disappeared below the surface.

Again under way, with *Newton Beech* panting along behind the warship, Captain Langsdorff congratulated all hands for a truly successful operation. Only a report that the Arado needed a new engine spoiled a perfect day. Fortunately, they had a replacement engine on board but the landing problem persisted.

Newton Beech, although handy as a holding ship, impinged on *Graf Spee's* mobility. Captain Langsdorff decided on October 8 to sink the doughty freighter. A demolition crew removed useful materials, including a powerful Marconi radio, and implanted explosive charges throughout the ship. *Graf Spee* piquet boats brought her prize-crew and prisoners to the warship.

At 1830hrs, explosions rocked *Newton Beech* but she did not go down. Like a stubborn old dowager she hunkered lower in the water. In the gloaming dusk she sat, lit up like a Christmas tree, sinking slowly at her own leisurely pace, with dignity.

Graf Spee could not leave her to be discovered by another ship nor could the Germans risk further violent action in the darkness. Impatiently Langsdorff waited the freighter's final departure.

Hours later, a dim light showed on the horizon. *'action stations'* sounded and all hands scampered to their posts. In response to a Morse signal, the distant ship identified herself as *Pollan Laut*, a Dutch neutral bound for Padang. She continued her course unaware of *Graf Spee's* identity or the last gasp of *Newton Beech*. At 2330hrs, the freighter disappeared below the surface leaving a blinking salvage buoy as her grave marker.

Freed of the encumbrance of *Newton Beech, Graf Spee* cruised WNW at fourteen knots for a full day. On October 9, she changed her course westward and on October 10, took a bearing southeast. Prowling her beat in the empty, lonely seas belied *Graf Spee's* position in the busy Capetown-Freetown shipping lanes. Hawk-eyed lookouts and the rotating optical range finder in the foretop found nothing on the horizon.

Afternoon leaned toward evening and a wisp of smoke wafted into view. In minutes, a freighter appeared above the horizon and *Graf Spee* sprang into action. A shrill whistle sent the prize-crew into their familiar routine. Five short buzzes on the alarm signaled *'action stations'*. Steel doors slammed shut, sending muffled clangs resounding through the ship.

With sea-spray splashing over her railings, *Graf Spee* raced toward the freighter. Less than a mile separated the ships when *Graf Spee* turned broadside, lost way and sent her signal:

'STOP, DON'T USE RADIO, WE ARE SENDING A BOAT.'

Captain A.H. Brown, in command of SS*Huntsman*(8,300BRT) was taken completely by surprise. Sixty-three years old, Brown expected to retire when his ship arrived in England. Diverted from Suez, Brown had anticipated a safer route than passing through the Mediterranean.

He had sailed around the Cape, carrying tea, carpets, leather and general goods from Calcutta. Now, his ship faced a powerful battleship flying a German naval ensign and his Lascar crew ran around the deck like maniacs.

Within seven minutes Schünemann and his prize-crew boarded *Huntsman.* In the radio room a distress signal clattered out, advising all ships a surface raider had attacked *Huntsman.* Transmission stopped abruptly when the armed Germans burst into the room. Who was listening? How much time before hunters came after *Graf Spee?*

Huntsman *crewmembers in* Graf Spee *launch.* – Gilbey Collection

Langsdorff wished to keep *Huntsman* as a holdall but he knew British warships would be hot on his trail. *Graf Spee* must immediately quit this location and seek new hunting grounds. Swiftly the prize-crew assumed full control of the freighter and the ships set off toward the southwest. *Graf Spee* led the way with her crew on full alert.

Among *Huntsman's* papers, *Graf Spee's* analysts discovered secret instructions to British warships. Telegraphist Chief Petty Officer Herbert Fröhlich painstakingly broke the cipher code and later received an Iron Cross 1st Class for his effort:

> *1) DON'T SCATTER NAVAL FORCES. PROTECT MAIN MERCHANT POINTS OF CONCENTRATION.*
> *2) SEPARATE SHIPPING LANES BY 100 MILES.*
> *3) DON'T LOSE TIME SEARCHING IN OPEN WATERS IF POSITION OF ENEMY UNKNOWN. WEIGH PROBABILITY OF SUCCESS WITH DANGER OF NEGLECTING MORE IMPORTANT TASKS.*[1]

Langsdorff decided to transmit these instructions to High Command in Berlin. Radio silence fell into second place assuming the British were already aware of a raider in these waters. To confuse the British Admiralty regarding the number and type of raiders in the region he ordered his wireless operators to send a false message. They used the Marconi radio taken from *Newton Beech* and sent a Morse signal.

'SSS POSITION 7°20'S 7°57'W NEWTON BEECH TORPEDOED.'

This message reported a submarine attack at a position more than 100 miles northeast of *Graf Spee's* current position.

Graf Spee's wireless-men listened for confirmation. They heard nothing but the red herring might divert some British warships. Good luck sailed with *Graf Spee* as she led her captive away from the shipping lanes. Only the naked sun, in a cloudless sky, saw their lonely progress.

On October 11, radio news featured Mr. Chamberlain's answer to Hitler's Reichstag speech. Peace talks would not be considered until German troops left Poland. France had also delivered the same message to Germany. Although inaction persisted along the western front, expansion of the war seemed inevitable.

Next day, October 12, High Command sent a long communication to Captain Langsdorff. Intelligence highlighted the location of British capital ships. None were close enough to cause concern but Allied warships gave extra protection to the Capetown-Freetown routes.

At the daily meeting of officers, maintenance staff reported the Arado repaired and ready for service. Langsdorff ordered the plane included in a camouflage program. They could paint her with British/French roundels sufficient to fool any neutral ships that saw her on patrol.

Arado spotter plane in camouflage. – GILBEY COLLECTION

Graf Spee's crew had already added some artistic painting to the major structural upper-works of the warship. Langsdorff needed assurance that neutral merchant ships did not recognize his ship and report her position.

He advised his officers they would meet *Altmark* October 14. Meanwhile, *Huntsman* would split and regroup on October 16 with *Graf Spee* and *Altmark*. Lieutenant Schünemann, in command of *Huntsman*, received his orders and the ships parted company.

○ ○ ○

October 14, *Graf Spee* lookouts sighted smoke at 0824hrs, and soon identified *Altmark*. Wattenberg and Höpfner had again proved their expertise in navigation. As the warship closed the distance *Altmark* suddenly sent out dense clouds of smoke from her funnel and tried to move away.

Langsdorff realized that, due to her effective camouflage, Captain Dau had mistaken *Graf Spee* for an enemy warship. Quick work with searchlight signals prevented a disaster: Dau was ready to scuttle his ship.

Following a meeting between Captain Dau and Captain Langsdorff, *Graf Spee's* prisoners were transferred to *Altmark*. Langsdorff insisted that Dau treat the men well. The merchant captain complained that lack of space denied accommodations for these extra people on his ship. Nor did he have men available to guard and service prisoners. However, Langsdorff offered an officer and some *Graf Spee* sailors to tend the prisoners and Dau grudgingly agreed.

Fate had brought these men together in war. Vast differences in their physical appearance reflected the philosophical gap between the two captains.

Sixty-year-old Captain Dau, had experienced prisoner-of-war conditions in England during World War 1. Unpleasant memories continued to hatch into a consuming dislike of everything English. The big, crusty veteran believed pocket battleships should bombard coastal installations besides raiding commercial vessels. Dau grumbled that submarines were far more effective and less costly raiders than pocket battleships – a view widely shared in German military circles.

Captain Langsdorff in contrast held a great professional respect for the Royal Navy. He countered that submarines were practical but their best use, striking without warning, still attracted an aura of dishonor.

Dapper Langsdorff and rumpled Dau, though incompatible in many ways, were nevertheless dedicated to a common cause: To serve their nation faithfully.

At 1100hrs *Graf Spee* began taking fuel and continued until almost nightfall. Simultaneously, the ship's mechanics attended the diesel engines. Wear and tear caused by two months of constant running needed urgent repairs.

Besides a full-scale clean-out of the exhaust system, twelve piston-rings must be replaced. One main diesel engine had a cracked piston – an ominous sign. Chief-Engineer Klepp had brought the deterioration of the engines to Langsdorff's attention. They needed careful monitoring. Klepp temporarily disconnected three main and two auxiliary engines to enable repairs.[2]

War news from the homeland reported a great naval exploit on the front pages. Guenther Prien had taken his U-47 into Scapa Flow, sank the battleship HMS*Royal Oak* and escaped back to the open sea. Another warship, possibly HMS*Repulse*, was torpedoed in the action. Such an incredible feat that Prien had breached this impregnable naval bastion in Scotland and escaped! Some officers recalled meeting Prien when *Graf Spee* and U-47 were visiting Ceuta in the Spring. He had impressed them with his unassuming deportment.

Two days later, October 16, *Graf Spee* and *Altmark* met *Huntsman.* From early morning till late afternoon the piquet boats ploughed to and fro among the three ships.

Eighty tons of supplies from *Altmark* replenished *Graf Spee's* lockers. The prize-crew sifted *Huntsman's* cargo of tea, Indian carpets, white shoes, pith helmets etc. They transferred anything useful to the German ships. Lieutenant Diggins, Captain Langsdorff's adjutant, confiscated a few boxes of cigars. Captain Langsdorff, an inveterate pipe smoker, loved a rich cigar. In a quiet moment, a glass of good Scotch, with a cigar, always brought a glow of serenity to the Captain's face.

Huntsman was cleared in the evening of October 16 when two explosive charges sent her to the bottom. Like *Newton Beech* she went reluctantly. It was 2300hrs when she finally sank below the surface. *Graf Spee* and *Altmark,* in mid-Atlantic, then cruised southward through the night.

Captain Langsdorff now sought a new area of operations. *Graf Spee's* code specialists had broken secret codes found in *Huntsman* documents. They now deciphered much of the wireless traffic between British stations and ships at sea. Also the High Command in Berlin regularly reported movements of Allied capital ships able to out-gun and out-pace *Graf Spee*.

Renown and *Ark Royal* were in Freetown, *Strasbourg* had arrived in Dakar, and *Malaya* and *Glorious* were en route to Capetown. Four hunting groups, operating along the African and South American coasts, sought to destroy the German raider.

Berlin advised Langsdorff that a meeting was set for November 17 at 30°S/30°W with *Dresden*. The German freighter was carrying carbonic acid that Langsdorff had requested for cooling the powder magazines. Another freighter, *Emmy Friedrich*, waited Langsdorff's orders in Tampico, Mexico. She also had carbonic acid and reserve supplies of fuel oil if needed.

On October 18, *Graf Spee* split from *Altmark* and headed due east. Langsdorff hoped to find target ships in the route between Capetown and Saint Helena. In the early morning, October 22, the Arado flew off on her first patrol with a new engine. At 0930hrs, she returned, breaking through the clouds.

Lieutenant Spiering signaled he must land but seas were too high. Captain Langsdorff brought *Graf Spee* around in a huge circle. This formed a lagoon of calmer water where the Arado could land. Slowly the plane lost height and speed and landed in a cloud of sea-spray. Even in the 'duck pond' it remained impossible to bring her down without soaking the engine cowling.

Soon the plane and her crew were back on board. Spiering reported sight of a merchant ship, one-hundred-miles northwest. *Spee's* navigating officers calculated a course intended to intercept the target. At 1400hrs, a column of smoke rose on the horizon. Lookouts, using the foretop range-finder, identified a freighter painted all gray. British ships in wartime favored this color. '*Action stations*' rang out. Bulkhead doors slammed shut and the boarding party ran to their places as *Graf Spee* raced toward the freighter.

Flying a French tricolor, *Graf Spee* took station close to the merchant while running parallel. The freighter responded and gave her name,

M.V. Trevanion*: 5,350 BRT. Captain J.M. Edwards.* –Gilbey Collection

Trevanion. At this point *Graf Spee* hauled down the Tricolor, replaced it with the German battle flag and signaled, 'STOP, DON'T USE WIRELESS.'

Captain J.N. Edwards, on the bridge of MV *Trevanion* (6,321BRT), reacted with remarkable aplomb. Ignoring the guns trained on his ship, he calmly gathered his ship's papers, placed them in weighted bags and dropped them into the sea. As he marched briskly toward the wireless room he heard the harsh rattle of a machine gun.

Inside the wireless room, operator Martinson stopped using his wireless. Simultaneously, the machine-gun fire from *Graf Spee* stopped. Edwards asked Martinson if he had completed the S.O.S. Martinson glumly replied 'only half'. Grim faced, Edwards told Martinson to send the complete message while he, Edwards, stood between the operator and the warship's guns.

When the wireless crackled again, the machine gun opened up. Tracer bullets wrecked the bridge, raked the ship's deck and tore into the wireless room. Bullets knocked over furniture, sending the radio officer and his Captain to the floor but the message was completed. Immediately the wireless cut out, the machine gun stopped firing.

Minutes later, an armed boarding party seized the ship. The prize-crew gave Captain Edwards time for his men to take some clothes and personal belongings before clearing the ship.

Aboard *Graf Spee*, Captain Langsdorff asked Captain Edwards if any of *Trevanion's* men were injured. With an expression of admiration for Edward's audacity and bravery he apologized for taking the ship. 'War is war and we must sink her,' he explained.

Two explosive charges blasted holes in *Trevanion* and she settled stern-first into the water. Slowly she filled and finally sat straight up. Her bow paused high in the air and she slipped reluctantly into the deep. Most seamen feel saddened when a ship goes down. Watchers on *Graf Spee* felt a mixture of elation and sorrow as the fine ship disappeared. Langsdorff, aware that *Trevanion's* explicit wireless transmission would bring hunters, set off at top speed westward.

On October 24, *Graf Spee's* radio operators intercepted a ship-to-shore wireless message. It advised Freetown of a submarine sighting between Saint Helena and Capetown. The position reported coincided with *Graf Spee's* location. It comforted Langsdorff that the British were hunting a nonexistent submarine but proved he must vacate this area quickly.

October 28, in mid-Atlantic northwest of Capetown, *Graf Spee* met *Altmark*. In a cocky spirit of bravado they flew at the masthead flags of *Graf Spee's* victims, like totem scalps on a war spear. But no time was lost

Trophy flags flying from Graf Spee *masthead.* —Gilbey Collection

transferring their latest prisoners and taking on supplies. With hasty farewells, *Graf Spee* steered southeast at full speed on full alert. Langsdorff hoped to evade enemy warships and find new targets in the Indian Ocean.

At the end of the month, October 30, *Spee* cruised in calm blue waters under a comfortable sun. She had been further camouflaged. Large areas painted white helped break up her lines. Good news from Berlin advised total tonnage losses inflicted thus far on Allied shipping – 80,000-tons of warships and 475,000-tons of freighters. Everyone realized Germany needed more to bring the Allies to a bargaining position but the news brought encouragement.

In the afternoon Captain Langsdorff addressed the full crew gathered on the after-deck.[3] The Navy High Command had awarded one hundred Iron Cross medals to *Admiral Graf Spee* in recognition of their success to date. Langsdorff stressed that every man on board deserved a medal and those who received them must recognize that they carried this great honor for all of their comrades. [After The Battle of the River Plate, Iron Cross decorations were awarded to all officers and men.]

Langsdorff told his men that their sister ship, *Deutschland,* would return to the homeland at the beginning of November. *Gneisenau* and *Scharnhorst,* the battle cruisers, would protect her through the North Atlantic. If all went well, *Graf Spee* would return to base at the end of January. A great cheer greeted this information. Two months at sea stirred a longing for land and home.

CHAPTER 5

Friends at War

Pulsating with positive energy and anticipation, *Graf Spee* criss-crossed the shipping lanes between Australia and Capetown, South Africa. Langsdorff expected intense traffic running in these waters but nothing was sighted. Sailing through calm and turbulent seas, always alert for enemy warships, the pocket battleship passed the first week of November without incident.

Captain Langsdorff told his officers their ship carried a large part of the German war effort at sea. Only two battle cruisers and six submarines were in action in the North Atlantic. *Graf Spee* and *Altmark,* alone, operated below the equator.

To confuse the enemy, they would conceal their identity in the Indian Ocean and use *Admiral Scheer's* signals when they returned to the South Atlantic. Meanwhile, they needed a victim to register their arrival in the Indian Ocean.

Inaction on a warship can breed boredom. All hands kept busy ensuring the ship remained in top condition. Gun crews practiced until their actions became automatic. They simulated unusual breakdowns and found resolutions. Their lives and everyone on board might depend on their efficiency. It seemed unlikely they would return to the Fatherland without firing their guns in anger.

British wireless news reported German losses of thirteen freighters captured and sunk. The reported list included *Emmy Friedrich,* sunk in the Caribbean. *Emmy Friedrich* had carried a shipment of carbonic acid needed to cool *Graf Spee's* ammunition magazines.

On November 8, the Arado made a short patrol. Blue skies, sun and an empty sea welcomed the airplane. Only a lone whale, sending spray flying into the air, broke the blank void to the horizon. Landing problems continued to plague the Arado's engine. Every flight presented a challenge.

Graf Spee now left the barren shipping lanes and searched for victims off the coast of Portuguese East Africa. Old salts smelled floral perfumes on the warm breezes. Some claimed they had seen parakeets landing in the rigging. Langsdorff hoped to find a target in this area but the main purpose was to show the flag.

On November 13, Captain Langsdorff called a meeting of all hands on the after-deck. He explained that they must find action in the Indian Ocean to help divert attention from *Deutschland.* Their sister ship, on the last stage of her homeward journey, had almost reached the Norwegian coastline.

Langsdorff congratulated the crew on their effort to date. Again, he stressed the iron cross awards and their distribution. Everyone awarded must realize they wore them as representatives of the entire crew. It was important they regarded themselves as members of a close-knit team. A spontaneous round of applause assured the Captain. These young men were together in their call to duty and total commitment to their Captain.

Through the night, a fierce storm came down on the ship. Shrieking winds whistled through the rigging and doused the decks with rushing water and foam. All day long heavy seas crashed over the rails. A distant landfall let the navigators certify their measurements, and verified their incredible accuracy.

At 2300hrs next day, they sighted a light and *Graf Spee* moved closer to investigate. The ship did not respond to a Morse signal. *Graf Spee* lit the wayward vessel with bright searchlights and she immediately identified herself as *Holland*(895BRT), running between Beira and Laurenco Marques. A merchant officer on *Spee's* staff recognized the Dutch coaster and she went on unmolested.

November 15, about 300 miles northeast of Durban, *Graf Spee* cruised off Mozambique. At 1115hrs a ship appeared through the mist, close to the coast. *Graf Spee's* well-rehearsed crew sprang into action. Setting a course to cut off the freighter from the neutral limit, the warship ploughed toward her target. It looked like a large tanker.

Captain Patrick Dove, on the bridge of MV*Africa* Shell(706BRT), saw the warship racing toward his ship. Dove could not identify her flag. Acting on a strong hunch, he decided to play safe and head for the coast. Better to beach his new tanker in soft sand than lose her to an enemy. Anyway, if he could enter the Portuguese three-mile limit, he could claim immunity from attack. Dove rang for full speed and *Africa Shell* churned out ten knots – her best effort.

M.V. Africa Shell: *706 BRT. Captain P. Dove.* – GILBEY COLLECTION

Captain Langsdorff saw the tanker striving to reach the neutral zone. She appeared much smaller than at first sight but would serve his purpose. *Africa Shell* ran unreadable flag messages up and down her poles but continued at full speed toward the coast.

Langsdorff ordered a warning shot fired. An 11-inch shell boomed from the forward turret and sent a great column of water into the air, astern of the fleeing tanker. Immediately, she lost way and a pennant signaled the warship to 'CLOSE UP'. *Graf Spee* swung broadside, showing her battle-flags.

When he saw the German ensign, Dove took defensive action. As the tanker lost way, he ordered his Second Officer to take a bearing from Cape Zavora and Quessico Point lighthouses. It appeared they were inside the three-mile limit. Dove quickly rechecked the measurements and confirmed his officer's calculations. While the warship's launch sped toward his ship, Dove ran to his cabin and tore open the safe. Grabbing the ship's confidential papers, in weighted bags, he rushed outside and tossed everything into the sea. *Graf Spee's* launch, carrying two officers and twelve men, came alongside and in moments the prize-crew seized the tanker.

Lieutenant Herzberg saluted Captain Dove and apologized for taking his ship. Dove complained that the ship was in neutral waters.

'Sorry,' replied Herzberg. 'We believe differently and we must sink her.' The German told Dove to gather some belongings. He could leave with his men or come with Herzberg to the warship. Dove continued to press home his argument and showed Herzberg his charts.

On board *Graf Spee,* Langsdorff signaled to the prize-crew that another ship was sighted. They must complete the demolition of *Africa Shell* at once and return to the ship. The Captain ordered Herzberg to bring Captain Dove to *Graf Spee* and set explosive charges to sink the tanker.

Two explosions rocked *Africa Shell* but she did not sink completely. Langsdorff saw water pouring out of the tanker and realized she was empty and in ballast. *Graf Spee* did not have time to finish her off nor wait out her end. He needed to check out the ship they had sighted on the horizon. Two lighthouses, which they could see from the ship, would report the capture of *Africa Shell* to the British Admiralty. *Graf Spee's* action in the area would draw attention.

When Lieutenant Herzberg and his men clambered aboard *Graf Spee,* a sentry escorted Captain Dove to Commander Kay's cabin. Full speed rang out and the ship ploughed through the rolling seas toward the shadowy shape of the distant freighter.

Captain Patrick Dove's world had altered swiftly. An hour earlier he stood on the bridge of a new ship happily looking forward to sailing these coastal waters for many months. Now, dressed in a white shirt, shorts and knee length stockings the Englishman stood in a large cabin of a German warship. Dove was a big, heavy man who carried his authority with dignity. Another officer, even taller than Dove, though less meaty, greeted the Englishman.

Commander Walter Kay spoke English and invited Dove to sit. Kay, an imposing figure with a jet black beard and mustache, made small talk while a steward served drinks. The German Executive Officer was friendly and promised to supply Dove with warmer clothes when they reached southern latitudes.

As they chatted, a telephone rang on Kay's desk. Following a brief conversation in German, Kay put Dove in care of the master-at-arms and left the room. While Commander Kay hurried to his action post an armed guard escorted Captain Dove to a small cabin in the rear of the warship. The master-at-arms said he would return soon, locked the door and left an armed sentry on guard.

Dove surveyed his tiny room. Lit with a dull blue light, it had two portholes fastened with watertight steel covers and a locked steel door. Vibrations from the racing propellers directly below the cabin shook the ship. *Graf Spee* was at action stations. Captain Patrick Dove wondered what his fate held in store.

Graf Spee closed the distance rapidly. Lookouts soon identified the ship as *Tihuku Maru*, a Japanese freighter. *Graf Spee* came close enough to see her name, signaled *'bon voyage'* and turned east-north-east toward Madagascar. Aware that curious eyes were watching from the coast, Langsdorff maintained this course until they lost sight of land, then he abruptly swung southward.

Within an hour the master-at-arms returned to Dove with a young artillery officer. Dove learned that the emergency was over and he would occupy this officer's cabin. While the young officer removed his gear, the Germans chatted with Dove in stilted English. The English captain was pleasantly surprised to find them friendly.

Around 1700hrs, a steward served a basic meal. Later, in company with the sentry, Captain Dove mingled with some officers taking leisure on the afterdeck. Lieutenant Diggins, Langsdorff's adjutant, found him there and with a smart salute and the Captain's compliments invited him to meet Captain Langsdorff immediately.

Two sentries, one on each side of the door, guarded the Captain's cabin. Feet placed apart, arms folded with a dagger pointing to the ceiling in the right hand, they made a formidable impression. Diggins knocked, opened the door and announced the English Captain. Dove entered the large cabin.

Captain Langsdorff stood at his desk facing the door. Dove's practiced eye recorded the service medals, including the Iron Cross, attached to Langsdorff's white tunic. The English captain saluted the German Commandant and Langsdorff came forward with a pleasant smile.

'Good evening, Captain Dove,' he said. 'I'm sorry to have to sink your ship. But, it is war. First there is a little business we must settle, then you and I will have a drink.'

Dove was surprised that Langsdorff had spoken near-perfect English and his demeanor seemed friendly. A smaller man than Dove, Langsdorff had fair hair including a moustache and a tiny spade-type beard. The German captain effused confidence and elegance. He showed Captain Dove to a large chart table where Dove's chart, taken from *Africa Shell*, lay spread out.

'My boarding officer reported that you made a protest about my seizure of your ship,' he opened. 'You say you were in territorial waters. If you were, that is going to be difficult for me.'

'Not half so difficult as it is for me already,' Dove retorted. 'I have lost my ship and everything else. And, I'm convinced that I was in Portuguese territorial waters. I was watching my position carefully the whole time you were chasing me. I took bearings, and there is not the slightest doubt in my mind that I was well inside the limit. Nothing will alter that opinion.'

Langsdorff smiled apologetically. 'I'm afraid, Captain, your calculations and mine do not agree. I have not only taken bearings, as you have done, but with range-finders which measure almost to inches. And I have taken soundings inshore from your vessel recording a depth of twenty-five meters. That depth on this coast shows that I could not be within the three-mile limit.'

'I don't think your soundings mean anything,' argued Dove. 'I know this coast like the back of my hand. I was at least half a mile inside territorial waters.' Both Captains pored over the chart discussing the issue.

Finally Langsdorff turned to Dove. 'It is plain that we cannot agree over this,' he said. 'So we will compromise. I have sunk your ship, but you can make a protest and I will sign it. I will give you a copy to keep and then you will have a record of your protest. I will ask you six questions and you will answer them in your own words. I will give you paper and pencil and you can take plenty of time.'

'That depends on what the questions are,' protested Dove. 'But if they are not of naval importance, I shall be quite willing to answer them.'

'You have no need to worry about that.' said Langsdorff. 'Come, sit and have a drink. What will you have?'

Dove noticed a bottle of Scotch whisky on a table nearby. 'I'll have Scotch, sir,' he replied.

'Good,' said Langsdorff. 'I enjoy good Scotch and a fine cigar.'

Soon the two captains were chatting comfortably, mainly about the sea. Dove had sailed in sailing ships and his animated chatter showed clearly his love of ships and the mariner's life. This was a common bond and Langsdorff said it saddened him to sink ships, but he was obliged to do his duty.

They talked about the war. Dove agreed with Langsdorff that women and children of the warring nations would suffer most. Langsdorff expressed his admiration for 'civilian sailors'.

'Merchant ships, manned by men without adequate war training, are attacked first. While the western front is dormant many merchant ships have gone to the bottom. Unfortunately, but necessarily, we will take more before returning to Germany.'

Captain Dove was astounded how much information the German captain had regarding the position of the hunters looking for *Graf Spee.* He also knew that the British were not exactly sure of his identity. He planned to take *Graf Spee* on a wide pass of the Cape of Good Hope to avoid searchers.

The tropical clothes Dove wore were inadequate for the journey into the 'roaring forties'. Langsdorff promised to have the ship's tailor modify an officer's uniform to fit Dove. He also told Dove to list any essentials he needed. The ship's canteen stocked most items.

Dove asked what would happen to him. Langsdorff explained that when they returned to Germany, Captain Dove and other officers would probably be exchanged, through the Red Cross, for German captains held by the Allies. Dove remarked that the Royal Navy might prevent *Graf Spee* from returning to Germany. Langsdorff agreed it was possible but first they had to find him. Then, only three British warships, *Repulse, Renown* and *Hood* were fast enough and powerful enough to force him to action. Some bravado had crept into the German's tone. Dove responded that the situation may be true, but only on paper.

Time passed comfortably in pleasant conversation. Eventually Langsdorff called for Dove's guard to return the English captain to his cabin. There he found a selection of English books taken from captured ships. This showed another thoughtful gesture.

Captain Dove copied the British Seafarers Society serial numbers, stamped in each book, onto the reverse side of a photograph. Perhaps, if he were rescued, the information might help trace the fate of the previous owners.

Next morning, November 16, about 0800hrs, a steward knocked on

Dove's door and brought breakfast. It consisted of four slices of bread, margarine and a mug of coffee. It was skimpy for Captain Dove but the same ration as *Graf Spee's* officers.

After breakfast the sentry asked Dove if he would like to go on deck. The British captain gladly accepted but *Graf Spee* was taking weather in rough seas and he felt cold in his tropical uniform.

Later in the morning, his escort took him to the tailor shop. Captain Dove was a big man. At 230 solid pounds, nothing off the rack came close. So, the ship's tailor removed the braid and naval buttons from a petty officer's uniform. Then he added some material and fastened civilian buttons to the jacket. With the suit came a shirt and underwear. Dove felt warm and respectable in his ersatz suit.

In the afternoon, the master-at-arms, Albert Jerichow, escorted Dove to the prize-officer's cabin. Lieutenant Herzberg sat behind his desk awaiting their arrival. He rose to greet Captain Dove and invited him to sit. Jerichow sat in a chair beside Dove and a sentry posted himself outside the closed door.

Dove saw the recovered papers from *Africa Shell* spread out on Herzberg's desk. The ship's articles, register, certificates of class and a plan of the ship lay on the desk. Herzberg, sitting behind his desk, addressed Dove.

'Captain, I have invited you here to write down the protest you made verbally yesterday.'

Dove complimented the German officer on his perfect English. 'I'm amazed that you speak English without an accent.'

'Ah, but I'm a merchant officer like yourself,' Herzberg replied. 'I have visited English ports for many years. You see, until the war broke out, I was Chief Officer of a Hamburg-America Atlantic liner. Strangely enough, we have another former merchant captain aboard this ship who actually knows you. He's a friend of yours, or was in the peace days.'

'Who on earth can that be?' blurted Dove.

Herzberg smiled. Captain Heinrich Schünemann of the coasting steamer, *Refugix,'* he replied, 'sailing on the same trade route as yourself, Captain.'

'How on earth did Captain Schünemann get on board this warship?' asked Dove.

'In the same way as I did, Captain. We were home on leave when

England declared war on us. As officers of the reserve, we were called up immediately.'

Captain Dove had heard the phrase 'when England declared war on us' from other German officers. Like a litany the phrase rang out when talk of the war arose. Now Herzberg produced a receipt for *Africa Shell's* documents and asked Dove to write his protest on the document. Captain Langsdorff would countersign it later.

When the business was done, Schünemann came into the cabin. Friendly greetings quickly developed into tale swapping from the old days. Merchant seamen together, experienced in the same East African coastal waters, they exchanged yarns. Soon the cabin was ringing with laughter and drama as they recalled old stories. Jerichow, caught up in the moment, laughed with the merchant officers, although he did not understand much of the conversation.

Eventually, the master-at-arms looked at his watch and told Dove he must return to his cabin. The officers shook hands, said goodnight and Jerichow took Dove to his cabin. It was late afternoon and Dove dropped into a deep sleep.

Shrill alarm bells ringing a five-stroke alert jolted him out of his nap. Orders crackled from the loudspeaker system as men clattered to their action stations.

Jerichow poked his head into Dove's cabin, and called. 'The alarm has gone. You will be locked in but you will be all right. Now I go to my station.'

He then locked the steel door and rushed to his post. Dove felt as though trapped in a bank vault. The small steel cabin vibrated as *Graf Spee's* propellers picked up speed. What lay before him now?

On *Spee's* bridge, Langsdorff focused his binoculars on the distant ship. As she drew closer her Dutch colors became evident. *Mapia,* running from Amsterdam to Medan, Sumatra responded to *Graf Spee's* signals. A prize-crew officer recognized the ship and verified her data. Following formalities, she continued her voyage. *Graf Spee* coasted north until *Mapia* disappeared over the horizon then resumed full speed southward toward the 'roaring forties'.

Jerichow soon returned and unlocked Dove's cabin. In answer to Dove's question he gave details of the brief encounter with *Mapia.* When asked why *Graf Spee* had not transferred him to the neutral vessel

Jerichow said they would soon meet their supply ship and Dove would join other British officers.

○ ○ ○

Several long days passed. The seas heaved and sank in mountainous waves. Gale force winds sent green, foam-lashed water crashing over *Graf Spee* and drew shrill shrieks from the rigging. The 'roaring forties' proved true to form and hammered the ship relentlessly. Dove had relative freedom to leave his cabin at will. When he went on deck the sentry stayed behind him but kept a discrete distance. On occasion, when weather allowed, Captain Langsdorff joined Dove for a walk.

On one such occasion, Langsdorff, smoking a cigar, asked Dove if he smoked. Dove affirmed and mentioned he had lost his pipe and fixings when his ship was taken. Langsdorff offered him a cigar.

As they walked, Langsdorff asked if there was anything Dove needed. The Englishman thanked him for his suit but apologized for not having money to pay for it. Langsdorff smiled and said Mr. Churchill would pay, his country could afford it. Dove remarked that the lean pickings in these trade routes would not cover the bill. Langsdorff admitted he could not understand why ships were not sailing in the Australia to South Africa routes. [Later the Germans discovered that a late wool clipping season had held ships waiting for cargo.]

Next day, to Dove's surprise, Lieutenant Diggins brought a package to his cabin with the compliments of the Captain. Dove unwrapped the

Captain Langsdorff sunning on the after-deck with his "prisoner" Captain Dove.

– Diego M. Lascano

parcel and found a straight stemmed briar, four ounces of tobacco, matches and two pipe cleaners.

To keep him busy, copies of English newscasts from New York and Rugby arrived each day for Dove to read. Captain Langsdorff often highlighted in pencil naval news of interest. Several times Langsdorff invited Dove to his cabin for a chat. Sometimes they would relax outside, taking advantage of the tropical sun.

As they became more friendly the two Captains found they had much in common. Both were extremely patriotic regarding their national interests. Occassionally, their discussions touched on subjects where it was impossible to agree:

Langsdorff defended the Nazi regime because it united the German nation in common cause. Previous attempts to govern the German republic had failed. Germany had lost World War 1 and her prestigious place in the World community. German self-esteem throughout the nation had diminished. A Republican system, forced into place by foreign powers, could never satisfy ancient feudal instincts, especially in conditions of worldwide depression.

Dove wondered how a system which disallowed criticism of any kind could last. The Nazi state demanded unconditional authority and destroyed all opposition. Even pastors, like Niemoller, were thrown in prison if they dared to condemn the system.

Langsdorff, aware of Niemoller's heroic war record as a submariner in World War 1, believed the jailed pastor held it in his power to be free. Niemoller insisted on mixing religious instruction with affairs of the state. If he stopped criticizing the regime from the pulpit he would not be in trouble. Hitler had promised, when he took power, that religious freedom would continue parallel to the state.

Dove remarked that Hitler's promises were fragile. To make his point he mentioned the German-Soviet Non-Aggression Pact, a mutual assistance package between two sworn enemies.

Langsdorff took a long time to respond. He believed this Pact was only a means to guarantee supplies of strategic materials. Germany's national need overplayed the animosities of the past.

Dove could not resist finessing that Hitler's word was therefore not sacrosanct. The Führer would seize any opportunity to advance his cause despite accepted codes of honor or morality.

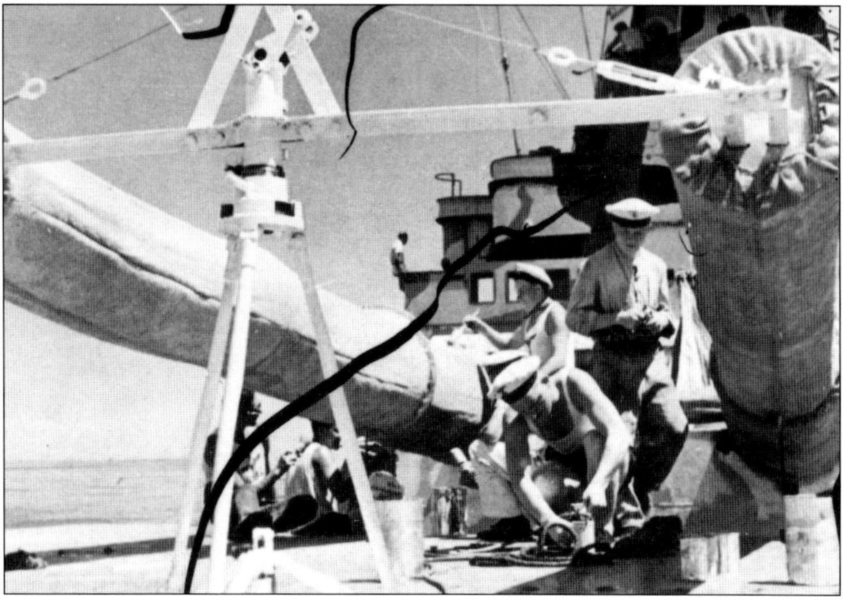

Crewmen affix false turret to Graf Spee. – Gilbey Collection

The German quickly changed the subject and Dove sensed he had touched a raw nerve in the Captain's personal philosophy.

Langsdorff switched the topic of discussion to magnetic mines that had scored multiple successes in the North Sea. He believed their effect would shorten the war. Many years of German research had developed this deadly weapon and there seemed little chance of an easily found antidote. They themselves had not found an effective counter measure.

Dove could only remind him of the British saying – 'nothing is impossible, it just takes a little longer'.

On November 22 *Graf Spee* completed her sweep past Capetown and turned northwesterly into the Atlantic. Great news came from the Homeland: *Spee's* sister ship *Deutschland* had arrived safely in Gdynia. *Deutschlands's* supply ship, *Westerwald,* also anticipated returning home soon.

Nostalgia for home enveloped the crew of *Graf Spee.* They had reached the last stretch of their tour but many miles of dangerous ocean still lay ahead.

At the officer's meeting next afternoon, Captain Langsdorff produced his copy of *Jane's Fighting Ships*. This internationally accepted 'bible' described the warships of all nations in service before the war began. Langsdorff pointed out the British battle cruiser *HMS Repulse*. The British warship had twin funnels and two gun turrets forward. She was three times the size of *Graf Spee* but her silhouette was quite similar. If they could build a false funnel and gun turret it would be an excellent disguise.

Captain Langsdorff chats with crewmen.
– Diego M. Lascano

Spee's officers caught onto the idea with enthusiasm. Steps to make the change began immediately. Wood and canvas resembling gun barrels to match the forward turret were nailed and tied into place. Everyone on the ship found entertainment and interest in the task.

A spirit of renewal enlivened the ship and on November 24 Captain Langsdorff broached a subject that had simmered among some of his officers. Until now, the operation had run strictly according to orders. Hit and run had proved successful but some officers felt the need to prove the ship's fighting capacity.

Langsdorff told the gathered officers at the daily meeting that their mission was almost completed. *Graf Spee* needed a major overhaul. If an opportunity arose to add significantly to their raider success, they would engage a protecting warship. This change in tactics uplifted many young officers and they addressed their daily chores with new vigor.

November 26, in a cloudless beautiful morning, *Graf Spee* met *Altmark*. Work began immediately to overhaul the engines and take on fuel. Constant running had developed serious flaws in the prototype diesels. Twelve pistons needed ring replacement for the second time. Some pistons were out of round. Fifteen cracks in the supports of the auxiliary engines could not be repaired at sea: *Graf Spee* urgently needed dock repairs.[1]

All day long and far into the night the men drew provisions from the supply ship. At the end of the day's activities, when the ships were

Time out for Altmark *and* Graf Spee. – Gilbey Collection

quiet and lit by a tropical moon, a small chorus sang traditional shanties. Visitors from *Altmark* joined the *Graf Spee* crew. Captain Dove and the German seamen, thousands of lonely miles from wife and home, joined in song with the choir.

Captain Langsdorff, smoking a cigar, listened to the music wafting in the tropical night. On his desk lay the Captain's daily war diary and a small glass of scotch whisky. Langsdorff sipped from his glass and quickly scanned the entries. He read a segment that outlined his plans for the continuation of the cruise. Divided into two sections, the entry was headed:

> *Operating order and supplementary instructions for the conduct of war at sea.*
> *1. Graf Spee should for as long as possible persevere in damaging or at least harassing enemy trade, so that as many fighting forces as possible have to be employed for the protection of commerce . . .* [2]

Langsdorff's eyes fell rapidly to the last paragraph:

> *5. The condition of the engines makes a dockyard overhaul necessary. Already on 23.X. this was proposed for January 1940. Moreover, the duration of the trade war is approaching its end. Thus, it is not*

necessary to consider to the same extent as before the possibility of action with a warship.

If Graf Spee closes the range, it can be reckoned that the heavy artillery of the armored ship can at the very least so damage any adversary, with the exception of the Renown, that it would no longer count as a shadower, that on the other hand the hits to be expected could not materially prejudice the intended homeward-bound voyage.

Against this, there remains the impossibility in the bright moonlight nights of the South Atlantic to attain any decisive successful action or shake off a rapid shadower.

Captain Langsdorff read the entry again, slowly. This was a divergence from his successful tactics thus far. If an opportunity arose to add significantly to their objective, he would engage a warship. Instead of taking a defensive role he would aggressively attack a faster warship. This change of tactics may alarm some of his senior officers but most of them hoped for an opportunity to prove their mettle in action.

Captain Langsdorff in informal mode. – Diego M. Lascano

Next day, Dove took his daily walk. The work on the dummy guns and funnel drew his attention. Captain Langsdorff met Dove and took him on an informal inspection. He explained the need to remain *incognito* in the shipping lanes. Most neutrals would alert the British Admiralty if they identified *Graf Spee*.

Langsdorff told Dove that some fellow British officers would join him in the morning. Makeshift accommodations were ready to receive them from *Altmark*. Langsdorff advised Dove he must move out of his cabin and accompany the others but he hoped they would be reasonably comfortable.

Naval news of the day, November 27, reported that Captain Prien with his famous U-47 had sunk a British cruiser. Other news from Britain mourned the loss of *Rawalpindi*. The news item reported that the 17,000-ton British auxiliary had valiantly fought a one-sided battle against *Deutschland* in the North Atlantic.

Captain Langsdorff told Dove that the armed auxiliary was downed by vastly superior firepower. *Rawalpindi* had been sunk under tragic circumstances. Langsdorff considered it an execution rather than a battle. Reports did not state how many survivors, if any, had escaped death – a truly sad affair.

Langsdorff did not tell Dove that *Deutschland* had already returned home. The German captain knew that *Scharnhorst* and *Gneisenau*, a fearsome team, prowled the North Atlantic.

Dove moved early next morning into a midshipman's flat fitted with extra bunks and a couple of tables. Dove saw his name marked in chalk in a corner of the flat. This was his new home.

Later in the morning, Dove stood on deck when the launches brought the British officers from *Altmark.* A full load of luggage filled the first boat. Trunks and sundry suitcases bore labels tagged with every world port imaginable. In the second launch a collection of captains, chief officers, second officers, radio officers, and engineers crowded together. As they came aboard, Dove moved forward to greet them but was swiftly diverted by the sentry and taken to the prisoner's flat.

As the new arrivals trooped into the flat they ignored Captain Dove. Wearing his tropical whites, Dove appeared to them as a *Graf Spee* officer. When he greeted them in his rich English accent, they bustled around him asking questions. It quickly became a question and answer contest as they exchanged their experiences.

On November 29, *Gráf Spee* left *Altmark* to resume her tour. The warship was dressed in gray British colors and sporting her false superstructure. High Command had advised that a campaign to avenge *Rawalpindi* had concentrated British warships in the North Atlantic. Langsdorff decided to prowl the sea routes south of Saint Helena before heading across the Atlantic on his way home.

Chapter 6

Heading Home

The British Admiralty responded typically to the loss of *Rawalpindi.* Winston Churchill vowed Britain would wash the North Atlantic clean of German pillagers. Every available warship was assigned to the task.

Meanwhile, Berlin High Command had given Captain Langsdorff a detailed disposition of Allied warships operating in the South Atlantic. *Exeter* and *Cumberland* stood in the Falklands. *Achilles* patrolled near Rio de Janeiro and *Ajax* steamed en route to the River Plate from the Falklands. *Neptune* and four destroyers backed by the submarine *Clyde* guarded the narrows between Brazil and Freetown. *Renown, Ark Royal, Provence, Bretagne, Hermes, Dupleix, Albatross* and *Foch,* with several destroyers and submarines operated from Dakar and Freetown. *Shropshire* and *Sussex* protected the Cape of Good Hope. In all, these ships comprised an enormous defense to counter a lone pocket battleship.

December 1, *Graf Spee* cruised toward the lucrative Capetown to Freetown shipping lanes. The sea-war in the South Atlantic had relapsed into tense calm. Since October 10, when *Huntsman* was captured, nothing had stirred. Captain Langsdorff had drawn attention into the Indian Ocean. Now he wished to attract interest again in the South Atlantic.

Langsdorff envisioned a strike off Africa followed by a speedy flight across the Atlantic to molest the River Plate traffic. Then he would take his ship and his men home. Weather conditions in December, when a full moon lit the night like a stage, prevented an easy crossing of the narrows. In January, with the light of a new moon, Langsdorff hoped to bring his ship and his men back to home base and honorable acclaim. If all went well, he expected a return to Germany at the end of January.

At dawn, December 2, the Arado sprang from her catapult and flew off, looking for a target. She soon returned with nothing to report. At midday Langsdorff sent her out again. She had barely lost sight of the ship when lookouts, at the foretop range-finder, caught signs of smoke.

Thirty sea-miles separated the smoke from *Graf Spee* but she changed course to intercept the distant ship. As *Graf Spee* sped toward the sighting the smoke trail vanished. Perhaps it was a mirage, a phenomenon familiar to all deep sea sailors. But the range-finder again located smoke. Twenty-three sea-miles away, a red-funneled merchant ship steamed a parallel course to *Spee*. Probably a neutral but it must be checked.

As *Graf Spee* closed, the merchant increased speed to escape over the horizon. '*Action stations*' rang out and *Graf Spee* jumped to full speed. While still at long range, Captain Langsdorff ordered a warning shot fired over the freighter and flashed 'STOP' with a searchlight. Now under attack, the merchant sent an S.O.S. on her radio. Langsdorff flashed 'NO WIRELESS' and ordered another heavy shell placed near the escaping ship. A huge spume of water rose into the air, close to the speeding vessel. Her wireless signal stopped, for a moment, then resumed her frantic S.O.S. Another 11-inch shell landed close. *Graf Spee's* wireless operators tried to block the signal using the Marconi radio taken from *Newton Beech*. It proved too weak to stop the telltale Morse. All ships in a vast area now knew a German warship had gunned a British merchant at 19°15'S/5°5'E.

Graf Spee's prize-crew raced toward the ship and at 1431hrs seized control of *Doric Star*(10,100BRT). Captain William Stubbs, in command, had obeyed Admiralty orders perfectly. The liner's engines were wrecked and all secret papers thrown into the sea. Some crewmen had already left the ship in sea-boats but Herzberg's men headed them off and herded them back to their ship.

On board *Doric Star*, the prize-crew with practiced ease searched their prize. The liner, routed from Australia and New Zealand to Britain was packed to the gunnels with wool, minerals, grain and frozen meat. Herzberg allowed the crew, mostly Lascars, to pick up personal belongings before taking them to *Graf Spee*. This surprised the merchant's crew. They had feared annihilation instead of the mild treatment they were receiving. Lieutenant Herzberg told them to take a blanket and eating utensils to the warship. Sixty-four additional prisoners would stretch *Spee's* 'guest' accommodations beyond the limit. *Doric Star's* display of courage against the awesome shell-bursts of the warship, drew congratulatory comment from Langsdorff and his men.

*S.S.*Doric Star*: 10,093 BRT. Captain W. Stubbs.*

– Gilbey Collection

Knowing that the hunters already knew his position, Langsdorff broke radio silence and signaled Berlin. He advised the High Command his intention to continue the raider campaign on his homebound voyage.

While Herzberg and his men worked on *Doric Star* an S.O.S. came to *Graf Spee* from the Arado. The plane had force landed in the open sea. Using her emergency transmitter she had signaled her position. Captain Langsdorff immediately flashed a signal to Herzberg. 'URGENT, FINISH WITH LINER. RETURN TO SHIP.'

However, Herzberg had found *Doric Star's* cargo holds smothered with sand bags and needed time to access the cargo. Herzberg had also found nineteen large ingots of silver bullion hidden behind a false wall in the captain's cabin. The prize-officer wanted these dug out and taken to *Graf Spee.* While Captain Langsdorff puffed angrily on his cigar, Herzberg calmly stretched time with the evacuation process until the silver ingots ended in *Graf Spee's* launch.

When the liner was cleared and demolition charges failed to sink her, Langsdorff used the main guns. Seven eleven-inch shells and a torpedo hammered into *Doric Star* and sent her to the bottom. At 1635hrs, while the liner slid under the surface, *Graf Spee* at full speed began a search for the warship's missing air crew. Every man on the ship knew of the drama unfolding. Somewhere in that great ocean two men clung to a tiny waterlogged plane. The Arado had sent her S.O.S. at 1445hrs. Now, in late afternoon, the crew's fate depended on their discovery before darkness.

At 1715hrs, a bright flare appeared ahead of *Graf Spee.* Lookouts spotted a tiny dot bobbing in the waves. The Arado lay low in the water with her port float submerged and waves washing over the wing. Spiering and Bongardts, standing in the cockpit, waved happily at the approaching ship. The light began to fade and at 1858hrs they climbed aboard *Spee,* groggy but in good fettle.

In debriefing, the aircrew reported sighting a ship before they ditched the plane. Spiering estimated the ship's speed and gave its course. Handlers quickly winched the Arado aboard and *Graf Spee* changed course to intercept the new target. Spiering then told his story.

Due to a battery failure they missed *Graf Spee's* signal when she changed course to catch *Doric Star*. When the Arado returned from her patrol, Spiering scanned a twenty-mile radius trying to find the warship. Forced to land when fuel ran low, the Arado found trouble in a moderate sea; the port float caught a wave that ruptured the pontoon. Soon the punctured float filled with water and dragged the Arado onto its side. The crew used their emergency rations, including a snort of cognac and made light of their ordeal. A curious shark swimming around the slowly sinking wreck gave them added concern. *Graf Spee,* appearing from the semi-darkness was a welcome gift from Providence.

Captain Langsdorff, while content the aircrew was saved, now posed some strong questions to Lieutenant Herzberg. Why such delay in evacuating *Doric Star*? The prize-officer lamely argued that he recognized his duty to account for all merchant crew members. This time, it took a little longer than usual. Herzberg insisted that the silver bars were incidental to the general evacuation of the ship.

As he presented his case, Herzberg knew Langsdorff was not accepting his argument. The Captain listened to Herzberg's tale with a grim half-smile. Finally, he reminded the prize-officer in a stony voice that a boatload of silver could not replace a single life. Fortunately for all concerned, in this instance, providence had served them well.

While *Graf Spee* sped through the night her wireless operators

*S.S.*Tairoa: *7,983 BRT. Captain W. B. Starr.* – Gilbey Collection

intercepted transmissions beamed to British ships. Two land stations in South Africa were relaying *Doric Star's* distress signal. Also, in the early hours of morning another intercepted signal showed the British had picked up the transmissions between *Graf Spee* and the Arado. Langsdorff must clear this area without delay.

○ ○ ○

At 0430hrs on December 3, Captain W.B.Starr stood on the bridge of the freighter SS*Tairoa*(7,983BRT). Starr was en route from Melbourne to Freetown to join a convoy to Britain. The 63-year-old Captain had heard *Doric Star's* signal and changed course westward to avoid contact with her attacker. A veteran of World War 1, Starr had hoped to miss further action. It was not to be. A fast-moving warship came out of the colorful dawn and bore down on his ship. She looked like a large battle-cruiser with twin turrets forward and two funnels. Starr could not read her pennants but thought she was French.

Captain Langsdorff watched the freighter come closer. At ten hectometers *Graf Spee* turned broadside to the merchant, hoisted her war flag and signaled 'STOP. DON'T USE RADIO OR WE WILL FIRE.' Although *Spee's* guns menaced the slowing ship her wireless immediately crackled through the airwaves. In response, as the prize-crew raced toward her, gunfire from *Graf Spee* raked the bridge and deck of the stopped ship.

Tairoa's wireless stopped for a few moments and then resumed transmitting. Instantly, *Graf Spee's* machine guns again opened up. Like an operatic duet the wireless crackled its telltale message and the machine guns rattled in response. When the wireless stopped, the guns stopped. Langsdorff was using 37mm guns, the smallest caliber on his ship.

Finally, *Tairoa's* superstructure was wrecked but sand bags piled around the wireless room protected the operator. Lying on the floor, P.J. Cummins continued sending the S.O.S. until his wireless was smashed into silence. Still, Cummins managed to get the message abroad, RRR 21°38'S/3°13'W Scheer [sic].

Langsdorff had no time to lose. *Graf Spee's* 37mm gunfire had immobilized *Tairoa's* steering gear. The ship was inoperable and must be sunk. Herzberg quickly cleared her and transferred eighty-four crew members, mostly Lascars, to *Graf Spee*. In the cargo holds, twenty-five hundred cases of frozen turkeys lay stowed beneath a cargo of frozen meat and wool. Mountains of sandbags covered the holds making them difficult to access. Christmas fare for the coming season was unattainable but a welcome gift came to *Graf Spee* from *Tairoa's* refrigeration equipment: Eighteen bottles of carbonic acid bolstered her depleting stock. This relieved the problem of keeping the powder magazines cool in the tropic heat. Also, in the captain's wrecked cabin the prize-crew found secret routing papers showing ports of call for merchant ships in the Indian Ocean. *Tairoa* was a valuable addition to *Graf Spee's* tally.

Without delay, the medium guns roared and shells crashed into *Tairoa's* waterline. To speed the process, a torpedo joined the assault and she sank like a stone. Langsdorff knew the hunters were aware of his position for the second time in two days. *Graf Spee* must make distance from this point immediately. Every fibre of the ship vibrated as the screws drove the pocket battleship southwesterly at full speed. Langsdorff had a rendezvous with *Altmark* in mid-Atlantic on December 6 and must leave no trail.

When time allowed, Captain Langsdorff invited Captain Starr to his cabin. He apologized for sinking *Tairoa* and using his guns to stop the wireless. Starr had given him no choice with the brave actions of his crew. Four young men, boys slightly older than Langsdorff's son, were wounded in the action. Three of the lads needed hospitalization. Langsdorff assured Captain Starr they would get the best medical treatment in the ship's hospital from Doctor Franz Kertzendorff.

Captain Starr complimented Langsdorff for using the smallest caliber guns to achieve his purpose. It was a merciful consideration given the German's obvious choices. Langsdorff explained he believed in the intent of the Geneva Conventions to humanize war. In his view, merchant seamen were civilians unless they took part in the action.

Langsdorff asked Captain Starr to sign a statement saying that *Graf Spee* had not fired on his ship without just cause. *Tairoa's* wireless message had menaced the safety of *Graf Spee* and her crew. Captain Starr, impressed by the sincerity of the young German commander, signed the statement.

Captain Langsdorff requested the name of the radio operator who had courageously risked his life. He invited P.J.Cummins to his cabin and commended him for his brave actions. Cummins gave Langsdorff the names of the wounded deck boys. The youngsters, Leedale, Farmer and Dixon were amazed when *Graf Spee's* Captain personally visited them in the ship's hospital. Langsdorff visited the lads several times as their wounds healed.

On December 4, *Graf Spee* slackened speed and altered course eastward to meet *Altmark.* Crew members began removing her false superstructure. Stripped of the extra funnel and gun turret, *Graf Spee* would make her way home.

Next day, English news from Rugby announced that a German warship had stopped *Mapia* in the Indian Ocean. *Graf Spee's* wireless experts intercepted British radio signals crediting the *Doric Star* sinking to this incident. The Admiralty assumed the German raider had returned to the Atlantic. Confident of their assumption, the British reopened the Mozambique Channel. This ended a three-week closure.

In the evening of December 5, Captain Langsdorff shared a special dinner with his officers. In a festive scenario, Commander Kay and Lieut-Commander Ascher were presented with Iron Crosses, first class, and promoted into a higher grade. Langsdorff admitted that he too had received Iron Cross honors, second class on October 6, and first class on November 11. The officers congratulated him and commented that these medals matched the awards he had earned in World War 1.

Langsdorff said he accepted the awards as the representative of everyone who had shared in the actions. He as Commandant, and Kay and Ascher, as the most senior officers on the ship, carried the honors for the entire ship's complement. The Captain expressed his content with the camaraderie so obviously shared on his ship. Thoughtfully, he remarked that perhaps this would be tested fully before they returned to Germany.

As the meal progressed, Langsdorff advised his officers of future plans. After replenishing supplies from *Altmark* they would head for Santos Bay, Brazil. At this point below Rio de Janeiro, merchant ships hugging the coast en route to Pernambuco, often left neutral waters to cross the bay. If *Graf Spee* could catch a ship or two in these international waters and then move toward the River Plate they might equal the legendary *Emden's* tally. Captain von Müller had sunk close to 100,000 tons during World War 1 and won acclaim for honorable conduct. If they had no success, they would stop a neutral ship to give the false idea they were making for Cape Horn, then head home to Germany. *Scharnhorst* and *Gneisenau* would help them through the North Atlantic like they had covered *Deutschland.*

Next day, December 6, at 24°17'S/19°45'W, *Altmark* met *Graf Spee* as casually as old friends meeting at a street corner. They exchanged cursory greetings and Langsdorff handed over one-hundred and forty-four prisoners. *Graf Spee* retained the most senior officers to take with them to Germany. Five merchant captains, six chief officers, five chief engineers and other radio officers, combining a total of twenty-six men, stayed on *Graf Spee.* Three wounded lads from *Tairoa* also remained aboard.

Captain A.H. Brown (*Huntsman*) and Captain W.B. Starr (*Tairoa*) asked Captain Langsdorff if they could accompany their crew on board *Altmark.* They had many Lascars in their crews and wished to assure their peace of mind. Langsdorff readily approved this humanitarian request. Provisions were transferred on the run and the ships headed westward. *Graf Spee* continued fueling under way.

In the gloom of early night, *Graf Spee* practiced searchlight exercises using *Altmark* as a target. They could not imagine another ship within miles of this isolated spot. At 2242hrs, when the exercises had finished and the men were stowing their gear, '*action stations*' rang out. Everyone rushed to their post. *Spee* lookouts, at 24°37'S/21°52'W, had noticed a faint shape in the distant darkness: A merchant ship sailing without lights. Tension mounted in the warship. Gunners, their sights coordinated, awaited the order to fire.

Captain Langsdorff faced a cruel decision: Had the passing freighter identified the warship and her supply ship? Anyway, the ghost ship, traveling without lights, risked a legitimate attack without warning. Should *Spee* shell her with enough force to prevent any wireless signal? But this ship could be a German, slipping home along an isolated route. If *Spee* challenged her in Morse, using customary *'au clair'* English, she may scuttle herself. Besides, using wireless would betray *Graf Spee's* presence to every listening ear within range. Maybe the 'ship in the night' had missed identifying the warship and her companion. Langsdorff decided to bypass the martial expedient of destroying the ship. Best to continue *incognito* westward with all haste.[1]

Through the night *Graf Spee* and *Altmark* coasted in company. At 0800hrs, December 7, they parted and *Graf Spee* resumed her search pattern. At 1746hrs, five continuous bursts on the alarm sent *Spee's* men to action stations. *'Smoke on the horizon'*, at 25°1'S/27°50'W. Automatically, at full speed, *Graf Spee* raced toward the sighting while prize-crews prepared for action. As *Spee* drew near the gray painted freighter they saw her boats swung out.

SS*Streonshalh* (3,895BRT), was carrying wheat from Montevideo to join a convoy at Freetown. *Graf Spee* pulled parallel with the freighter, 2,000 meters off her starboard beam, and signaled 'STOP. DON'T USE WIRELESS OR WE FIRE'. With hostile guns trained on his ship Captain J.J.Robinson had no choice but obey. Grabbing his secret documents, contained in two canvas bags, he heaved them over the side.

Armed Germans soon boarded and took control of his ship. Lieutenant Herzberg's men tore apart the captain's cabin, looking for documents or contraband of prime value. It was customary to take papers of any kind, even the contents of wastebaskets; *Graf Spee's* experts analyzed them for anything interesting. A sharp eyed seaman had spotted a canvas bag floating in the water near the ship and added it to the haul.

Soon, *Streonshalh's* thirty-two crew-members lined up on *Spee's* deck for roll call. Immediately the tally was verified her anti-aircraft guns opened up, striking along the freighter's waterline. In a short time *Streonshalh* slipped below the surface.

Roll call of Streonshalh *crew on board* Graf Spee. – Gilbey Collection

Captain Robinson and his men first lunched on coffee and sandwiches. Then a sentry escorted Robinson and Mallinson, his chief officer, to meet Commander Kay and prize-officer Herzberg. The Germans, speaking excellent English, shared a beer with the English officers while trying to garner information. They asked about the routing of merchant ships from the River Plate but learned nothing.

Meanwhile, *Graf Spee's* specialists had screened the papers taken from *Streonshalh.* A copy of the Buenos Aires Herald gave specific sailing dates for merchant ships from the River Plate. In the general flotsam they found enough information to learn the routing of allied merchant ships leaving the Plate. Instead of following the coast to Pernambuco the Royal Navy escorted the ships to mid-ocean, 300 miles off the coast of Uruguay. The ships then continued solo to Freetown for convoy to Britain.

According to the captured Buenos Aires Herald, *Highland Monarch,* a large British mail-boat, would sail December 5 from the Plate. On December 10, another liner, *Andalusia Star* would leave Buenos Aires.

Shipping information from the High Command the same day, December 7, included an item that added spice to this information. On December 5, four freighters were reported readying to leave the Plate. Specific names and tonnages gave Langsdorff pause for thought – *Highland Monarch* (14,000BRT), *Marconi* (7,400BRT), *Ashbury* (3,901BRT) and *Southgate* (4,862BRT).[2]

Langsdorff noted the difference in class between *Highland Monarch,* a mail steamer, and the others. It seemed unlikely she would travel in convoy with these slower freighters. Still, if *Graf Spee* searched around the dispersal point, about December 9, they might find something. With good luck they could add significantly to their tonnage. Alert to any opportunity, Captain Langsdorff revised his initial plan and decided to sweep the mid-ocean dispersal point.

The information from High Command on December 7, also gave current dispositions of Allied warships. On December 6, *Barham* with two destroyers had left Gibraltar heading west, and the same day *Provence* and *Royal Sovereign* with two destroyers had arrived at the British naval base. HMS*Neptune,* and part of the *Hermes* hunting group, had moved south from the Dakar area toward Freetown. High Command's shipping information to date had proved remarkably accurate.

On December 9, another update from High Command gave a wider picture: *Renown and Ark Royal* were operating from Capetown. A large fleet of warships was operating in West Africa between Dakar, Freetown and Natal, Brazil. Four cruisers, *Exeter, Cumberland, Achilles* and *Ajax* were protecting the east coast of South America. *Achilles* was now in Montevideo. No information was provided regarding previously reported destroyers or the submarine *Severn.*

While Captain Langsdorff initiated his restructured plan, the British Admiralty coordinated information from every source to pin down the German raider. Commodore Henry Harwood, in command of the cruiser squadron protecting South American shipping, had received a signal on December 2, advising the attack on *Doric Star*. Next day, another signal reported an attack on an unidentified ship one-hundred and seventy miles further to the southwest. The Admiralty had advised him specifically that only one pocket battleship was operating in the South Atlantic. Harwood believed she was coming his way. What should he do?

The anniversary of the Battle of the Falklands was near. On December 8, 1914, Graf von Spee and his two sons had gone down with their ships in the German defeat. An attack on Port Stanley close to this date would be a propaganda asset for Germany. Harwood estimated a travel speed of fifteen knots and figured that the German warship could arrive around December 12/13 somewhere in his zone.

Harwood knew the reputed prowess of a pocket battleship. With 11-inch guns and 26-knots she could outrun a battleship and outgun a cruiser. Supposedly, only Britain's battle-cruisers *Renown and Hood* had enough speed and armament to bring a pocket battleship to action. But Harwood had argued for years that two heavy cruisers, properly engaged, could give a pocket battleship a strong fight. In 1936 he had lectured senior naval officers at Greenwich and outlined specific tactics.

Commodore Harwood now had two heavy cruisers and two light cruisers under his orders. He preferred to meet the pocket battleship with two heavy cruisers but *Cumberland,* his heaviest ship, needed urgent maintenance. Still, temporary protection of the Falklands and maintenance could be achieved simultaneously if he sent *Cumberland* there and kept her on short notice. However, this precaution must not hinder Harwood's main responsibility: to protect the River Plate traffic. In addition, German merchant ships waiting to exit neutral South American ports must be countered. Commodore Harwood had an awesome task for his small squadron.

Harwood decided to concentrate his three active ships near the dispersal zone where most merchants passed en route from the River Plate. This focal point was about three-hundred miles east of Uruguay. While patrolling this vulnerable area, he could swiftly reach any vessel under attack in the zone. Harwood reasoned, if a pocket battleship appeared, his cruisers could engage the larger warship with hopes of success. To activate his plan Harwood sent a signal at 1315hrs December 3, 1939:

> *TO THE SOUTH AMERICAN DIVISION. IN VIEW OF REPORT POCKET-BATTLESHIP, AMEND PREVIOUS DISPOSITIONS. CUMBERLAND, SELF-REFIT AT FALKLAND ISLANDS AS PREVIOUSLY ARRANGED BUT KEEP ON SHORT NOTICE ON TWO SHAFTS. ACHILLES, LEAVE RIO DE JANEIRO AREA SO AS TO ARRIVE AND FUEL MONTEVIDEO 0600(ZONE PLUS 2) 10 DECEMBER. EXETER, LEAVE FALKLANDS FOR THE PLATE AM 9 DECEMBER COVERING SS.LAFONIA WITH RETURNING VOLUNTEERS. AJAX, ACHILLES CONCENTRATE IN POSITION 35°S.; 50°W. AT 1600(ZONE PLUS 2) DECEMBER*

10. EXETER TO PASS THROUGH POSITION 090° MEDANOS LIGHT 150 MILES AT 0700 DECEMBER 12. IF CONCENTRATION WITH AJAX AND ACHILLES IS NOT EFFECTED BY THAT TIME FURTHER INSTRUCTIONS WILL BE ISSUED TO EXETER. OILER OLYNTHUS IS TO REMAIN AT SEA RENDEZVOUS UNTIL SITUATION CLEARS INSTEAD OF PROCEEDING TO FALKLAND ISLANDS.[3]

Thus, Commodore Henry Hardwood drew the fateful British hand. He would play it bravely and wisely in the coming Battle of the River Plate.

Meanwhile, Captain Langsdorff's run of good luck began bogging down. On December 11, the Arado spotting plane finally lost her engine. The ingenuity of her skilled mechanics could not repair the cracked cylinders. They had already proved their competence in keeping the inept plane operating so far into the cruise. This loss dealt a deadly blow to *Graf Spee's* mission.

Chapter 7

Action! The Battle of the River Plate

Precisely as planned, the three cruisers of the South American Squadron concentrated at 0700hrs on December 12, and steered for 32°S/47°W. Commodore Harwood had marked on his plot the Allied ships sailing in his zone. He had selected the most advantageous staging area to contact the pocket battleship. Perhaps the raider would make an aggressive move and reveal her presence. If she attacked one of his merchant ships he should be within striking distance to retaliate.

Harwood was taking a huge gamble that the pocket battleship would show up near the dispersal point off Uruguay. In fact, Langsdorff had passed far north of this area on his way to Santos Bay. But using information gathered from *Streonshalh* on December 7, he changed his plans. Even then, if the Arado had lasted two more days and warned him of the concentrated cruisers, history may have evolved differently.

However, positive thinking was Henry Harwood's forte. To ensure his crews were properly prepared to fight a pocket battleship he sent a signal at 1200hrs, 12 December:

> TO SOUTH AMERICAN DIVISION: MY POLICY WITH THREE CRUISERS IN COMPANY VERSUS ONE POCKET BATTLESHIP. ATTACK AT ONCE BY NIGHT OR DAY. BY DAY ACT AS TWO UNITS, 1ST DIVISION (AJAX AND ACHILLES) AND EXETER DIVERGED TO PERMIT FLANK MARKING. FIRST DIVISION WILL CONCENTRATE GUNFIRE. BY NIGHT SHIPS WILL NORMALLY REMAIN IN COMPANY IN OPEN ORDER. BE PREPARED FOR THE SIGNAL ZMM WHICH IS TO HAVE THE SAME MEANING AS MM EXCEPT THAT FOR DIVISION READ SINGLE SHIP.[1]

Later that day, at 1813hrs, Harwood added a further signal:

MY OBJECT IN THE SIGNAL ZMM IS TO AVOID TORPEDOES AND TAKE THE ENEMY BY SURPRISE AND CROSS HIS STERN. WITHOUT FURTHER ORDERS SHIPS ARE TO CLEAR THE LINE OF FIRE BY HAULING ASTERN OF THE NEW LEADING SHIP. THE NEW LEADING SHIP IS TO LEAD THE LINE WITHOUT FURTHER ORDERS SO AS TO MAINTAIN DECISIVE GUN RANGE.

During the evening of December 12, and again in the early hours of the next day, the three cruisers practiced these maneuvers.

Predawn exercises were second nature to the seamen serving on British warships. In the dark on Wednesday morning, December 13, a series of bugle calls – DOH-SOH-SOH – followed by -G- sent the men scampering to their action stations. Rattlers sounded throughout the ships adding a note of urgency. Boilers were flashed and made ready to deliver full speed. When the dawn light brightened, lookouts scanned the horizon. They saw nothing. Crews were dismissed and the boilers trimmed back to conserve fuel.

Over the horizon from Harwood's squadron, to the northwest, a few minutes before 0600hrs, *Graf Spee* sliced through the calm seas at fifteen knots. Cruising on course 155°, she would swing about to 335° at the change of watch. Captain Langsdorff was criss-crossing the area where he had learned the merchant ships from the Plate made their course change.

Information from *Streonshalh* indicated that the Royal Navy herded merchants 300-miles eastward from the Plate to the dispersal point. Single freighters then continued alone, 30-miles apart to Freetown.

High Command had advised, in a wireless dispatch, that four merchants totaling 30,000-tons were preparing to leave the Plate on December 5. One of these ships, *Highland Monarch*, would probably not accompany the others. Still, Langsdorff hoped to find all or part of a small convoy, perhaps escorted by a cruiser.

If good luck prevailed, and they found a convoy, Langsdorff planned to attack on sight. A swift aggressive attack, before the escort generated enough speed to escape *Spee's* main guns, could be successful. A rapid dispatch of the escort would also restrict the freighters from scattering.

Gunnery Officer Ascher and his men thirsted to test their heavy guns and prowess in battle conditions. *Graf Spee* had never been involved in action with a warship. Langsdorff's standing orders prevented this prospect unless it advanced their specified task: to disrupt commercial traffic.

Graf Spee now depended totally on the optical range finder to find her prey. Two days earlier, the Arado had lost her engine. Although *Spee* had fulfilled her task brilliantly many technical problems had caused concern. Four months of cruising without major maintenance had taken a heavy toll on the engines. Multiple cracks in the auxiliary engine foundations, and out of round pistons, could not be repaired at sea. Their mission had provided valuable field testing but *Graf Spee* now needed urgent dock repairs.

However, Langsdorff had agreed they should battle-prove the advanced technology of their armament if it enhanced their mission. A small convoy, even if guarded by a cruiser or auxiliary, would be a providential gift too good to refuse.

Gray light was showing on the horizon at 0552hrs, turning the lazy sea into an endless vista of steel gray ripples. A change of watch and a change of course would occur at 0600hrs. Suddenly, the lookouts called an alarm. *'Mast-tips on starboard prow.'*

Lieut-Commander Wattenberg and Lieutenant Schiebusch had arrived on the bridge to take over the new watch. A check of the horizon through binoculars revealed nothing. However, the officer of the watch decided to maintain the present course for a few minutes before swinging round to continue sweeping the pre-assigned zigzag.

Within moments the range-finder on the foretop located the tiny tips of two masts on the distant horizon and instantly found two more. Wattenberg picked up the telephone and appraised Captain Langsdorff of the situation. 'Sir, two mast tips were sighted on the horizon, then nothing. After a few moments we saw four. Now, we see only two, but it appears to be a warship.' Wattenberg's words were crisp and clear.

Langsdorff, in his day cabin, pondered for a few seconds and made his decision. 'Maintain present course. Ring full speed and clear the ship for action.'

As the buzzers called all hands to action stations and the ship surged forward Langsdorff swiftly made his way to the bridge. In the quickening light it was possible to see the smoke and twin masts of a cruiser. Look-outs had already identified the British heavy cruiser *Exeter* and believed she was in company with two destroyers.

Wattenberg, a cautious, careful officer had a premonition of danger. 'With respect, My Captain, should we ignore our standing orders to avoid conflict with warships?'

Langsdorff and Wattenberg had mutual respect for each other. Their excellent cooperation had been significant in making the cruise successful. The Captain noted Wattenberg's concern but felt confident they had luckily found a small convoy. 'I believe they are protecting a convoy,' he said. 'We have not yet been fully tested. Now we shall see. They will put up a good fight but we shall swallow them.'

Over the horizon from *Graf Spee*, shortly after 0600hrs, Commodore Henry Harwood's flagship, *Ajax*, led the three cruisers at fourteen knots. Leading Signalman Swanston saw a faint wisp of brownish smoke abaft the port quarter. He reported his sighting to Lieutenant Lewin who shared the bridge with Lieut-Commander Pennefather.

Casually, the two officers brought glasses to bear on the smoke. They anticipated meeting a friendly merchant ship in the area. Leisurely, the Officer of the watch, Lewin, leaned into the voice pipe and advised Captain Woodhouse and Commodore Harwood of the sighting.

The Commodore, roused from his bunk, ordered Lewin to send a flag signal to *Exeter* 'INVESTIGATE'. If the ship was a British freighter, *Exeter* could pass her dispatches for delivery to the British Consul at Montevideo or Buenos Aires.

Meanwhile, on board *Achilles*, steaming second in line, Captain Parry and Lieutenant Washburn were chatting on the bridge. A sharp call from the lookout interrupted their words. 'SMOKE, BEARING RED ONE-DOUBLE-OH, SIR.' Parry brought his glasses to bear and Washburn, the ship's gunnery officer, looked through the target position indicator.

Instantly, they recognized the silhouette of a pocket battleship scudding toward them, black smoke trailing in her wake. Chief Yeoman of Signals, Lincoln Martinson, called that *Exeter* had hauled off the line and hoisted a yellow flag 'N', signifying 'ENEMY IN SIGHT'.

Without a pause, Captain Parry ordered the engine room alerted. Lieutenant Cowburn immediately replaced Washburn as officer of the watch. *'Action stations'* rang out throughout the ship and Washburn lost no time climbing to his post in the D.C.T.(director control tower).

On board *Ajax,* the pace had quickened sharply. Lewin, at Swanston's insistence had taken a harder look at the smoke on the horizon. He now saw a cloud of black smoke drifting back from the small shape in the distance. It was definitely a pocket battleship. Commodore Harwood had come to the bridge and his prearranged battle plan swung into play. *'Action stations'* rattled through the ship and men ran swiftly, with practiced ease, to their posts.

Luckily, the cruisers' boilers, still charged from the morning exercises, quickly built steam for maximum speed. *Ajax* and *Achilles* thrust ahead. Every turn of their screws building additional speed until their bow waves rose in churning white arcs. They planned to make a wide sweep ahead of *Graf Spee* and come up on her lee side. *Exeter,* racing toward the German's smoke, signaled 'ENEMY IN SIGHT. I AM GOING TO ATTACK'.

On board *Graf Spee,* Lieutenant Diggins arrived on the bridge to join his captain. The lookouts had just reported they faced *Exeter* and two *Leander*-class light cruisers. Captain Langsdorff realized he had serious trouble on his hands. He had gambled on finding three or four freighters with an escort over the horizon. Never did he expect to fight three cruisers. Now he faced the South American Cruiser Division, in company, and it was too late to refuse action: He must play out the hand that fate had dealt.

Langsdorff turned to Diggins. 'Let's go up to the foretop. We'll see better from that point' he said.

Diggins knew this high point on the ship. It had no special armored protection. With typical *sang-froid,* he asked, 'Shall I bring some 'groceries', Sir?'

Lieutenant Diggins knew the captain loved to smoke an occasional cigar at this normally calm location. It was the highest platform position on the ship and allowed a magnificent panoramic view.

Langsdorff's blue eyes twinkled. 'But of course, Lieutenant,' he said.

So, in quickening dawn light, December 13, 1939, *Graf Spee* rushed at full speed toward a potent squadron of British cruisers. *Exeter, Ajax* and *Achilles* in company made a formidable force:

HMS Exeter: *8,390 BRT. Captain F.S. Bell.* – Central Press

HMS Ajax: *7,050 BRT.(Flagship for Commodore H. Harwood). Capt. C.H.L. Wooodhouse.* – Central Press

Exeter (8,390BRT) a heavy cruiser, carried six 8-inch and four 4-inch guns, six 21-inch torpedo tubes and two spotter planes. Around 175m long, with two funnels she could run at 32 knots. Lightly armored, with 2.75-inch sides, and 2-inch decks and turrets, *Exeter* alone should not present any problem against the powerful 11-inch guns of *Graf Spee*.

Ajax and *Achilles* (7,050BRT) were low-slung, single funneled light cruisers, easily mistaken as destroyers at a distance. Sister ships, they carried eight 6-inch and eight 4-inch guns plus eight 21-inch torpedo

HMNZS Achilles: *7,050 BRT. Captain W.E. Parry.* – George Deacon Collection.

tubes. About 170m long they could make 32.5 knots. Fully loaded with one spotter plane they weighed in close to 9,000 tons. Protected by 4-inch steel around the sides and 2-inch decks, they added a deadly augmentation to *Exeter's* heavier guns.

Unknown to Captain Langsdorff the British warships and crews had prepared to give him the battle of his life. Through the previous day and night, the tough cruiser-crews of the Royal Navy had strenuously practiced Harwood's tactics to handle a lone pocket battleship. To add to Langsdorff's misfortune the supposed convoy did not exist. On the contrary, merchant ships were accumulating in Montevideo.

Harwood's gamble had paid off better than the British commodore could ever have hoped. He could have used his small squadron dispersed over a wide area. On contacting the raider, he could then have shadowed her till heavier ships came to his aid. It was a courageous strategy to concentrate the squadron and plan to attack on sight a warship that could clearly outgun his largest unit.

On board *Graf Spee,* Captain Langsdorff in his position high on the foretop saw the three cruisers clearly. Langsdorff sought to close and disable the cruisers before they could generate their greater speed. He believed they might back out of his gun-range and shadow *Spee* till help arrived. At this time of morning, with hours of daylight to come, the prospect of losing fast, shadowing cruisers seemed remote. The British ships could trail him, outside his range, and call in bigger warships to annihilate *Graf Spee*. Best to close and put them out of action as quickly as possible.

Langsdorff's anticipation that the British warships, if protecting a convoy, would be caught napping on low steam instantly vanished. They were already thrashing out twenty knots and building extra speed every minute. He had expected the cruisers to fall back. It puzzled the German captain that *Exeter* charged toward him on a parallel course. Could the squadron be supported by submarines or heavier warships?

At this point Langsdorff felt secure that his armor could withstand 8-inch shells without sustaining critical damage. The British cruisers soon shattered this illusion. With Gunnery Officer Ascher in his D.C.T., Wattenberg and Schiebusch in the wheelhouse and Langsdorff and Diggins in the foretop, at 0617hrs *Graf Spee* opened fire on *Exeter.* Three 11-inch shells burst from 'B' turret and screamed toward *Exeter.* 'A' turret remained silent. Ascher reported a problem with the elevation system on the forward turret.

Inside the ship, at his control panel, Lieutenant Rasenack almost burst a blood vessel. He held responsibility for the electronic and mechanical control of the main armament. Stemming any inclination to panic, Rasenack reasoned, correctly, that an earlier problem had recurred. A loose magneto screw in the middle gun had fouled the height control mechanism. In a few minutes his mechanics disconnected the middle gun and formed a bridge to allow the turret to operate. In short time they fixed the magneto and the turret resumed normal fire.

Aboard *Exeter,* before she hauled off to investigate smoke, the engineers had idled half her boilers to conserve fuel. When action stations rang out, they quickly flashed up and connected all boilers. Navy gunners raced to 'A' and 'Y' turrets and Royal Marines took their places in 'B' turret. Lieut-Commander Jennings, the gunnery officer scrambled into his D.C.T. and damage control parties reported at the ready.

At 0620hrs, Captain Bell called for full speed and with battle-flags snapping at the halyards *Exeter* raced toward the pocket battleship. *Graf Spee* had straddled *Exeter* with 11-inch shells and Bell wanted to get his licks in quickly.

As the cruiser picked up speed Jennings let fly with his first salvo of 8-inch shells from turrets 'A' and 'B'. Two-and-a half minutes later 'Y' turret joined the chorus. The Gunnery Officer was exuberant. At 18,700yd he had straddled *Graf Spee.* Simultaneously, *Achilles* opened up with her 6-inch shells at 0621hrs and at 0623hrs *Ajax* joined the attack.

Bloody and brutal action developed rapidly. *Graf Spee* had found the range. At 0624hrs an 11-inch shell burst in the water close to *Exeter's* starboard side. Showers of fragmented metal, flying at the speed of sound, swept the after length of the ship. Shrapnel smashed the number one torpedo tube and killed the crew. All gun-ready lamp circuits and fall-of-shot hooters went dead. The near miss knocked out communications and searchlights at that end and wrecked one aircraft.

Seconds later another 11-inch shell hit the front of 'B' turret with devastating results. Bursting on impact the shell destroyed the gun turret and killed the crew. Shrapnel and splinters instantly wrecked the wheelhouse, killing everyone on the bridge except Captain Bell and two other ranks. Bell soon discovered that this hit had disabled the wheelhouse communications. To control the ship, he must move to the after conning position.

Temporarily out of control, *Exeter* swung to starboard. Torpedo officer Lieut-Commander C.J. Smith noted that the ship would close its 'A' arcs and the main guns would not bear on the target. Struggling to a buckled voice tube, he yelled a change of course to the after steering position. The ship swung to port and Smith released his three starboard torpedoes.

When Captain Bell, bleeding from a face wound, arrived at the after conning position he could not raise contact with the helm. Bell quickly organized a manual line of sailors to verbally pass instructions from the commander to the helmsman. Despite great difficulties within the damaged ship, Bell had *Exeter* under control.

Graf Spee, 13,000yd off to starboard, began a sweeping turn to port. *Exeter* had landed a direct hit on the starboard side of the pocket battleship. The 8-inch shell sheared through an anti-aircraft gun-shield, passed through two decks and burst in the funnel area that housed the fresh water apparatus; the blast dislodged an engine silencer. Chief Klepp ordered the engine throttled until repairs were completed. *Graf Spee's* other diesels picked up the slack and a slight loss of speed went unnoticed.

As the German warship turned to run on the same line as *Exeter* she fired an 11-inch volley at *Ajax* then released a smoke screen. *Ajax* and *Achilles*, now running on *Graf Spee's* starboard side, prepared to close the range.

Exeter continued firing with amazing speed and accuracy. When *Graf Spee* completed her turn, the cruiser landed another 8-inch shell in the midships of the German. This shell crashed through *Graf Spee's* armored side, passed through three bulkheads and burst in the galleys. Another 8-inch bulls-eye pierced the upper part of the bridge and continued without exploding.

Exeter now made a dramatic swing to starboard. Lieut-Commander Smith had called for the turn to release his three port torpedoes. The torpedo salvo was barely away when two 11-inch shells crashed into the cruiser.

One shell pierced the navigator officer's cabin, passed through the armament office and traveled another 60ft before bursting on a starboard 4-inch gun. It knocked out 'A' turret, and the foremost ready use locker, loaded with 4-inch shells, caught fire. Exploding ammunition sent showers of splinters and debris slicing through the air to add to the carnage. The other shell smashed through the C.P.O. flat, went through three bulkheads and exploded on the lower deck, above the 4-inch magazine and torpedo gunner's store. It blew a massive 16ft x 14ft hole inside the ship. *Exeter* disappeared from view behind a huge smoke screen.

Cautiously, anticipating the re-appearance of the damaged heavy cruiser, *Spee* turned her 11-inch guns toward the light cruisers off her starboard quarter. *Graf Spee* had stuck her head into a hornet's nest. She would need all her skills and good luck to avoid disaster.

On board *Achilles*, gunnery officer Washburn in his D.C.T., focused *Graf Spee* on the range-finder. Because of the broken lines on the pocket-battleship's foremast, he concentrated his effort on the rear mast. It was difficult to get a good bearing because of the intense smokescreen that shrouded the German warship. Washburn gave thanks for *Graf Spee's* high foretop as it showed above her smokescreen.

As *Spee's* main guns turned from *Exeter* and searched for a new target she straddled both light cruisers. A near miss landed fifty yards astern of *Ajax*, then an 11-inch shell burst close to *Achilles'* port side. White-hot shrapnel whizzed through the bridge like hundreds of tiny lightning bolts. Captain Parry and Chief Yeoman of Signals Martinson received minor wounds. In the D.C.T., five of Washburn's ten men took hits - three men died instantly. The ship's wireless faded and went dead.

Captain Parry ordered *Achilles* to break off the concentrated attack with *Ajax.* They would continue the fight under individual control until they re-established communications.

Lieutenant Washburn, with wounds to his head and shoulder, surveyed the bloody carnage in his control tower. It was essential to get back to business without delay. His guns were now pointing away from *Graf Spee*. Obeying the Captain's orders, the helmsman had steered into the splash of the near miss. This tactic had proved immensely successful during their attack.

Now Washburn needed to steel himself and his men to work in the midst of the slaughter left by the shell splinters. It was incredible how calm and matter of fact they behaved. True professional warriors turn automatically to their training in the worst of circumstances.

Both light cruisers fired their guns furiously as they targeted *Graf Spee*. Lieutenant Lewin, had taken off in his plane while *Ajax* fired her guns. Now he passed spotting information to the flagship's gunnery control. Mistakenly, he accorded *Achilles* fall of shot to *Ajax* and the flagship adjusted her sights to Lewin's information. This caused *Ajax* to overshoot the target. The misunderstanding caused a loss of accuracy for some minutes but the problem ceased at 0703hrs when *Achilles* regained wireless contact with *Ajax.*

At 0700hrs *Exeter* reappeared from a bank of smoke, off *Graf Spee's* port quarter, firing only her after-turret. On the ship, Lieut-Commander Jennings stood on the roof of 'Y' turret yelling his spotting corrections down a manhole. Chief Ordinance Artificer Johns, inside the turret, in turn directed the fire. Captain Bell, grim and determined, took his bearings with a simple boat's compass and steered from the after position. HMS*Exeter* would fight till her last gasp.

When *Exeter* reappeared, Captain Langsdorff immediately brought his 11-inch guns to bear again on the heavy cruiser. Shells rained on the hapless warship as she fought her valiant fight. Explosions erupted in the sea as shells overshot the cruiser but flames engulfed her, licking as high as her masts. She developed a ponderous list but continued to fight. Finally, about 0730hrs, her electrical circuits gave out and the guns stopped firing. Captain Bell had no recourse except to turn away in a mixture of flames and smoke.

With her guns now silent and listing 7 degrees to starboard, *Exeter* continued at twenty knots. Captain Bell resolved to ram *Graf Spee* if given an opportunity. Tradition in the Royal Navy dies hard.

Exeter's defiant grit impressed Langsdorff. He could imagine the horrors taking place in the enemy warship. The British cruiser's guns had stopped firing and she sat nakedly in *Graf Spee's* sights. It needed only his command to give the helpless warship the coup-de-grace. Lieut-Commander Ascher in his gunnery control tower waited grimly for the order to continue fire.

This order did not come. Instead, Langsdorff ordered the heavy guns swung round to target the light cruisers attacking his starboard rear quarter: Senseless slaughter was not his style.

Ajax and *Achilles* swept close at full speed. Using drifting clouds of smoke to great advantage, they darted here and there, always closing the range. Working in perfect coordination, like well-trained sheepdogs, they showered *Graf Spee* with 6-inch shells.

Graf Spee absorbed serious punishment. Captain Langsdorff, standing in his lofty perch in the foretop, received shrapnel wounds in his right arm and shoulder. A few moments later a powerful blast of furnace-like heat knocked him unconscious. Lieutenant Diggins, standing at the Captain's side, had his uniform singed by the blast.

With the Captain prone on the deck, Diggins called for *Graf Spee's* Executive Officer to take control of the ship. Commander Kay left his post in damage control and headed for the foretop. While Kay clambered up the steel ladder to the high platform, Langsdorff regained his senses. Seeing Kay's head and shoulders at the top of the ladder he smiled and said he would continue in command.

Graf Spee's firing at this time seemed uncoordinated. The British gunners thought they had damaged the German's computerized sighting system. In fact, swift changes of position taking place between the cruisers had caused confusion between the range-finders and their directors. This was soon corrected and the big guns resumed their former accuracy.

Ajax and *Achilles* now closed to 9,000yds from the pocket battleship. Every available gun blasted away as fast as they could fire. *Ajax* let fly with four torpedoes and *Graf Spee* turned sharply to port, thus hampering her own effort to fire a torpedo volley - she fired only one tube. A minute later, *Spee* scored a direct hit on *Ajax* with an 11-inch delayed action shell. The shell pierced the after superstructure, went through some cabins and 'X' turret's trunk, then exploded in the Commodore's sleeping cabin. Part of the shell smashed into the 'Y' turret barbette and jammed the mechanism. It killed four men and wounded six others in 'X' turret and put both turrets out of action.

Twisting and turning to avoid hits the three great ships churned the water into foam. Like furious hounds, the cruisers snapped at the heels of the pocket battleship. Coming from the starboard quarter they crossed her wake, firing all the way, and finally poured their screaming metal onto her port quarter. Direct hits and shrapnel struck the length of the German ship. *Graf Spee's* conspicuous control tower made an inviting target.

Graf Spee now landed her shots with great accuracy. *Ajax* lost her top mast at 8,000 yards; *Achilles* forward halyards came crashing down, leaving the New Zealand flag flying from her main mast.

Commodore Harwood had no way of knowing how effectively his shots had hurt *Graf Spee*. When he received notice that ammunition was running low, he decided to withdraw. It made sound sense to trail the pocket battleship and wait for a better opportunity during darkness.

At 0742hrs, under cover of smoke, the cruisers withdrew outside *Graf Spee's* range and took station on each side of her wake. *Graf Spee* continued westward, at twenty-three knots, under the sharp-eyed vigilance of the British cruisers. Meanwhile, Captain Langsdorff took advantage of the lull in the action to check his damage and receive medical attention.

CHAPTER 8

Serious Damage

There is little to compare to the hellish brutality of a sea-battle. Men are entrapped in a tight steel box, a warship beyond sight of land, floating in untold fathoms of sea-water. Separated by miles of rolling ocean, combating warships throw tons of high explosives at each other. It seems an unreal fantasy. Eventually, like a thunderbolt, a shell pierces a ship. A deafening explosion sends lethal particles of shrapnel and flying debris ricocheting off the ship's interior panels. Unfortunate men are cut down instantly in death or mutilation. Fire, fumes and flooding, in darkened confined spaces, summon terror to the survivors. Exercises can never equal the real thing. In battle conditions the spirit of man is forced to new levels. Heroic deeds are executed courageously in response to critical need. Tales of valor and bravery are carried forward, timelessly adding depth to old traditions.

Damage from 6-inch shell on Graf Spee's *port bow.*
– F.W. RASENACK

Such was the case in HMS*Exeter* and *Admiral Graf Spee* in the historic Battle of the River Plate. HMS*Ajax* and HMNZS *Achilles* suffered fatal casualties and provided many heroic deeds but the larger ships bore the brunt of the

Close-up of Graf Spee *funnel indicating abscence of armored protection: Crucial steam system located within this area.*
– Diego M. Lascano

action. In *Exeter,* sixty-one men lost their lives and twenty others were wounded; Captain Bell struggled to keep his mangled ship afloat. *Graf Spee* suffered thirty-six men killed and more than fifty wounded.

Graf Spee had taken a surprising beating. The widespread, serious effect of flying shrapnel astonished Captain Langsdorff. Direct hits had easily penetrated *Graf Spee's* steel protection. One 8-inch shell had pierced her armored belt like it was cardboard. Only the turrets of the 11-inch guns and the face of the control tower, weathered the punishment unscathed.

When Langsdorff moved through the ship inspecting the damage, he received summaries from each section officer. They reported extensive structural damage including a gaping hole in the port bow above the waterline. The most serious news came from Lieut-Commander Klepp. The Chief Engineer had reported that a shell-burst had wrecked installations that produced high pressure steam. *Spee's* engines depended on this steam, generated in the funnel area, to clean fuel and lubricating oil. Fresh water distillation, and the galleys and the laundry, depended on the same steam facility. Klepp now advised Langsdorff he could not repair this vital system with materials on board: *Spee* was using pre-cleaned fuel from a holding tank that carried less than one day's supply. Langsdorff accepted Klepp's report stoically and continued his inspection.

When he arrived at the ship's hospital, Langsdorff waded into a section flooded with sea-water and blood. Doctor Kertzendorff and his staff were working tirelessly in sorrowful conditions tending the wounded. The Captain offered words of encouragement to the suffering men. Some horribly wounded lads were young reservists barely older than Langsdorff's son.

After completing his damage inspection Langsdorff walked smartly to the Captain's bridge. Lieut-Commander Wattenberg rose to greet him as he entered the room. Langsdorff's face was haggard and his manner brisk. 'We cannot repair our damage with means on board. We must run into port for repairs. Ascertain whether Montevideo or Buenos Aires comes into question.'

Wattenberg was shocked to hear the ship must go into port, but did not question the Captain's statement. Langsdorff ordered Lieutenant Diggins to bring him the 'red book' which showed German Naval Attache's in residence in South America. *Spee* would need material and political help wherever they landed. Lieut-Commander Ascher now joined the small group in the Captain's bridge.

Diggins found the 'red book' and handed it to Langsdorff. The Captain flipped through the pages. He quickly discovered that Buenos Aires and Montevideo were the only ports in South America with a Naval Attaché available.

Wattenberg's navigation charts highlighted and warned of notorious muddy shallows in the Punta Indio Channel leading into Buenos Aires. Montevideo seemed a better haven. Langsdorff decided to get there as quickly as possible.

Later, in the chart room, Ascher asked Wattenberg why they were going ashore. Wattenbeg told him it was the Captain's decision. Neither senior officer had a penchant to take the ship into port but it was not a time for explanations. They were still on high alert and Captain Langsdorff must have a good reason for his decision.

On the the British side, Commodore Harwood's light cruisers now shadowed *Graf Spee*. One vigilant ship covered each flank of the German, abaft and well out of her range. What would the pocket battleship do?

Harwood had no indication that the German warship had taken serious damage. She was speeding westward in purposeful fashion. British lookouts could easily see *Graf Spee's* high, bulky control-tower in the perfect spring morning. They intended keeping the enemy in view and attacking when daylight faded. Harwood could afford to bide his time and take care of other matters as the ships steamed westward.

Ajax had lost wireless communications when *Graf Spee* shot off her masts. *Achilles* filled the gap in communications and advised the Admiralty and all freighters in the area *Graf Spee's* position, course and speed. Shortly after 0900hrs, *Ajax* brought her aircraft aboard and around 1000hrs the flagship regained wireless contact with the squadron.

Harwood immediately signaled HMS*Cumberland* to leave the Falklands and close the River Plate at full speed. Luckily, *Cumberland* had already sailed when the message arrived. Wireless operators on the heavy cruiser had overheard a transmission during the battle that suggested the squadron had found action. Captain Fallowfield, on his own initiative, broke off repairs and took his ship to sea. When he received Harwood's signal *Cumberland* had a running start and promptly turned on full speed.

A few minutes after 1000hrs *Achilles*, on *Graf Spee's* starboard quarter, closed to 23,000yd from the alert German. She smartly turned away when an 11-inch shell landed 500yd from her bow. Moments later a second shell blew a rising column of water high into the air in *Achilles'* wake.

Commodore Harwood's worries about *Exeter's* fate lessened at 1105hrs. Captain Bell's wireless signaled he had one 8-inch gun in 'Y' turret operating on local control and one 4-inch gun still serviceable. Bell had redistributed his fuel to balance the ship's list but she lay three feet down at the bows. Lack of air circulation caused suffocating conditions on board. The engines continued running and she could cruise at reasonable speed but steering remained difficult. Bell continued using a boat's compass to navigate from the after conning position. Commodore Harwood could expect no further help from the gallant cruiser. He ordered her to close the Falkland Islands.

Meanwhile, on board *Graf Spee*, Commander Kay and his damage control men worked frantically. Leaks in the hull demanded urgent repair. Wounded men, trapped in wreckage throughout the ship needed immediate help. Salvage units collected dead comrades for identification.

Kay was a hard man who had often stirred resentment in the crew. In the midst of the horrors around him he maintained a calm business-like demeanor that encouraged his men to address their miserable task with resolve and courage.

Ignored in the heat of the battle, the British prisoners aboard *Graf Spee* had survived a strange experience. The British merchant seamen were prisoners aboard a German warship in mortal combat with a British cruiser squadron. Was friendly fire really friendly?

During the action a shell tore a hole in the roof of the officer's prison-flat. Debris from the near miss flew around the room and slightly wounded a *Tairoa* lad still recovering from an earlier wound. Through the torn gap in the roof the prisoners could see a damaged anti-aircraft gun and a distant view of the sea. However, they were securely locked in the flat, unable to participate in any way.

The merchant officers could not see *Spee's* attackers but they heard hits striking the ship. As the pocket battleship turned and rolled in the antics of combat, the men held onto lockers, bunks or anything fastened down. To help relieve the tension Captain Dove and B.C.McCorry, Huntsman's radio officer, gave a mock running commentary on the battle. Peeking through two small holes in the steel door of the cabin, they reported anything they could see in the passageway. When a dry thud vibrated the ship, or muffled, gravel-like ricochets rattled along the sides, everyone cheered in appreciation. This totally irrational behavior, typically British, diverted attention from the peril they all faced.

About 0800hrs, the warship stabilized and the guns stilled. *Graf Spee* shuddered as she sped westward at high speed. No doubt, the Royal Navy was following on the heels of the German. Once engaged they would not quit until they had resolved the conflict, one way or another. Action could start again at any moment. What would happen to them? As the morning passed, they heard nothing and their fears abated.

On *Graf Spee's* bridge Captain Langsdorff, his right arm bandaged and supported in a sling, was ready to counter any move from the cruisers. Langsdorff had signaled to High Command in Berlin his intention to enter Montevideo for repairs. Berlin responded affirmatively. Langsdorff, a keen student of naval history, remembered the World War 1 story of the British cruiser *HMS Glasgow.*

Damaged in the 1914 Battle of Coronel, *Glasgow* had gone into Rio de Janeiro for repairs. Neutral Brazil had allowed the warship one week for repairs. Immediately after her refit, *Glasgow* had joined the battle cruiser group that defeated Graf von Spee in the Battle of the Falklands. Perhaps Langsdorff could arrange a dock repair in Montevideo for *Graf Spee.*

His musing was abruptly interrupted. A lookout saw smoke ahead on the horizon. *'Action stations'* rang out and men took their familiar combat places. Soon the lookouts identified the British freighter *Shakespeare.* Langsdorff realized he could easily sink this ship before the cruisers tailing him could intervene. As the distance between the ships shortened *Graf Spee's* flags signaled, 'STOP. ABANDON SHIP.' To ensure the ship understood the message a 5.9-inch shell whistled over the freighter's bow.

Shakespeare slowly lost way and the ship's boats dangled out on their davits. However, the crew made no effort to leave the ship. Langsdorff, anticipating the crew would evacuate the ship, had sent *Ajax* a wireless signal to retrieve the men. The German captain knew the rules of war. This daring freighter had refused his command. A couple of torpedoes, as they passed, could legally send her to the bottom. But he did not attack the ship. Did Langsdorff fear the subsequent consequences in Montevideo, or did his conscience refuse to allow a deadly strike against civilian sailors? He took the answer to this question to his grave. *Graf Spee* serenely sailed past *Shakespeare* without further molestation.

Over the horizon from *Graf Spee,* to the southwest, the 10,000-ton French liner *Formose* intercepted *Spee's* signal to *Ajax.* A little later, the liner heard *Ajax* transmit the pocket battleship's position, speed and course. Realizing he lay in *Graf Spee's* path Captain Buron altered his course to enter Uruguayan territorial waters. At 1500hrs *Formose* reached a position five miles from Cape Santa Maria and followed the coast toward Montevideo.

Meanwhile, Commodore Harwood's cruisers doggedly followed the German pocket battleship. Aboard *Achilles,* the medics had treated and bandaged the wounded men. Damage control had cleaned up the D.C.T. and made it as shipshape as possible. The ship's parson had organized the burial of four casualties.

In the traditional manner, as in the days of Nelson, the carefully wrapped bodies in their canvas shrouds were committed to the deep. The minister spoke the time-honored words and the remains of men, switched instantly from vibrant life to bloody death, slid into the sea. Shipmates, still on high alert, with bared heads lowered in respect gave their last farewells. Similar scenes would take place on *Ajax* and *Exeter* when conditions allowed.

But the relentless shadowing of *Graf Spee* continued. Around 1600hrs *Achilles* signaled an alarm that sent all hands scrambling to action stations. A ship in the far distance looked like a *Hipper*-class heavy cruiser. This type of German warship had eight 8-inch guns and over thirty-two knots in speed. In company, *Graf Spee* and such a cruiser would outmatch the two light cruisers. With rising concern lookouts watched the distant ship draw closer. Captain Parry and his men relaxed when they identified the British liner *Delane* on track for Montevideo.

Commodore Harwood, a seasoned sailor in the Atlantic waters of South America, anticipated that *Graf Spee* would enter the River Plate Estuary. Harwood was familiar with a political controversy over the international status of these waters:

In 1828, when Uruguay became an independent state, she assumed authority of the northern bank of the River Plate. The Republic had claimed a nine-mile limit off the coastline of the estuary. An imaginary line, drawn southwesterly between Punta del Este and Cabo San Antonio, separated the Estuary from the Atlantic. Argentina claimed jurisdiction for the balance of the internal waters. Later, the two countries mutually agreed to joint jurisdiction over the whole Estuary. Argentina and Uruguay presented a submission to the World Conference of Maritime Rights. They claimed that the waters involved were 'internal waters' and therefore should be considered territorial waters of the riparian states. A decision was never reached on this submission and the British Admiralty in 1939, as in 1914, recognized only a three-mile territorial limit from the coast of both countries. Most international maritime nations followed Britain's assumption.

○ ○ ○

Punta del Este is a renowned vacation resort located 83-miles east of Montevideo. On a high point overlooking the town, a lighthouse flashes her signal seaward. A few minutes before 5pm(local time)on December 13, the lighthouse keeper saw the national cruiser *Uruguay* leave Maldonaldo harbor. The Uruguayan warship headed out to sea and picked up unusual speed, obviously bent on an urgent errand. Captain Fuentes, in command, had received orders from the Ministry of Defense to investigate a reported incident off the coast.

Uruguay sped southeasterly until Fuentes sighted *Graf Spee* at 60° on his beam. Continuing this course, Fuentes soon identified *Achilles* at 45° and Ajax at 90° on his beam. The British warships were converging on *Graf Spee*. Fuentes closed toward *Ajax* then swung about, and set course for territorial waters, in the direction of Punta Negra.

Close to 1900hrs, *Ajax* cruised eighteen miles south of Punta Jose Ignacio. *Graf Spee* was running ahead, twelve miles southeast of Punta del Este. A small island, Isla de Lobos, lay in the calm sea between *Graf Spee* and the mainland. To ensure *Graf Spee* did not reverse course around the tiny island, Harwood ordered *Achilles* to steam between the island and the coast. This would place the cruiser inside Uruguayan waters but in 'hot pursuit' of a belligerent. Commodore Harwood gave Captain Parry instructions to 'take advantage of territorial waters'.[1]

Harwood then ordered Captain Woodhouse to close the distance toward *Graf Spee. Ajax,* her battle flags flapping at the halyards, swept past *Uruguay's* stern, heading toward *Graf Spee;* Captain Fuentes had a grandstand view.

Lookouts on *Graf Spee* had spotted the Uruguayan cruiser in the distance. An alarm rang out and the crew sprang to action stations. Lieut-Commander Ascher, the gunnery officer, picked up the small, twin-funneled warship on a range-finder and recognized her Uruguayan flags. Moving at high speed, *Uruguay* crossed *Graf Spee's* wash. Luckilly, the alert paid a dividend. Langsdorff had warned his men to keep close watch for submarines. Hydrophone operators now picked up a torpedo track approaching the ship. The Captain called for a swift change of course to present *Spee's* stern to the danger.

Then *Ajax* came into view, closing quickly. *Graf Spee's* rear turret swung into line. From 26,000yds, two 11-inch volleys, at short intervals, whistled toward *Ajax*. *Spee's* shells fell too close and gave Harwood second thoughts. He ordered Woodhouse to take *Ajax* south of English Bank, a massive sandbar southeast of Montevideo, and await developments. *Ajax* immediately threw out a huge smokescreen and turned off. *Graf Spee* altered course to pass near Isla de Lobos and resumed her westward line.

Thirty minutes ahead of *Graf Spee*, the French liner *Formose* passed the point at Punta del Este. Captain Buron had seen *Graf Spee*, further out to sea, running a parallel course and overtaking his ship. When *Spee's* big guns barked, Buron feared he might be a target. Choosing caution, he ordered all passengers to don life-belts. *Formose* experienced no threat but her passengers observed the distant action.

Sitting in his high post, the Punta del Este lighthouse keeper heard *Graf Spee* fire on *Ajax*. Grabbing his binoculars, he focused on the action. It looked like a giant German battleship was engaged in a running fight with two small British cruisers. The German warship, running westward, would likely enter Uruguayan territorial waters. No doubt the British would follow and continue the fight. Anxious to spread the news, the keeper phoned a major newspaper in Montevideo. Word moved along the coast like a drum beat and people scrambled into position to watch the action.

Achilles now steamed along the Uruguayan coastline. Daylight had begun to soften and bright visibility would quickly fade into darkness. Captain Parry hoped to make another attack on *Graf Spee*, silhouetted against the setting sun, if she kept on her western course.

As daylight turned to dusk and the setting sun dropped behind the horizon the lighthouse keeper kept the Montevideo newspaper up to date. Crowds gathered in front of the newspaper's building to read the latest news from a handwritten message pinned to a board on the wall.

On board *Graf Spee* Langsdorff stood in the chart room, watching over Lieut-Commander Höpfner's shoulder. Wattenberg stood at the other side of Höpfner. The German navigators hoped to take the ship directly into Montevideo harbor. Höpfner, before his Naval service, had served as navigating officer on merchant ships plying the River Plate. He knew very well the treacherous shallows in the eastern roads and the dredged channel leading into the inner harbor. The German officers also recognized the political implications in entering the Plate Estuary.

Captain Langsdorff removed the pipe from his mouth. 'So, can we take her directly into the harbor?'

'I believe it is possible, Sir,' replied Höpfner. 'Fortunately the tides are in our favor.'

Wattenberg added a comment. 'We must reduce speed for the shallow water but with luck we can find anchorage without pilot assistance. If this is your plan, Sir, we can be anchored about midnight in Montevideo harbor.'

A note of uncertainty in the chief navigator's voice brought a sharp word from Langsdorff. 'We need major repairs,' he said. 'The closer we are to shore facilities the better.'

'Of course, my Captain,' replied Wattenberg. 'If we must go ashore, it is best we enter the harbor under our own power.'

Langsdorff smiled apologetically. 'Don't worry, Gentlemen, we'll find a way out of this mess,' he said, as he left the chart-house for the bridge.

'Yes Sir,' the navigators murmured, without conviction.

On the bridge Lieut-commander Ascher waited for Captain Langsdorff. 'Sir, the light is fading rapidly. We will presently be high-lighted against the setting sun and the afterglow. No doubt, the cruisers will use this to advantage.'

'Thank you, replied Langsdorff. We will start using smoke now. It appears one of our friends has detached, probably to cover any southern escape possibility. I'm anticipating the other cruiser will try an attack when the light fails.'

'Yes Sir,' agreed Ascher. 'And it will be difficult to get her range while she stays between us and the shadow of the land.'

Langsdorff puffed on his pipe thoughtfully before replying. 'I don't wish to engage inside the Plate territorial waters unless provoked. But, if they fire on us we can range on their gun-flashes.'

'Yes Sir, I'm keeping my men on high alert in readiness.'

Ascher left the bridge to climb into his D.C.T. and *Graf Spee* shrouded herself with a smoke screen large enough to cover her silhouette against the western sky.

This tactic was successful until 8.48pm(local time), when the unmistakable crack of gunfire boomed across the still waters. *Achilles,* illuminated by the flash of her own guns opened a five-volley barrage. Shrapnel rattled along *Graf Spee's* hull.

Dodging into a thicker cloud of smoke she responded although Ascher could only guess the range. Somehow he managed to land his shots close to *Achilles,* forcing her to turn away under a smokescreen. To ensure *Achilles* kept her distance, *Graf Spee* fired three single shots at 9.32pm, 9.40pm and 9.43pm. Very poor visibility made it impossible to mark the fall of shot.

Montevideo's lights shone ahead and Höpfner prepared to guide the ship into the tricky entrance channel. At 10pm, *Graf Spee* slid past the northern point of English Bank.

Achilles had maneuvered to within five miles of the pocket battleship. Captain Parry saw *Graf Spee* clearly against the glow of electric lights but declined any further attack. At 10.17pm Commodore Harwood ordered *Achilles* to withdraw.

With a dual feeling of relief and concern Harwood reviewed the situation. He found it incredible the fabled pocket battleship had run into Montevideo. Why had she done so? How long would she stay? How could he ensure she did not escape his vigil?

All these questions ran through Harwood's mind as he planned his next move. He had already signaled the Naval Attaché in Buenos Aires and the Admiralty, appraising them of the situation. 'Thank God for the excellent relationship we have with the Uruguayan authorities', he murmured. 'Millington-Drake's efforts over the last umpteen years as British Minister to Uruguay will stand in good stead.'

Militarily, Harwood's nearest help would come from *Cumberland* now closing the Plate at full speed from the Falkland Islands. Additional help would come from the nearest source the Admiralty could divert to the Plate. Now, he must guard the immense expanse of the River Plate Estuary to keep *Graf Spee* from slipping out in the darkness. It gave Commodore Harwood a sense of *déjà vu* when he recalled a practice session with the Uruguayan corvette *Huracan* in 1937. Commander Varela, then in command of the corvette, had been most cooperative in staging the scenario of an enemy warship seeking refuge in Montevideo.

Commodore Harwood now ordered his two cruisers onto station.

Achilles would patrol from Punta del Este to a point 120° from English Bank. *Ajax* would cover from that point to the Argentine coast at Cape San Antonio. Harwood believed his ships, patrolling this line, would see *Graf Spee* against the lights of Montevideo if she left in the night. In the morning the cruisers would resume their vigil inside the Estuary. Harwood would position them to negate the backdrop of eastern light. Commodore Henry Harwood felt he had covered all points and looked forward to a successful conclusion of the action: *Graf Spee* had retreated into a military and political trap.

Chapter 9

Hello Montevideo!

At 11pm (local time) December 13, hundreds of curious spectators gathered in Montevideo to watch a strange arrival. A German warship, with a massive, triple gun-turret fore and aft, was creeping into the inner harbor. Among the crowds on the quays, a young American broadcaster tingled with growing interest. Mike Fowler recognized the lines of a pocket battleship. Fowler's employer, The Red Meat Packing Company of Chicago, had sent him to Uruguay to study wild birds and enhance public relations. The Company had provided a portable radio system and a generous budget to record the local bird life. When Fowler saw the German warship, intuition told him a unique opportunity was coming his way.

United States had declared neutrality in the war now festering in Europe. However, powerful newspaper dailies in New York, Chicago and other American cities had warned that the war could easily expand into Continental-American trade routes. Strong political lobbies in the

Graf Spee *seeks sanctuary in Montevideo.* – Malvin Maritime Museum

States supported a 300-mile neutral zone along the entire Atlantic coastline; they did not wish American shipping dislocated or molested. The 300-mile proposal was currently in negotiation. Great Britain had formally rejected the proposal unless United States warships guaranteed non-violation in the whole area, including South America. What impact would the intrusion of a German battleship into neutral Uruguay make on these negotiations and North American public opinion?

As *Graf Spee* set anchor in Montevideo, special editions spilled onto news-stands around the world. Front page headlines reported a dramatic sea-battle involving *Admiral Graf Spee:*

At dawn on December 13, she had engaged three British cruisers off the South American coast. Heavy cruiser HMS*Exeter* had retreated to the Falklands naval base. Light cruisers, HMS*Ajax* and HMNZS*Achilles*, had trailed *Graf Spee* into Montevideo and awaited her exit: The European War had expanded into the western hemisphere.

Realizing his good fortune, Fowler swiftly organized a deal to broadcast the live action from Montevideo. Consequently, the American would play a key role in a death watch on the pocket battleship. Meanwhile, the Royal Navy, in close cooperation with the British Foreign Service, planned to end the German raider's successful campaign. For the next four days, *Graf Spee* and Uruguay would dominate world news.

○ ○ ○

Safely harbored in Montevideo, in the early hours of December 14, Captain Langsdorff expected a visitor from the German Legation. He had signaled his ship's imminent arrival in Montevideo and awaited the German Minister and the Naval Attaché. Throughout the previous day, Langsdorff had fought a desperate sea-battle. Now he must enter the world of politics.

Langsdorff had previous political experience in his career. In 1935 he had returned to sea-duty after four years shore service in Berlin. Personal disquiet in the offices of the Ministries of Defense and the Interior had motivated him to transfer back to sea.

At the dock in the harbor, *Graf Spee's* launch met an automobile from the German Legation. Soon the German Minister was piped aboard the warship. Captain Langsdorff, in company with some senior officers, greeted Herr Otto Langmann with a smart Naval salute to which the Minister replied with a casual Nazi 'wave'.

Langmann, a stocky little man wearing steel glasses on his round face, walked briskly with Langsdorff to the Captain's cabin. Lieut-Commander Ascher and Lieutenant Diggins accompanied them to the meeting. It was not an occasion for small talk.

They took their seats and the Minister promptly opened the discussion. 'I wish I could say welcome to Uruguay, Gentlemen,' he said gruffly. 'You have made a serious error to bring your ship here seeking aid.'

Langsdorff flashed a quick glance at his officers. He sensed the politician's annoyance. 'I'm truly sorry to cause problems, Your Excellency,' he said, 'but my ship is seriously damaged and we have little choice.'

Langmann's voice was calm but his face flushed. 'In this hotbed of English and French sympathizers you will get nothing to help you. Why on earth do you come here?'

Langsdorff, incensed by the Minister's hostile reception, snapped back. 'Your Excellency, my 'red-book' shows only two ports in this hemisphere with a naval attaché on station – Buenos Aires and Montevideo.' He paused briefly then continued. 'This port offers strategic advantages over Buenos Aires.'

Herr Langmann grasped the fact that Langsdorff knew nothing about the political situation in Montevideo. 'I should inform you Captain Langsdorff, that our Naval Attaché for Montevideo and Buenos Aires is the same. Captain Niebuhr will come from Buenos Aires on the first plane. Furthermore, I must warn you,' Langmann continued, 'The British Government holds strong political clout in this country. Their representative will strive to have your ship interned.' Langmann paused. 'Or, they may delay your departure and call in enough naval power to annihilate your ship if you try to break out.'

A sentry knocked on the cabin door and announced the arrival of the Attaché from Buenos Aires. Captain Dietrich Niebuhr exchanged salutes with the group and shook hands all round, starting with Herr Langmann. 'It's good you're already here, your Excellency,' he said, and sat in a chair beside the Minister.

Captain Niebuhr, a well respected naval officer and a skilled politician, was a decorated veteran of World War 1. He instantly sensed the tension in the room; it lingered like a sour smell.

Captain Langsdorff rapidly briefed the Attaché and made a suggestion. 'We must request the longest possible time to make repairs,' he said. 'We shall need favorable weather and knowledge of enemy strength to attempt a breakout.' He looked toward Lieut-Commander Ascher, 'Have you any ideas, Commander'?

Ascher responded. 'Yes Sir,' he agreed. 'We need time to choose further action – perhaps thirty days would be good.'

Otto Langmann's round face turned red. The eyes behind his round spectacles blazed. 'Thirty days!' he shouted, 'Are you mad?' He smacked his fist on his knee. 'British warships regularly use this port on a forty-eight-hour turnaround. For the honor of the Fatherland we must do the same, or better.'

Captain Langsdorff was almost spent from recent events and lack of sleep. 'Your Excellency, this is not a pleasure cruise.' His blue eyes glowed like a cutting flame. 'I have dead and injured men on my ship and the vessel is not seaworthy.' He glared into Langmann's eyes. 'We must stay in this port the longest time possible.'

Langmann reacted angrily to Langsdorff's ferocious tone but Captain Niebuhr cut into the charged atmosphere with cooling logic:

'We have brought a skilled naval constructor from Buenos Aires. He is inspecting the ship with *Spee's* Chief Engineer. They will quickly make a detailed damage list and we can estimate a reasonable repair time.' With a hint of reprimand he added, 'Gentlemen, we can expect enough problems from the enemy without adding disagreement among ourselves.' A big bulky man, Niebuhr sat easily in his chair: cool and precise. 'The Minister makes a viable point,' he continued. 'We can expect at best, very slow response to our request for aid. The only major shipyard in Montevideo is Reguschi & Voulminot, a family venture with strong French connections.'

Herr Langmann wished to prove his full support. 'We'll offer them a blank check,' he said, crisply. 'I have never known a Frenchman to refuse a chance to make quick money.'

Niebuhr was not convinced. 'Anyway, we will lay groundwork for aid to come from Buenos Aires.' The Attaché addressed Langsdorff understandingly. 'Captain, you and your men should get some sleep and leave these details in our hands.'

Langmann stood up to suggest the meeting be ended and said to Niebuhr: 'Bring me your list of repairs and we'll ask the Government of Uruguay's indulgence.' The group exchanged salutes, and the Attaché accompanied Langmann to the waiting launch.

○ ○ ○

In the British Legation in Montevideo, the lights had burned all night as the Minister worked at his desk. A signal from the Admiralty had alerted him, in the afternoon of 13 December, that a damaged German warship might demand sanctuary from the government of Uruguay. In that case, Eugen Millington-Drake wished a front and center position in the political action; he had passed the night carefully screening the fine print of the Hague Convention.

A consummate professional politician, Millington-Drake had cultivated the trust of the Uruguayan government and its people over many years; in 1934 he had founded the Anglo-Uruguayan Cultural Association. Genuinely popular, he returned the Uruguayan friendship with a heartfelt fondness for the people and their beautiful country.

Now, in the early hours of Thursday, December 14, Millington-Drake phoned Captain H.McCall, the British Naval Attaché in Buenos Aires. The Minister knew a leak existed in telephone communications but his news could never remain secret:

'I'm so sorry to disturb you Captain but we have a unique situation in Montevideo.' He paused to let the Attaché gather his thoughts then continued. 'The *Graf Spee* has shown up in Montevideo harbor. She needs repairs and will seek asylum.'

McCall responded quickly. 'Aha, good morning, Your Excellency, thanks for calling. Damned good show by Bobby Harwood and his boys,' he said. 'Bye-the-bye, I've been notified of the action. I'll fly over to join you on the first flight.'

Millington-Drake had assumed McCall would already know his news; one can never upstage the navy. Into the phone he said, 'That'll be perfect, Captain. I look forward to seeing you again.'

He hung up the phone and flipped through a listing on his desk. Captain H. Daniel was a friend of the Minister and agent for the Houlder

Line. Millington-Drake dialed the number and spoke into the phone without fanfare. 'My apologies' old boy,' he said. 'We have important work to do. The Germans have sailed *Graf Spee* directly into the harbor and we need to keep a constant eye on her doings. Can you arrange a 24-hour vigil, beginning immediately?

Captain Daniel, accustomed to the Minister's outlandish requests, already knew of the warship's presence in Montevideo. Without exclamation or query he answered slowly, 'Good morning Your Excellency, I'll look into it right away.' Then he hung up the phone.

Millington-Drake replaced his dead phone on the cradle. 'Amazing fellow,' he chuckled, shaking his head slowly from side to side.

The British Minister now composed an official protest to another old friend, Doctor Alberto Guani, the Uruguayan Minister for Foreign Affairs. Great Britain would demand Uruguay order the German warship to leave neutral waters within twenty-four hours. If she failed to obey, Uruguay must intern her, as ruled in the Hague Convention of 1907. This strategy was obvious – no need to wait for official orders from the Foreign Office.

Millington-Drake's 'official note' to the Uruguayan Minister of Foreign Affairs already lay in a red-sealed envelope when the British Minister's instructions arrived by cable from Whitehall:

> *H.M. MINISTER MUST USE EVERY ENDEAVOR TO GET SPEE INTERNED. ARGUMENTS TO BE USED ARE (A) IF SHIP IS SEAWORTHY, HAGUE CONVENTION DOES NOT PERMIT REPAIRS AND SHE MUST LEAVE AFTER TWENTY-FOUR HOURS OR BE INTERNED, (B) IF SHE IS NOT SEAWORTHY, SAME IS TRUE, AS THERE IS WIDE SUPPORT FOR THE VIEW THAT NO SHORE FACILITIES OR EXTENSION OF TIME MAY BE GRANTED FOR REPAIRS AND DAMAGE SUSTAINED IN ACTION. IF URUGUAYAN GOVERNMENT WILL NOT ACCEPT THESE ARGUMENTS WE PREFER THE SHIP REMAINS FOUR OR FIVE DAYS.*[1]

Millington-Drake was steering the right course, well ahead of his instructions.

○ ○ ○

Aboard *Graf Spee,* Captain Langsdorff felt obligated to cover another duty before resting. He ordered Captain Dove brought to his cabin. Langsdorff wished to appraise the Englishman of the prisoners' impending release.

Dove's escort knocked on the door, and announced the arrival of the English captain. Langsdorff's haggard appearance shocked Dove. 'My God Captain, you look like you've had a bad night.' The huge, bear-like, Englishman bit back his friendly greeting. Dove realized, the German Captain was not in his usual jocular mood but the silly words were out.

Langsdorff gave a tight grin and responded seriously. 'Ah Captain, I'm sorry you had to be in this action. I'm glad none of you people are injured.'

Dove looked at the tired face of the German. He noticed the slight shrapnel wounds on his clean shaven face (Langsdorff had previously worn a mustache and a tiny spade-type beard). The Englishman gestured toward the sling supporting Langsdorff's right arm. 'But you're wounded, Captain,' he said. 'Weren't you under cover.?

Langsdorff shrugged. 'It was impossible,' he said. 'I had three enemy ships to watch and I could not take my eyes off one of them.' He went on to express his appreciation of the skills and courage of his opponents: 'They were magnificent splendid fighters. When you fight brave men like that you cannot feel any enmity. You only want to shake their hands. The *Achilles* and *Ajax* came at me like destroyers. I thought they would never do this unless supported by big ships or submarines.'

The Captain's fair-minded decency always impressed Dove. 'What will you do now,'? he asked.

Langsdorff took a moment before replying: 'The Uruguayan authorities will probably allow me forty-eight hours to repair my ship. That is not enough time. It will take many days to repair the damage. This is not a friendly port to Germany. So, the workers will work very slowly for me.' He pursed his lips, then added, 'We shall see what can be done.'

Dove did not press the point further but asked about his release and the rest of the British prisoners.

Captain Langsdorff responded typically: 'Of course Captain, you will all be released later today. The German Legation in Montevideo will arrange everything.' He reached into his desk and pulled out two hat-bands. The bold gold letters read, *Panzerschiff Admiral Graf Spee*. 'I would like you and Captain Pottinger to have these,' he said. 'They belonged to two of my fallen men.' [*Ashlea's* captain had impressed Langsdorff with his courteous qualities.]

The merchant captain could not find words to reply. With suppressed emotion, the two men shook hands, exchanged salutes and Dove left the cabin.

When the door closed, Langsdorff filled one of his pipes, lit it and slowly paced the large space in his cabin. As he puffed the pipe he picked up a family picture from his bookcase. It showed his two sons, Jochen and Kläuschen, smiling happily. Jochen's protective arm cradled his little brother.

Three years ago the younger boy had suddenly died of a childhood illness. Twelve-year-old Jochen had suffered heartbreak when he lost his seven-year-old brother. Langsdorff carefully replaced the photo. 'Happy birthday my son,' he murmured. Today, December 14, Jochen turned fifteen.

○ ○ ○

Lieut-Commander Klepp, *Graf Spee's* chief engineer, and the constructor from Buenos Aires soon compiled a comprehensive damage report. Armed with specific details of the ship's damage, Captain Niebuhr went ashore to report to Herr Langmann. In the Embassy, he found the German Minister in a foul mood. Niebuhr saluted, shook hands and sat in a chair facing the ornate wooden desk of the Minister.

Langmann chose his words carefully. 'The plot has already begun,' he said glumly. 'The French shipyard refused us any assistance. We told them to name their price but they wouldn't even discuss the work.'

Niebuhr was not surprised. 'We're flying workers and materials from Buenos Aires,' he said. Then he placed a short list on the desk and slid it toward Langmann. 'Here is the damage list affecting the seaworthiness of the ship. We must insist on a fourteen-day minimum stay to effect repairs.'

Graf Spee's list of damages included a conspicuous four-square-meter hole in the port bow. The ship needed extensive repairs to a high pressure steam system that served the kitchen, the laundry, and a condenser apparatus that produced fresh water. These facilities were essential to sail the high seas.

Otto Langmann had scant knowledge of ships or life at sea. The Nazi Party had posted the former Lutheran Pastor to Uruguay for services rendered. Niebuhr did not wish to confuse the minister nor present him with political ammunition that might embarrass the navy.

Langmann examined the damage list intently. '*Graf Spee* has clearly received heavy punishment,' he commented. 'She has nine holes in her structure.?

Niebuhr quickly cut in. 'There are more but we see no need to tell the enemy. The major hole in the bow is enough to argue the point of sea-worthiness.'

Langmann nodded. 'I understand the crucial nature of the item regarding fresh water, but, I have problems with the kitchen equipment and laundry.' He waited for Niebuhr's explanation.

The Attaché looked lamely at the Minister. 'There is a major problem with the fuel and lubrication system associated with this damage. High pressure steam used for the kitchen is also essential to clean the fuel and lubricating oil for the engines. The enemy would relish this vital information.'

Langmann sighed. 'Ah! Our difficulties multiply every hour,' he said. 'The enemy is watching us from eight British merchant ships anchored in the harbor. Other spies are working ashore. Millington-Drake is applying great pressure to urge the Uruguayan Government to the British side. His contacts include many friends in important positions who can help his efforts.'

Niebuhr understood Langmann's problem. Millington-Drake was highly popular in Uruguay. The clever Englishman would use this opportunity to advance his political career. The British Minister embodied a formidable opponent in the political arena. 'We too have friends, in Argentina' Niebur said, wishing to console Langmann. 'We can enlist help from this direction'.

'Of course,' replied Langmann. 'But the BBC (British Broadcasting Corp.) is already gloating about a great victory. They claim large warships are nearby to prevent *Graf Spee* from escaping Montevideo.'

Niebuhr shrugged. 'Any news of this type is probably false,

especially coming from the BBC. We must assess all information closely.'

Langmann agreed, then asked. 'What about Langsdorff's report claiming poison gas burns on some of his men? There was uncertainty in the Minister's tone.

Captain Niebuhr took a moment before answering: 'I questioned Captain Langsdorff about this inclusion in his initial report. Personally, Langsdorff could not believe the British used mustard gas in the battle. However, strong medical evidence supported gas burns on his men that he could not ignore.' Niebuhr then added, 'I agree with Langsdorff's opinion. The British had no reason to use such a weapon. I suggest extreme caution in any propaganda until we have proof.'

Langmann nodded in agreement. 'I'll include the item in my talks with Doctor Guani and demand an investigation. Perhaps it will gain us extra days in port.' He took a gold pocket watch from his vest pocket and checked the time. 'At noon, we have an appointment with the Uruguayan Foreign Minister. We'll ask for a minimum stay of fourteen days.'

Niebuhr rose from his seat. 'Very well, Your Excellency, if you'll excuse me, I must check the men and materials coming from Buenos Aires.'

Chapter 10

Needs 14 days!

Early morning, on December 14, soon after *Graf Spee* anchored in Montevideo, General Alfredo Campos, the Minister of National Defense telephoned the President of Uruguay. General Alfredo Baldomir listened attentively while Campos appraised him of the arrival of a German warship in their country. Campos advised Baldomir he had confined the Uruguayan army to barracks pending further orders. He had also mobilized transportation units and placed the Navy and the air force on high alert.

Baldomir congratulated Campos on his fast reactions and instructed him to consult immediately with Dr. Guani, the Minister for Foreign Affairs. President Baldomir then placed a call to Franklin D. Roosevelt, the President of the United States: He wished to ensure neutral support in case of need. Roosevelt, already informed about the incident, had ordered a close surveillance of the situation.

General Campos lost no time in calling Dr. Alberto Guani. The foreign minister, roused from his sleep, listened to Campos' story. When the General hung up, Guani thought about calling Eugen Millington-Drake. The British Envoy and Dr. Guani had first met socially in 1914. They made further friendly connections in 1925 when Guani was Uruguayan Minister in Paris. Their fellowship expanded in 1933, when he was Uruguayan Minister in London. They had become close friends.

A few days earlier, Dr. Guani told his friend he had closed his apartment in Paris. All his magnificent furniture, accumulated since 1925, had left Le Havre on the French steamer *Formose.* Guani had received a shipping date and estimated arrival in Montevideo. *Formose* was due any day in Montevideo from Santos, Brazil, her last stop en route to the Uruguayan capital.

Guani had talked again with Millington-Drake while the sea-battle raged off Punta del Este. Guani fretted that *Formose* might get involved in the action. Millington-Drake jokingly suggested the Royal Navy may have used *Formose* to attract the attention of the German warship;

Guani's furniture might become a small contribution to the British war effort. The Uruguayan Minister did not take the joke lightly.

Now trying to shake himself awake, Guani believed the British Minister would have information at his fingertips concerning *Graf Spee.* He decided against making the call. To talk privately with a belligerent power in these circumstances might raise questions of neutrality. Instead, he pulled out his books on the Hague Convention and read the familiar document to refresh his memory.

° ° °

Just before noon on December 14, the Uruguayan Minister of Foreign Affairs concluded his official acceptance of diplomatic notes from the Representatives of Great Britain and France. Mr. Eugen Millington-Drake and Monsieur M.Gentil were taking their leave in elegant style. Their official envelopes, red seals broken, lay on Dr. Guani's desk. Besides their official documents, both Ministers had presented their arguments verbally. They demanded immediate expulsion, within twenty-four hours, of the German pocket battleship anchored in the harbor of Montevideo, or, alternately, the vessel be interned. They quoted various acts and clauses of the Hague Convention to support their demands. While speaking elegant language with the politeness of skilled politicians, they left no doubt that their demands could not be denied.

Dr. Guani, no less accomplished in political elan, blandly informed them he would consider their arguments and respond officially, when possible. The three Ministers, in correct professional manner, smilingly shook hands and bid each other good-day.

In Dr. Guani's anteroom, precisely at noon, Herr Langmann and Captain Niebuhr waited their meeting with the Uruguayan Minister. Guani greeted them with customary politeness and received their official documents. Seated at his desk, with the Germans comfortably seated in front, the Minister asked for a verbal summary of their needs.

Herr Langmann explained, the warship *Graf Spee* needed fourteen days for repairs into seaworthy condition. In addition, he complained some German seamen had suffered poison gas burns during a sea-battle with British warships.

Guani responded that Uruguay could not approve fourteen days of sanctuary without justification. A Uruguayan Commission must inspect the ship and file a damage report. Captain Niebuhr agreed this was a reasonable condition. Guani then addressed the poison gas claim. An International Health Commission would check the injured men and publish a report.

Finally, he told them he would gather all the facts concerning *Graf Spee's* intrusion into his country and present them to his government. The Cabinet would discuss the matter and render a decision. Promptly, he would deliver the decision to the German Minister.

Captain Niebuhr asked the Uruguayan if thirty-six German casualties, still on board *Graf Spee*, might be buried in Montevideo. Dr. Guani agreed to this humanitarian request but to ensure security he must check with General Campos, the Minister of Defense. Guani telephoned the General who approved the funeral and offered a Uruguayan military escort. All agreed that the ceremony could take place December 15, which was next day. Cordially, with excessive politeness, the conference ended and the Germans left the Uruguayan Minister to his work.

Dr. Guani brooded about the German claim of poison gas wounds on their casualties. The Minister knew a respected eye specialist had treated the men in the Pasteur Hospital, Montevideo.

Dr. Walter Meerhoff answered the phone when Guani called:

'*Buenos Dias*, Doctor Meerhoff, Our German visitors claim the British used poison gas against their men. Can you help me in this regard?'

Meerhoff replied. '*Buenos Dias*, Your Excellency. I can certainly give you my professional opinion of the injuries I examined in this hospital.'

'Thank you, Doctor,' said the Minister. 'What exactly is your opinion of the injuries you examined? '

Meerhoff gently cleared his throat. 'I'm sorry to say the injuries I have treated are consistent with exposure to mustard gas, or a similar substance.'

'Are you certain? ' asked Guani. 'This is incredible.'

Dr. Meerhoff was adamant. 'Doctor Guani,' he growled, 'you requested my professional opinion. I have given it to you and it will not change.'

Meerhoff's mother, a Uruguayan, had married a German seaman, therefore, the famous eye specialist had German family connections. He knew of Dr. Guani's well-known leanings toward Britain and wished to make his position absolutely clear. 'I don't wish to aid or abet any political cause, or to fathom the source of these wounds. My professional integrity demands that I diagnose and treat an injury. The cause of an injury interests me only if it helps in treatment.'

Guani did not loose his cool tone. 'Of course, Doctor,' he said. 'I would expect nothing less from you. I will of necessity request the appointment of an International Commission to study the matter.'

Meerhoff was equally calm. 'As you wish Your Excellency,' he said. 'I bid you good-day.'

Guani then called General Campos and asked for a Commission of Naval Experts to examine *Graf Spee*. Also, he requested a scrutiny maintained on the German warship to ensure compliance with the Hague rules.

Campos assured him that the Uruguayan corvette *Lavalleja* was already on guard duty close to *Graf Spee* with orders to prevent violations. General Campos advised Guani that President Baldomir was depending heavily on the Minister's political expertise to guide the Uruguayan effort. They must unwaveringly follow international law in this unusual situation. Neutral countries all over the continent, including United States, were watching with concern Uruguay's handling of the situation. Guani realized the matter was in his hands. He must comply strictly with the law despite his personal dislike of the Nazi regime.

○ ○ ○

Aboard *Graf Spee* on December 14, thirty-six flag-draped caskets lay on the after-deck. A uniformed guard of honor ceremoniously kept watch on their fallen comrades. Meanwhile, repairs to the damaged ship progressed methodically and rapidly.

In mid-afternoon, the British prisoners held on *Graf Spee* during the sea-battle left the warship. They included merchant Captains, Chief Engineers, Radio Officers, the three lads from *Tairoa,* and finally, officers and crew from *Streonshalh.* In all, they numbered sixty-one men.

Everyone welcomed their release and praised the treatment they had received from their German captors. Captains Dove and Pottinger

Guard of Honor: Graf Spee *casualties in Montevideo.* – F.W. Rasenack.

had made friends with Captain Langsdorff and all hands noted the personal decency of the *Graf Spee* Commander. As they filed past the flag-draped coffins on the after-deck the British officers gave a solemn salute of respect.

When the ex-prisoners arrived ashore, British Intelligence immediately cornered them for interrogation. Captain McCall, the Naval Attaché, and his assistant, Captain Rex Miller[1] conducted searching interviews. They gleaned from the merchant seamen any information that might help the war effort against *Graf Spee.*

Later in the evening, Captain Dove gave a radio interview that angered some of his British compatriots. The British Merchant Captain reported the meticulous attention Captain Langsdorff had paid to the Hague Conventions in his operations.

In the interview, Dove gave several examples of the German Captain's humanitarian principles. Despite the loss of his own ship, which Dove saw as a legitimate act of war, the British Captain gave respectful praise to Langsdorff. Dove reminded listeners that commerce raiding embraced a legitimate wartime tactic; the Hague Convention outlined rules and guidelines. Captain Langsdorff had followed these rules to the letter and should be commended.

Soon after his broadcast Captain Dove received a visit from Captain Rex Miller. The Army Captain told Dove, leaving no room for doubt, that praising the enemy in battlefront conditions was not acceptable. Such behavior would not enhance the British war effort nor his personal career. Miller conducted the interview quietly, without anger. Dove agreed to add nothing to his comments while the *Graf Spe*e problem persisted.

On December 14, Thursday night, Captain Langsdorff called a meeting of his officers in the mess. They deserved to know their fate. The Captain appeared haggard and ruffled but his voice held firm and calm. Langsdorff praised the men for their speedy efforts to repair the ship's damage. He then explained:

'Complexity of the work involved or lack of materials still delayed essential repairs. *Graf Spee* might break out to the open sea or to Buenos Aires. It depends on the number and quality of enemy ships assembled to prevent our escape: *Graf Spee* must reach deep water in any breakout attempt.'

Langsdorff did not diminish the situation. He gave them the information, short and straight:

'It may be possible to break out to Buenos Aires into a less hostile political climate. Perhaps we could arrange something with Argentina to help the war effort. For example, in World War 1 *Goeben* and *Breslau* escaped a trap and entered Constantinople. Turkey bought the German warships and later joined Germany in the war'.

'Our position is very serious but it is not hopeless. We will weigh our best options when the ship is ready to sail. Meanwhile, our Minister is seeking political help from Berlin to gain enough time for flexibility of action.'

Langsdorff never failed to be optimistic. The officers listened and warmed to their charismatic Captain. They knew he would lead them out of this mess, somehow.

As Langsdorff spoke words of encouragement to his officers, the net around his ship closed tighter. HMS*Cumberland*, an eight-gun x 8-inch heavy cruiser arrived at 2200hrs to join *Ajax* and *Achilles* in the vigil. *Cumberland* had steamed 1200 miles from the Falklands in thirty-six hours making record-breaking time. The heavy cruiser, much more powerful than *Exeter,* brightened Commodore Harwood's chances of stopping *Graf Spee.*

CHAPTER 11

Report to Berlin

Captain Langsdorff completed his official battle report after midnight, December 14, in the German Legation. *Graf Spee* was the first pocket battleship to face enemy shell-fire and important details of the action must be conveyed to his superiors. Top naval authorities in the High Command appreciated the technical merits of the pocket battleships but were ignorant of some serious flaws. Langsdorff had learned the bitter truth that *Graf Spee's* orders held merit – do not engage warships even of inferior class. The pocket battleships, though brilliant commerce raiders, had skimpy armor protection. This would not surprise his superiors but Langsdorff had encountered other technical problems in his command. A disastrous lack of protection for the vital steam system led the list. Langsdorff must get this information to Berlin without revealing it to the enemy. Furthermore, fierce in-house rivalry between the army, air-force, navy and foreign office prevented clear communication. The pocket battleships held an aura of naval prestige that must continue: *Graf Spee, Deutschland* and *Admiral Scheer* represented a large portion of Germany's fleet in 1939.

Langsdorff read the report several times, made small corrections, and signed his name at the bottom. Dated December 14, 1939, the cipher was addressed to Naval Headquarters from *Admiral Graf Spee* Command 195 and transmitted to Berlin at 1am, December 15:

> *SEARCHED FOR CONVOY ASSUMING IT IS PROTECTED BY A CRUISER. EXETER SIGHTED ON DECEMBER 13 AT DAWN. SHE IS MOVING ALONG PRESUMED ENGLISH STEAMSHIP ROUTE. ACCOMPANYING VESSEL AT FIRST BELIEVED TO BE A DESTROYER, LATER IDENTIFIED AS TWO CRUISERS OF ACHILLES CLASS. AS SHAKING OFF THREE CRUISERS SEEMED IMPOSSIBLE, ATTACKED BEFORE ENEMY COULD GET UP STEAM FOR MAXIMUM SPEED SO AS TO CLOSE THE RANGE. ENEMY DIVIDES SO*

THAT ONE CRUISER AT LEAST IS NOT EXPOSED TO FIRE AND TRIES TO CLOSE THE RANGE. HEAVY DIRECT HITS CLEARLY OBSERVED ON FORWARD QUARTER OF EXETER, SILENCING BOTH FRONT TURRETS. DIRECT HITS ON THE BRIDGE, CAUSING SERIOUS FIRE, AND HEAVIER DIRECT HITS APPARENTLY DAMAGING BOILERS, WHEREUPON EXETER MOVES OFF. TO RELIEVE HER, LIGHT CRUISERS CLOSE THE RANGE ON GRAF SPEE AT FULL SPEED. NEAREST APPROACH 76H/M [4.1 Nautical miles] LIGHTCRUISERS FIRED RAPIDLY AND WELL. DEFENCE MADE DIFFICULT BY FAILURE OF FORWARD AMMUNITION SUPPLY OF GROUP M.A.[15cm] MEDIUM ARTILLERY AND OUR SHARP CHANGES OF COURSE IN ORDER TO MANOEUVER AWAY FROM HITS. AFT TURRETS ON ONE CRUISER SILENCED; MOREOVER ANOTHER S.A.[28cm] HEAVY ARTILLERY DIRECT HIT AND PROBABLY TWO X 10.5cm DIRECT HITS. THIRD CRUISER APPARENTLY UNDAMAGED. AFTER EXETER HAS MOVED OFF, LIGHT CRUISERS MOVE TO A GREAT DISTANCE AND REMAIN TO THE N.E AND S.E. TO BREAK OUT TO OPEN SEA AND SHAKE OFF THESE TWO CRUISERS IS OBVIOUSLY IMPOSSIBLE. INSPECTION OF DIRECT HITS REVEALS THAT ALL GALLEYS EXCEPT FOR THE ADMIRAL'S GALLEY HAVE BEEN BADLY DAMAGED. WATER ENTERING FLOUR STORE ENDANGERS BREAD SUPPLY WHILE A DIRECT HIT IN THE FORECASTLE MAKES SHIP UNSEAWORTHY FOR NORTH ATLANTIC IN WINTER. ONE SHELL PIERCED ARMOUR BELT WHILE THE ARMOURED DECK IS TORN IN ONE PLACE. DAMAGE IN AFTER PART OF SHIP. 36 KILLED, 5 SERIOUSLY WOUNDED, 53 SLIGHTLY INJURED, 14 OF THEM AFFECTED BY POISON GAS. AS SHIP CANNOT BE MADE SEAWORTHY FOR BREAKTHROUGH TO THE HOMELAND WITH MEANS ON BOARD, DECIDED TO GO INTO THE RIVER PLATE AT RISK OF BEING SHUT IN THERE. BECAUSE OF EXPECTED SUBMARINE ATTACK NEAR ENGLISH BANK WE MAINTAINED ZIGZAG COURSE AND HIGH SPEED.

ATTACK BY SUBMARINES SOUTH OF LOBOS ISLAND FAILED. AT 12 O'CLOCK AT NIGHT [11pm local time] XIII DECEMBER ENTERED MONTEVIDEO HARBOUR WITHOUT PILOT.[1]

(SIGNED) LANGSDORFF.

Captain Langsdorff needed sleep. Adrenaline alone had carried him through the last hours. Bidding Herr Langmann, goodnight, he left the Legation and returned to *Graf Spee.* When crossing the harbor, his launch passed a Uruguayan corvette lying between *Graf Spee* and the dock. Also anchored in the harbor, a German freighter offered a friendly face. *Tacoma* (8,268BRT) was ready to help the warship in any way possible.

Langsdorff climbed aboard his ship and headed for the mess room. *Graf Spee* hummed with activity. Lights were burning on every deck and spasmodic blue flashes sparked where busy men worked with welding equipment. In the mess room four officers awaited his return. Lieutenant Diggins poured the Captain a small whisky and the group clustered around a card table.

Commander Walter Kay, the Executive Officer, a giant with a black mustache and goatee spoke first. 'Well Captain, what news?'

Langsdorff sipped a tiny taste of whisky, gave an appreciative sigh and replied. 'Gentlemen, The Uruguayan Government is studying a damage report produced by their Expert Commission. We must wait their pleasure to tell us how long we can stay in port.'

Kay grunted with contempt. 'Damned banana republic. They will do exactly what the *Tommies* tell them to do.'

Langsdorff smiled, 'Perhaps you're right,' he said. 'But they must conform to the Hague Conventions, as indeed we are obliged to conform.'

'To hell with the Conventions,' spluttered Kay. 'We should show some muscle and take what we need to get out of this trap.'

Langsdorff sensed where Kay was heading. 'That would add to our problems and enrage every American state, including the United States.' He put his glass on the table and continued. 'No! This is a situation that requires careful diplomacy, not brute force. I believe, somehow, we will retrieve ourselves from this problem with honor, the same high level of honor that we have attained throughout our campaign.'

Kay remained unconvinced but switched his thought to a practical complaint. 'Then how should we deal with the port officials harassment of our men?' he asked. 'Every bolt and piece of machinery is being checked prior to shipment from the dock to the ship.'

'We will act with persuasion and patience,' replied Langsdorff. 'I will ask the Minister to give this matter special attention.'

Langsdorff picked up his glass, examined the contents and took another tiny sip. 'What is our latest status?' he asked. 'Is the problem with our medium artillery resolved?'

Lieut-Commander Ascher replied, 'Of course, Sir. My men gave this top priority.' Ascher, the gunnery officer, controlled *Graf Spee's* huge armament. 'But we have some bad news,' he continued. 'Damage to the main optical gun-sight on the foretop is serious. It is impossible to repair. We are reduced to the secondary gun-sights in battle conditions and of course the radar is ineffective as a gun-sighting aid.'

The high-powered special optics on the foretop had played a key part in *Graf Spee's* successful raider mission. Lookouts sometimes sighted ships' smoke from fifty miles. Added to the loss of the Arado spotter plane, such lack of vision would hinder *Graf Spee's* return home, if she escaped from Montevideo.

Langsdorff took the news calmly. 'Another item in our long list of problems,' he mused.

Lieut-Commander Wattenberg, the chief navigator and technical advisor, broke into the conversation. 'It's ironic we saw few British ships at sea but here we find eight of them sitting on our doorstep.' Wattenberg, a long, lean elegant man who enjoyed literature continued. 'It's obvious the enemy is watching us from those ships.' He shrugged, then added, 'We are naked in an uncovered fish-bowl.'

Langsdorff nodded, 'Yes, and the World will be monitoring our actions in this fish-bowl.'

The Captain switched back to Commander Kay 'How are the men holding up, Commander?'

'They are doing very well, Sir,' Kay replied. 'Moral is high, even among the men in the ship's hospital. Ashore, in the Military Hospital, our casualties are receiving good care. Today the burial party will go to the cemetery, as you know.'

'Yes, we will see the reaction of the local people,' mused Langsdorff. 'I feel they will be sympathetic to our fallen men.'

The Captain then drained his glass and put it on the table in a quick, decisive motion. 'Well, Gentlemen,' he said, 'If there is nothing else, I bid you good night.'

'Good night, Sir,' they chorused and saluted as the Captain left the room.

○ ○ ○

December 15 began early for Millington-Drake. A telegraph from Commodore Henry Harwood, commandant of the British cruiser squadron guarding the mouth of the Plate, arrived in his office. It was dated December 14, the previous day. Harwood's signal directed the British Minister to arrange that a British merchant ship leave Montevideo immediately. In his message he mentioned the '24-hour rule' (The Hague Conventions ruled that a warship must not sail until twenty-four hours after an enemy merchant ship had left port). A blatant violation of the Hague rule could bring international censure. The Minister recognized that Harwood wanted *Graf Spee* held in Montevideo until additional warships reinforced his squadron. On paper, *Graf Spee*, 12,000 tons, toting six 11-inch guns mismatched Harwood's two light cruisers. It was a useful though technically weak ploy to delay *Graf Spee*.

At Millington-Drake's request, Captain Daniel, the agent for the Houlder Line, persuaded port authorities to release SS*Ashworth* at 6.15pm that day. For good measure he organized a second ship, *Dunster Grange,* to sail next day, December 16. Captain Daniel also reported to Millington-Drake all activities observed aboard *Graf Spee*. Daniel had called in friendly pensioners to watch the warship around the clock. Several British freighters, accumulated in Montevideo harbor, provided ideal platforms for spying on the pocket battleship.

Meanwhile, a British Intelligence effort to intimidate *Graf Spee* made headway. Captain McCall, the Naval Attaché, had left his assistant, Commander Lloyd Hirst, in charge of the office in Buenos Aires. Hirst, a highly experienced intelligence officer, planned to spread as many rumors as possible purporting the arrival of large British warships to join the siege.

Commander Hirst, a veteran of World War 1, had served as intelligence officer aboard HMS*Glasgow*. This British cruiser, badly damaged in the 1914 Battle of Coronel, had escaped from Admiral Graf von Spee's victorious cruiser squadron. Hirst had played a vital role negotiating a dry dock session for his ship in Rio de Janeiro. Neutral Brazil had allowed *Glasgow* five days in dry dock plus two additional days re-fitting. Immediately after these extensive repairs *Glasgow* rejoined the British battle cruiser squadron that eliminated Graf von Spee's squadron in the Battle of the Falklands.

Now in Buenos Aires, with typical cheek and nerve, Commander Hirst requested an audience with Admiral Scasso, a high-placed officer in the Argentine navy. Playing with a poker face the British officer asked Scasso if Mar del Plata could immediately provision HMS*Ark Royal* and HMS*Renown*. Located one-hundred and fifty miles from Montevideo, Mar del Plata was not a regular port of call for British warships.

Admiral Scasso consulted a senior officer from Mar del Plata who happened to be in the building. Commander Hirst wanted assurance the entrance channel was deep enough to handle the British aircraft carrier and battle cruiser when they arrived within a day or so. The British officer asked specifically where the ships could be berthed and refueled. Leaving nothing to chance, he questioned the Argentine officer if large enough tugs were on hand.

Lloyd Hirst played his role perfectly. Special editions of Buenos Aires newspapers published a report 'from a reliable source' that *Ark Royal* and *Renown* would arrive in Mar del Plata within forty-eight hours.

Unwittingly, Commodore Harwood reinforced this ploy. In the first hours of daylight in the Estuary, Harwood prepared his squadron for a knockout blow on *Graf Spee*. RFA*Olynthus*, a 15,000-ton fuel tanker stood nearby. Harwood ordered his flagship HMS*Ajax* to refuel at sea. Under the watchful eyes of the other two cruisers, *Ajax* replenished her bunkers. High seas made the task hazardous but the British warships, barely in sight of Montevideo, completed the operation successfully.

○ ○ ○

Graf Spee crewmen at funeral in Montevideo. – DIEGO M.LASCANO

At the harbor in Montevideo around 10am, British watchers could easily see the happenings on *Graf Spee's* after-deck. Thirty-six coffins, each wrapped in a *kriegsmarineflagge*, were loaded onto a tug for transit to shore. The caskets had been ceremoniously guarded throughout the previous day and night. Now, with Uruguayan co-operation, the Germans would bury their battle causalities in Montevideo. The Uruguayan Government, thanks to General Campos, supplied transportation for a 300-man detachment of *Graf Spee's* crew to honor their fallen comrades.

Slowly, sadly, the funeral procession progressed up spacious *Avenida 18 de Julio*, Montevideo's main route. An automobile, overflowing with flowers, led the cortege. Various vehicles came close behind, carrying the coffins smothered with wreaths and flowers. Automobiles with the German Minister, Captain Langsdorff, Admiral Schröder(Uruguay's Chief Naval Officer) and some of *Graf Spee's* senior officers came next in line. In the rear, in a fleet of buses, *Spee* crew members with an escort of Uruguayan naval personnel completed the procession. A mounted Uruguayan guard of honor lined the edges of the parade.

Huge crowds had formed along the route in *'diez y ocho'* to see the procession. Most Uruguayans were simply curious to see the parade but nothing disturbed the hushed drama as the ceremonial cortege quietly advanced along the route.

Captain Langdorff's final salute to his fallen men.
– Diego M.Lascano - Eduard Schüler Collection

At the *Cementerio del Norte*, two German pastors, one Catholic and the other Presbyterian, performed the funeral rites. Captain Langsdorff said a few words and Herr Otto Langmann delivered a rousing speech. Captain Dove, representing the British merchant officers, laid a wreath at the grave-site. It said, 'TO THE MEMORY OF BRAVE MEN OF THE SEA FROM THEIR COMRADES OF THE BRITISH MERCHANT SERVICE.' A Uruguayan guard of honor raised their rifles to fire a final salute.

Captain Langsdorff, dressed in white tropical uniform, stepped toward the open graves. The Captain's smart uniform, complete with ceremonial sword and white gloves, could not cover or disguise the anguish emitting from his face. Langsdorff paused before each individual grave to pick up a small handful of soil. Slowly and deliberately he sprinkled the soil on top of each casket. Thirty-six times he repeated this ritual. Rifles upheld, the guard of honor waited to fire their shots. It seemed like a long, long time, but they and the entire assembly, patiently waited.

Finally, he stood back from the graves, pulled himself to attention and snapped a salute in farewell. Simultaneously, the guard of honor fired their volleys. Officers and officials raised their arms in salute while crew members and military personnel stood rigidly to attention. Langsdorff, grim faced, upheld his salute, forefinger to cap-peak, as the commands and shots of the honor guard rang out. His salute, similar to the Royal Navy's, contrasted sharply with the Nazi straight-arm mode used by Herr Langmann and dignitaries standing beside the Captain.

When news pictures of the scene appeared in the World's press, Allied propaganda experts made a great fuss. They offered sundry explanations, all critical of the Nazi regime. Otto Langmann could not contain his anger at Langsdorff's apparent political *faux-pas*. The Captain insisted there was no political significance to his action. He had used the Imperial Navy salute since 1912 and it was still standard practice in the German Navy in 1939. Langmann remained perplexed by this explanation while his chief in Berlin, von Ribbentrop, simmered with anger.

Captain Langsdorff speaks at funeral in Montevideo. – MALVIN MARITIME MUSEUM

Chapter 12

72-Hour Deadline

Immediately after the burial ceremony at the *Cementerio del Norte,* Herr Langmann, with Captains Niebuhr and Langsdorff, Lieut-Commander Ascher and Admiral Schröder, made a courtesy call on General Campos. They wished to thank the General for his help in the German funeral. Their visit was short and courteous and impressed Campos, especially the precise behavior of Captain Langsdorff. Campos offered the German captain additional help in caring for the wounded men still on board *Graf Spee*. The General assured Langsdorff the men would be well treated in the Military Hospital in Montevideo. In case of emergency they had a German interpreter available. General Campos found a professional rapport with Langsdorff and his officers but viewed the aggressive posture of Langmann with disdain.

Despite sympathetic assistance during the funeral, bad news greeted the Germans when they returned to their Legation. Uruguayan President Baldomir had signed a decree: *Graf Spee* had seventy-two hours to effect repairs. She must leave Uruguayan waters by 8pm Sunday, December 17, or face internment. To compensate for a delay in

Montevideo December 15: Captain Niebuhr, Herr Langmann, Captain Langsdorff & Lt-Cmdr. Ascher. – Gilbey Collection

organizing the Uruguayan Commission, the seventy-two-hour count-down began when the Commission left the ship.

Further disturbing news from Buenos Aires confronted the German officers. Argentine naval units at the naval base of Puerto Belgrano, close to Bahia Blanca, had identified HMS*Cumberland* on December 14, racing at full speed toward the Plate. Langsdorff and Ascher, fully aware of the 8-inch potency of *Cumberland,* realized the odds had seriously shortened against *Graf Spee.* To worsen their plight, Buenos Aires had also advised that HMS*Ark Royal* and HMS*Renown* had left Capetown on December 4, heading westward. These capital warships joined with Commander Harwood's cruiser squadron would eliminate any hope of *Graf Spee* escaping. Chartered spy-planes from Argentina, flying over the estuary December 14, had seen only two British cruisers. Now the picture had drastically changed.

Langsdorff and Ascher left the Legation immediately to rejoin *Graf Spee.* Repairs on the ship were going well but the large hole in the bow and the wrecked steam system still presented problems. Suitable plates to repair the bow were still unavailable and many hours of work remained. Port authorities continually delayed the free flow of materials and men to the warship. In spite of these hindrances, the work advanced at a furious pace.

Look-outs in the morning had reported seeing an aircraft carrier on the horizon. Ascher decided to check this sighting personally. *Graf Spee*'s gunnery officer had many years experience in optical observations at sea but his best tool, the range-finder on the foretop, was defunct.

Lieut-Commander Ascher climbed as high as possible on the control tower and scanned the horizon through binoculars. Visibility was poor but through the haze he saw obscure forms. Fiercely concentrating, adjusting the lenses, he trained his glasses on the ghostly dots in the distance. Two or three tiny shapes, close together in the misty distance, could be destroyers or cruisers. Ascher was certain he recognized the form of a large warship, bigger than the cruisers that engaged *Spee* in the battle. At greater distance he saw a tiny, shimmering apparition. Her shape was obscure but she was bigger than the first ship. Ascher looked for masts but could not see any. The blurry, indistinct shape seemed to have a flat superstructure. He strained to see more and convinced himself she was an aircraft carrier, as previously reported.

Recalling the intelligence from Buenos Aires, Ascher took another hard look. It was impossible to clearly identify the minuscule shapes but it seemed *Ark Royal* and *Renown* had arrived. This was serious news. Ascher reported immediately to Langsdorff who decided they should go at once to the Legation and discuss this development with Niebuhr and Langmann.

At the Legation, neither Langmann nor Niebuhr expressed surprise that Ascher had sighted the British capital ships. Captain Niebuhr immediately contacted the Embassy in Buenos Aires looking for fresh information. Intelligence had nothing new to report but would check their sources and advise promptly.

° ° °

In late afternoon that day, December 15, Millington-Drake, Captain McCall and Captain Miller gathered in the British Legation. Lloyd Hirst phoned from Buenos Aires:

Hirst read verbatim the 'planted' newspaper story of the impending arrival of the big British warships at Mar del Plata. *Renown's* speed and firepower joined with *Ark Royal's* aircraft canceled any hope of escape for *Graf Spee*. McCall, speaking with Hirst, passed the 'good news' to Millington-Drake and Miller. They made jubilant exclamations in keeping with the play, fully aware that enemy ears were listening.

When McCall hung up the phone, the three British officials compared notes. Captain Daniel's watchers had reported every detail of activity around *Graf Spee*. Experts had examined the exterior damage on the ship with high powered glasses. Millington-Drake had used all of his persuasive powers and significant influence to get the rumor mills working in favor of the British cause. Captain McCall had received secret information from Whitehall regarding the disposition of warships expected to aid the siege; *Ark Royal* and *Renown* were off the Brazilian coast at Pernambuco. Captain Miller had a copy of the Uruguayan Commission's Damage report and the gist of Langsdorff's battle report: The British officials had much to discuss.

Later, in the Uruguayan Foreign Ministry, Millington-Drake sat quietly as Dr. Guani shuffled papers lying on his highly polished desk. Alberto Guani, a small roly-poly man with a balding head, sat behind his large desk like a round dumpling. He had prominent black eyebrows that shaded expressive Latin eyes. Those eyes could be tearful in sympathy or hard in criticism, depending on Guani's intention. Totally dedicated to his profession, the politician had risen slowly and carefully to his present position.

The Uruguyan Minister knew he occupied the epicenter of his country's action in this strange drama. General Campos, the Minister of Defense, had affirmed he would follow Guani's guidance, as President Baldomir had instructed. Alberto Guani would not jeopardize his career in any foolish action. As Uruguayan Minister he must maintain neutrality despite his sympathies toward the Allies.

Guani valued his longtime friendship with Millington-Drake, now seated in front of his desk. However, the golden rule of politics insisted he protect his own interests, as would the British Minister. He had already felt pressure from Millington-Drake and co-operated as much as possible. General Campos's watchful eye would not overlook any obvious violations of neutrality; his career could also be affected.

The British Minister was complaining that materials and workers from Buenos Aires had boarded *Graf Spee*. He claimed technicians and hoisting parts, probably to repair ammunition delivery systems, had come from the Siemens Company. This being a contravention of the Convention, Millington-Drake demanded a picket placed aboard *Graf Spee* to prevent repairs to fighting equipment.

Guani made a phone call to General Campos who turned down this suggestion. Campos assured Guani, the corvette *Lavalleja* on duty in the harbor, approved all materials boarding the German warship.

Millington-Drake then advised the Uruguayan Minister that the freighter *Ashworth* had sailed out of Montevideo at 6.15pm. Uruguay must officially advise the German Legation. *Graf Spee* could not legally leave port until twenty-four hours after the British ship, according to the Convention.

Guani looked at his watch. It was 6.55pm. The German Minister and the Captain of the *Graf Spee* were waiting in the anteroom for their appointment. The Uruguayan pressed a buzzer on his desk and his secretary entered the office.

He rose from his seat and held out his hand to Millington-Drake. 'Please, you will excuse me now,' he said. 'You probably already know I have an urgent appointment at seven o'clock.'

'Of course, your excellency,' replied the British Minister, 'But there are other matters I need to clarify. Could you kindly give me and Captain McCall a few more moments of your time later this evening – perhaps at eleven o'clock?'

Guani gave an annoyed sigh. 'Minister, you are becoming a mosquito around my head. Can this not wait until morning?'

Millington-Drake knew he had tested Guani's patience. 'It would be considered a personal favor if we could see you tonight,' he said, 'But I know you must be tired.'

Guani looked glumly at the secretary, waiting to escort the British Minister to the door. 'Please book the Minister for 11.30pm tonight and show him out through the other door.'

The two friends then exchanged formal diplomatic farewells and the secretary accompanied Millington-Drake out of the office.

○ ○ ○

At 7pm, the secretary ushered Herr Langmann and Captain Langsdorff into Dr. Guani's office. Langmann saluted with a small raise of his right hand and Langsdorff gave his usual Naval salute.

Guani rose from his chair and came forward to greet them. '*Buenos tardes*, Gentlemen, I hope we will not be too formal in our discussion,' he said, smiling as he offered his hand.

Langmann shook the Uruguayan's hand, '*Buenos tardes*, Excellency,' he said, in excellent Spanish.

Captain Langsdorff also shook hands but spoke in English. 'Good evening, Your Excellency,' he said. 'Please excuse me, I am not able to speak Spanish.'

Guani smiled. 'Don't worry Captain,' he said, in English. 'I compliment you on your command of English. I listened to Captain Dove's radio interview last night when he described his frequent talks with you while a prisoner on board your ship.'

'You are well informed, Your Excellency,' responded Langsdorff. 'I hope we can have an acceptable communication.'

Herr Langmann, uncomfortable in English, preferred to show his political seniority and knowledge of Spanish. He addressed the Uruguayan Minister in his native language. 'Your Excellency, you have all the information before you and must be aware of our predicament.'

Guani pulled out a paper from the pile on his desk and said, 'Yes, indeed. I have here a copy of an official communique issued by the *Deutsches Nachrichtenbureau* that says:

'Early yesterday morning off Punta del Este, a naval battle took place. The German pocket battleship, *Admiral Graf Spee,* was engaged by three British cruisers, *Exeter, Ajax* and *Achilles.* In the course of this engagement, the German battleship gained a victory. The British cruiser *Exeter* was seen to be shot to pieces and the other British cruisers fled. The *Graf Spee* herself received a few minor hits . . . '

'Excuse me, your Excellency,' Captain Langsdorff interrupted. 'Could you repeat the last part in English?'

Guani smiled blandly, 'Of course Captain,' he said and translated the last sentence of the communique.

Langsdorff listened carefully and said, 'This is not true.'

Guani seemed surprised, 'Not true?' he exclaimed.

Langsdorff sensed Guani was playing games but continued, 'My ship has suffered serious damage. She is not seaworthy, and cannot be made seaworthy in less than fourteen days.'

Guani looked at the German Ambassador and spoke in Spanish. 'Your official agency quoted this information at 1315hrs Greenwich Mean Time yesterday. Are you saying that it is not the truth?'

Langmann adjusted his round steel glasses to a more comfortable position. 'Your Excellency knows that official news in wartime must consider the psychology of the people, the maintenance of morale, the . . . but, of course, Your Excellency is joking.'

Guani looked surprised. 'You think I would joke in such a serious matter?' he asked. Then he added, 'By the way, I am advised that a British merchant ship has just sailed from Montevideo in the course of her business. This means that *Graf Spee* cannot sail for at least twenty-four hours.' He paused for several moments then added. 'This should not have any effect, if, as you say, your ship is not fit to go to sea.'

Captain Langsdorff had previously experienced the political minuet. In the early thirties he had served four years ashore in Berlin. As an adjutant in the Ministry of Defense and later in the Ministry of the Interior he knew the farce of politics. It appeared no different in Uruguay. The 'word-smiths' could parry and thrust for hours, delighting each other with their skills, but the die was already cast and nothing would change.

Soon, the Germans were herded out of Guani's office, with emphasized courtesy. Nothing had changed. Only decisive physical action would break the siege.

Chapter 13
Berlin's Orders

In Berlin, Saturday morning, December 16, Admiral Erich Raeder waited patiently while his colleagues read copies of Langsdorff's situation report. Captain Langsdorff had presented a grim picture in a telegraph from Montevideo. Raeder wished to discuss the details with colleagues before sending instructions to Langsdorff. Following their discussion, Adolph Hitler, self-proclaimed Supreme Commander of the German Military, must approve Raeder's orders to Montevideo. Political friction between the branches of the Armed Forces demanded a cautionary approach. Any adverse publicity against the pocket battleship would strengthen current criticism of surface warships, and Raeder's Navy.

Raeder opened the meeting and read aloud the first item of Langsdorff's telegraph, dated Friday, December 15, 1939:

> *(1) RENOWN AND ARK ROYAL AS WELL AS CRUISERS AND DESTROYERS OFF MONTEVIDEO. CLOSE BLOCKADE AT NIGHT. NO PROSPECT OF BREAKING OUT INTO THE OPEN SEA AND GETTING THROUGH TO GERMANY.*[1]

'Are there any comments, Gentlemen?' asked the Admiral, concerned by the tone of finality in Langsdorff's message.

Commander Wagner, a highly respected senior officer in Naval Operations, immediately raised the question that *Renown* and *Ark Royal* were near the Plate. 'I don't believe it is possible, if our tracking reports are accurate,' he remarked.

Rear-Admiral Schniewind, another highly qualified member of Raeder's inner circle, brought the meeting's attention to Langsdorff's proven analytical talents. 'Langsdorff is on site. He must be certain of his facts to present them in this manner,' he said. 'We all know the vagaries of intelligence. Sometimes it is cleverly planted by the enemy. We must rely on observations at the scene, and of course, the Captain's judgment.'

After a short discussion Raeder agreed with Schniewind and continued reading:

> *(2) INTEND TO PROCEED TO THE LIMIT OF NEUTRAL WATERS. IF I CAN FIGHT MY WAY THROUGH TO BUENOS AIRES WITH AMMUNITION STILL REMAINING I SHALL ENDEAVOR TO DO SO.*[1]

Raeder raised his eyes from the telegram. 'Well Gentlemen?' There was instant, unanimous approval of this suggestion. Raeder nodded and carefully read the final item of the report.

> *(3) AS THE BREAK THROUGH MIGHT RESULT IN THE DESTRUCTION OF SPEE WITHOUT THE POSSIBILITY OF CAUSING DAMAGE TO THE ENEMY, REQUEST INSTRUCTIONS WHETHER TO SCUTTLE THE SHIP (IN SPITE OF THE INADEQUATE DEPTH OF WATER IN THE PLATE ESTUARY) OR SUBMIT TO INTERNMENT.*[1]

When Raeder stopped reading, the group broke into animated discussion that continued for over an hour:

They immediately ruled out internment as unacceptable for military, political and traditional reasons. *Graf Spee* was a sister ship to *Deutschland,* and *Admiral Scheer.* The advanced technology of the pocket battleships, especially the gunsights, must be protected.

In this respect, any plan to scuttle *Graf Spee* in these shallow waters presented major problems. Best to instruct Langsdorff to sail out and fight his way to deep water, no matter the cost. Perhaps he would sink a British warship en route. The discussion continued in this manner.

But Commander Wagner remained sceptical:

'*Admiral Graf Spee* draws 22ft draft. Our charts show 30ft maximum water depth in the Plate above English Bank. Dredged access channels to Montevideo and Buenos Aires are 33ft deep. Neither channel offers ocean space for battle conditions.'

Wagner spread a large marine chart of the River Plate Estuary on a table to prove his information and continued:

'When *Graf Spee* leaves Montevideo harbor, inadequate sea-room severely hinders her defense against attackers for at least ten miles. She will certainly take hits.'

Wagner paused to stress his next point:

'Remember, Gentlemen, the so-called pocket battleships were constructed under severe weight restrictions. At best, they are a compromise between a cruiser and a corsair. Armor protection, by necessity, was kept to a minimum. *Graf Spee's* armored belt, her heaviest body armor, is barely three inches thick.

Penetration of her shell would decrease flotation. Odds are high she would be grounded and totally at the mercy of the enemy. Such an event would be tragic in loss of technological equipment, lives, and of course, naval prestige.'

Admiral Raeder completely agreed with Wagner's concise analysis. To round off the meeting, he read a segment of a telegram from Otto Langmann in Montevideo. Sent to the Foreign Office, Langmann's report #184 was dated December 16, 1939:

> *(1) NO ARGUMENTS CONCERNING LEGAL RIGHTS CAN ALTER THE NECESSITY FOR AN URGENT DECISION REGARDING SPEE. SUPERIOR ENEMY NAVAL FORCES, WHICH HAVE BEEN CLEARLY ESTABLISHED FROM ON BOARD SPEE, MAKE IT APPEAR TO THE COMMANDING OFFICER QUITE OUT OF THE QUESTION TO SHAKE OFF SHADOWERS AND THUS ACHIEVE SUCCESSFUL BREAK THROUGH TO GERMANY. FROM THIS POINT OF VIEW A 14-DAY STAY WOULD NOT ALTER THE SITUATION AND WOULD ONLY ASSIST THE ENEMY CONCENTRATION.*
> *(2) I AM AT ONE WITH THE NAVAL ATTACHÉ IN REGARDING THE INTERNMENT OF THE VESSEL AS THE WORST POSSIBLE SOLUTION IN ANY CIRCUMSTANCES. IT WOULD BE PREFERABLE IN VIEW OF HER SHORTAGE OF AMMUNITION TO BLOW HER UP IN THE SHALLOW WATERS OF THE PLATE AND HAVE THE CREW INTERNED.*[2]

Raeder looked up from the telegram. 'Superior enemy forces have been clearly established from on board *Spee,*' he quoted.

The Admiral meticulously folded the telegram and placed it into the center drawer of his desk. 'Gentlemen, I will leave the option to Captain Langsdorff, whether to fight or scuttle.' In a lowered voice he added, 'May God guide him toward the correct choice.'

○ ○ ○

Saturday morning, December 16: Overcast weather in Montevideo gave perfect conditions for a break-out attempt. Langsdorff gathered his crew together to arrest any rumors. Throughout his mission, he had regularly addressed his assembled crew to keep them informed. Rumors now circulating among the ship's company covered every possibility. Some talked about a suicidal charge out of the harbor to reach open seas. Others thought the Captain would try to fight the ship to Buenos Aires. A possibility of scuttling the ship entered the discourse. No one, no one at all, envisioned *Graf Spee* turned over to the Uruguayan Government.

The Captain did not waste words in pretense but quickly summed up the desperate plight that faced them:

'*Graf Spee* is unfit for a long sea trip. An initial idea to request a thirty-day stay proved unrealistic. Officially we asked for fourteen days to make repairs. This has been refused.

'We must leave Uruguayan waters by 8pm tomorrow, December 17, or face internment. Every neutral nation on the American Continent will support Uruguay if we refuse to leave.

'British cruisers, with reported reinforcements, are guarding the mouth of the Plate. We are still making essential repairs. Sometime later today, when the ship is ready, we will decide our course of action.'

After the assembly, Langsdorff talked with some junior officers. He told them he was not disposed to serve as a target for a shooting match: 'I will not let us be shot to pieces at sea by an overwhelmingly superior force. To me a thousand young men alive are worth more than a thousand dead heroes. However, we must be prepared to sail at a moment's notice. We will continue repairing and provisioning so that our choices, such as they are, remain open.'

Langsdorff's address had not revealed any magic formula to ease their problem but the crew set to work with renewed spirit. He held the unqualified trust of his crew. Many were reservists, little older than teen-aged youths. Their Captain was like a father figure. Wherever he led, they would courageously follow. If providence demanded their death, so be it. *Graf Spee's* young, ambitious officers, also had faith in their captain that was almost spiritual. They believed he would lead them out of this predicament somehow, with honor.

° ° °

In Berlin, at 1pm (local time) December 16, Admiral Raeder had a meeting with Hitler, General Jodl and Commander von Puttkammer. Hitler was seldom at ease with Raeder: He constantly criticized the Admiral's wartime strategy with Germany's biggest warships; hit and run agitation was not Hitler's idea of fighting a war. Yet, he tolerated Raeder. The Führer, in 1939, was still wooing the pre-Nazi officer corps for their undisputed loyalty. Admiral Raeder, in these early days of the Second World War retained a relatively free hand to manage the navy as he saw fit.

Raeder brought Hitler and his staff officers up to date and showed them a draft of his instructions to Langsdorff. No one raised any objections. Following the meeting Raeder's staff cabled his instructions. The radiogram (1347/16) addressed to *Graf Spee* at 5.07pm (local time) was received in Montevideo on Saturday, December 16, soon after 1pm (local time):

> *'(1) ATTEMPT BY ALL MEANS TO EXTEND THE TIME IN NEUTRAL WATERS TO GUARANTEE FREEDOM OF ACTION AS LONG AS POSSIBLE.*
> *(2) WITH REFERENCE TO NUMBER 2: APPROVED. [possible breakout]*
> *(3) WITH REFERENCE TO NUMBER 3: NO INTERNMENT IN URUGUAY. ATTEMPT EFFECTIVE DESTRUCTION IF SHIP IS SCUTTLED.'*[3]

Meanwhile, telegraph messages zipped between the Foreign Office in Berlin and Herr Langmann in Montevideo. When Von Ribbentrop, the Foreign Minister, had received Langmann's first telegram he displayed cold anger. Joachim von Ribbentrop was incredulous that a tiny country like Uruguay should dictate terms to the Third Reich. This arrogant minister, whom some top Nazis labeled 'the champagne salesman', had negotiated the German Non-Aggression Pact with the Soviet Union in August and still glowed with new-found importance. Von Ribbentrop, never slow to leap into the limelight, immediately responded with sharp instructions:

> *'ACCORDING TO ENGLISH PRESS REPORTS THE ARK ROYAL IS IN THE PLATE AREA. AS YOU KNOW WE BELIEVE THE ARK ROYAL HAS BEEN SUNK. BY ORDER OF*

THE FÜHRER YOU ARE TO ATTEMPT TO TAKE PHOTOGRAPHS OF THE SUPPOSED ARK ROYAL. SIGNAL RESULTS AND FORWARD PHOTOGRAPHS.'[4]

Logistics to carry out this order can only be imagined. To fly close to operational warships, already poised for action, and take photographs was a tall order. Serious attempts to charter a plane in Montevideo failed. Finally, Lieut-Commander Wattenberg persuaded a sportsman to take him up in a tiny private plane. The Uruguayan pilot claimed the Government had banned flights over the Estuary and refused to approach the coast. Wattenberg's fifteen minute trip proved fruitless.

The Foreign Office then ordered Langmann:

'SEEK TO PROLONG THE AUTHORIZED STAY AND COUNTER WITH THE GREATEST POSSIBLE ENERGY THE INFLUENCE OF THE BRITISH.'[5]

Langmann tried every wile and threat to obey his instructions but ran against a stone wall. On Saturday morning, December 16, he met with General Campos the Uruguayan Minister of Defense, but could not move the General's position one iota. Langmann complained that Campos was completely in the English camp and mainly responsible for the unfavorable decision of the Uruguayan cabinet. However, Otto Langmann, a dedicated Nazi, was not easily dissuaded from his orders. The former Lutheran pastor, spellbound by Hitler's promises, firmly believed in the Nazi cause. But his haughty manner had not served him well in the past and stalled his efforts in the current situation. Against the suave professionalism of Millington-Drake and Guani he swam beyond his depth. Politically incompetent in this respect, Herr Langmann became totally frustrated.

In a last ditch attempt to change the deadline imposed on *Graf Spee* the German Minister arranged a 6pm meeting on Saturday evening with Dr. Guani. Herr Langmann's career and reputation were on the line. He intended using every weapon in his political arsenal in this final argument.

Precisely at 6pm, Guani's secretary heralded Langmann into the office of the Uruguayan Minister of Foreign Affairs.

Dr. Guani, rising from his desk, came forward with a smile and outstretched hand to greet his visitor. The courtly, mild mannered

Uruguayan expected a stormy meeting but offered civility. '*Buenos tardes* Your Excellency, please take a seat.' He motioned toward a comfortable chair placed before his desk. 'I hope we can have a friendly discussion.'

Herr Langmann gave his customary half wave, half Nazi salute, and took the proffered hand in a light handshake. '*Buenos tardes* Your Excellency. The spirit of our talk will depend on an adjustment of the time limit imposed on *Graf Spee.*'

The German was holding himself on a very tight rein. His gruff words were spoken softly. 'Anyone who has visited the ship must know she cannot be made seaworthy in the given time.'

Guani made a typical Latin American gesture - a shrug of the shoulders and extension of the palms of both hands. 'Your Excellency, the cabinet and President Baldomir have already made the decision based on expert examination of the warship.'

Herr Langmann sensed the first step of a futile political dance. 'It would be a humanitarian gesture if the Government of Uruguay extended the deadline for a few days. If necessary, the inspection team could check the progress of the repairs.'

Gauni smiled blandly,'I'm sorry to advise your Excellency that the matter is now out of my hands. The Presidential Decree carries the full weight of my country's law and I cannot rescind or adjust it in any way.'

Langmann's face betrayed his fake composure. Cold, grey eyes behind his round, steel spectacles flashed with anger. 'Dr. Guani, my country can be a good friend or a deadly enemy. Perhaps the political power of your laws may be lessened by the physical power of an enraged Germany.'

This undisguised threat shocked Guani. 'Be assured Sir, my country and her friends in democracy, will uphold our principles in any event.'

The Uruguayan was referring to the union of neutral American Countries, including the United States, still debating its position regarding the European war.

Nursing his anger, Langmann offered a final suggestion. 'Could you be so kind, Your Excellency, to arrange an interview with President Baldomir for my ultimate presentation?'

Guani could taste his victory. But always a professional, the slick politician wished to leave a chink in case of necessity. 'I believe an interview with the President is not possible,' he said. 'However, if Your

Excellency will put in my hands a formal agreement from your country that it will abide, without recourse, with the consequences of a Presidential meeting, I will submit your request.'

Langmann's fury boiled over. 'Señor Minister, I consider that proposal an impertinence. You must be prepared to answer personally for the consequences of this refusal. Uruguay may find an exploding wreck in the neighborhood of Montevideo.' Herr Langmann rose from his seat and tossed his Nazi 'wave' toward Guani. 'I bid you good evening,' he spluttered, and marched to the door.

The sad eyed Uruguayan watched the angry German leave the office. 'Chau!' he murmured.

Chapter 14
British Tactics

On Saturday morning December 16, light rain and heavy mist blanketed the estuary of the River Plate. British cruisers *Cumberland, Ajax* and *Achilles,* on high alert, guarded against *Graf Spee's* escape. Captain McCall, the British Attaché, visited *Ajax,* flagship of the small squadron. Commodore Henry Harwood and some senior officers snapped smart salutes as the bosun's pipe shrilled.

In Harwood's cabin, over breakfast, the Commodore and Attaché discussed the *Graf Spee* situation. McCall had vital information for Harwood. Captain Rex Miller, the Attaché's assistant, had worked vigorously since his arrival in Montevideo. Miller, a former infantry officer with the Manchester Regiment, was a combination strong-arm man, spy and runner.

McCall told Harwood that British agents had scrutinized the German warship's damage. Powerful glasses had scanned every scratch on the ship. Captain Miller's informants had supplied complex reports on visible damage to *Graf Spee.* Their precise information, coupled with details of materials imported from Buenos Aires, showed how seriously the cruisers had mauled *Graf Spee.* All agreed that *Exeter's* 8-inch shells had easily penetrated her armored belt. Also, the light cruisers' 6-inch shells had delivered spectacular damage to *Graf Spee's* superstructure. Splinter damage was serious and widespread. Miller had obtained copies of the German damage report submitted to the Uruguayan Commission, and also the Commission's official report to the Uruguayan Government.

The Attaché showed Harwood *Graf Spee's* submitted list:

1) Nine holes in the outer plating: including, two in the bows (2x2 meters) & (.70 x.60 meters) and one on the starboard waterline.
2) Installations for firefighting are of reduced efficiency.
3) Cracks in the stern.
4) Indispensable installations in the galley, the bakery and the laundry.
5) Repairs to the auxiliary boiler for the production of drinking water.[1]

In comparison, McCall gave Harwood corresponding details from the Commission's report:

> . . . after inspecting the reported damages to *Graf Spee* we came to the following conclusions:
> 1) There are twenty-seven holes on the ship. Fifteen on the starboard and twelve on the port sides, including large and small.
> 2) The apparatus for firefighting cannot be argued to affect seaworthiness.
> 3) Cracks on the stern were not observed.
> 4) With regard to the galley installations for cooking, baking and laundry, there was a shell-burst which destroyed one of the cauldrons and its piping as well as electrical installations.
> 5) With regard to the auxiliary boiler for the production of drinking water, repairs to this were necessary.
> The Commander when asked if he had any damage to his main engines, replied that these were below the armored deck and had suffered nothing, so they were not inspected.
> From all the foregoing we came to the conclusion, subject to your opinion, that these repairs could be effected in a provisional manner in three days.
>
> The report was signed and dated by Commander Varela & Lieut-Comdr Ing. Fontana, the Technical Commission to General Campos, Uruguayan Minister of Defense.
> Montevideo
> 15 December 1939[1]

Captain McCall told Harwood, that British Intelligence had puzzled over the high priority placed on damaged kitchen equipment. *Graf Spee's* large complement surely needed a secure food supply. However, she was not a transatlantic liner on a maiden voyage but a powerful warship that must extricate herself from a perilous trap. Intelligence also noted that the fresh water equipment appeared tied into the same system that produced steam for the kitchen. Really, what was the most critical item of damage? Was it kitchen equipment, fresh water supply or did another factor come into play?

In any case, the common problem arises from the installations in the funnel area. British Intelligence also believed the German's reluctance to show the engine rooms suggested another problem existed, perhaps entailing the engines.

McCall then updated Harwood on damage to *Graf Spee's* fighting equipment:

Main guns were undamaged and torpedo tubes seemed intact. One 5.9cm gun was inoperable. Atop the foretop, the range-finder had shrapnel scars. It was impossible to assess its operational condition. *Graf Spee's* airplane was wrecked, although the engine had been removed before the action.

Captain McCall carefully swirled the last dregs in his teacup. 'You know Commodore, we believe the Navy has overrated the *Graf Spee* as a fighting ship.' He gazed into the cup and continued, 'Metal peeling from the hole in her bow is about one-and-a-half inches thick. Eight-inch shells easily ploughed through her armored deck. Damage caused by your six-inch shells shows clearly that she is vulnerable to everything you can throw at her.'

Harwood laughed, 'Of course Captain, all we need do is slip underneath her 11-inch armpits and tickle her belly.'

McCall chuckled.'No! No! Commodore,' he exclaimed. 'I know it won't be easy but victory with *Cumberland* and the two light cruisers is highly probable.'

Harwood replied in a serious tone. 'I had calculated *Graf Spee's* chances of escape at 70% but you have convinced me her odds are much narrower.'

McCall then gave Harwood some disturbing news. 'The Admiralty has advised me that *Ark Royal* and *Renown* are now off Pernambuco.' He paused a second and continued. 'But they'll be moving rather slowly toward the Plate.'

Harwood, ready to take a sip from his teacup, paused in surprise. 'Why? Don't they want part of the kill?'

McCall smiled, '*Gneisenau* and *Scharnhorst* are somewhere in the North Atlantic. They represent the only logical help available to *Graf Spee.* It would be nice if we could bag those battle cruisers in the same net.'

As Harwood and McCall were talking, they heard the whine of *Ajax's* seaplane coming home. Poor visibility had aborted the spotter plane's mission over Montevideo harbor. McCall looked at his watch. It was 8.30am. Harwood reached for the teapot to offer the Attaché a refill.

McCall declined. 'No thanks Commodore, I'll hold off and celebrate *Graf Spee's* demise with something stronger.'

Commodore Harwood was pensive. 'From what you've told me, a couple of good puffs should blow out his candle.' The Commodore finished his tea and added, 'But he's still got those damned 11-inch thunderbolts to throw at us.' He put down the cup, gave McCall a hard look and said softly, 'We'll get the bugger somehow, no matter the cost.'

Harwood held out his hand to McCall. 'You have been a great help, Captain. Knowing we can hurt *Graf Spee* with every shot, besides torpedoes and 8-inch stuff, gives us an edge. In the Estuary, we'll have numbers, speed and shallower draft to our benefit.'

McCall shook the Commodore's hand, 'Yes, and like you say, *Graf Spee* must sail about ten miles in the dredged channel until she reaches deeper water.'

Harwood laughed. 'She'll really be in deep water when she moves outside the three-mile territorial limit.' Then he added dourly, 'We'll stop her in her tracks. You know those damn-fool Germans. Like ourselves, they'll never pull down a battle flag. We'll reduce the ship to scrap.'

When McCall left *Ajax,* Commodore Harwood ordered his squadron to action stations. Although the Attaché considered it unlikely *Graf Spee* would sail today, Harwood was taking no chances. The Admiralty had signaled Harwood to engage *Graf Spee* anywhere outside the three-mile territorial limit. This gave him authority to ignore the neutrality of the Estuary claimed jointly by Argentina and Uruguay.

Henry Harwood was very familiar with these waters. He had been sailing in them for many years. Taking a page from his letter pad, he wrote:

ENEMY'S COURSE OF ACTION:
(a) Exit north of English Bank.
(b) Exit between English and Rouen Banks.
(c) Exit between Rouen bank and Cabo San Antonio.
(d) Exit and double back on any track.[2]

Harwood closed his eyes, leaned back in his chair, thought for several minutes. Then he resumed writing:

SQUADRON COURSE OF ACTION:
(a) Action off whistle buoy politically impossible.
(b) Action immediately outside three-mile-limit unsuitable; lack of sea room and possibility of 'overs' into neutral zone.
(c) Position to east, to keep advantage of Montevideo lights in background, until dawn phase.
(d) Patrol north of English Bank within intercepting range.

TACTICS:
(a) Rely on getting Graf Spee's time of sailing and initial course from shore.
(b) Get Cumberland's aircraft up when Graf Spee sails.
(c) Initially, divisions spaced eight cables apart, with Cumberland placed to avoid masking her fire.
(d) Divisions to have complete freedom of action in engagement.

Commodore Harwood harbored no illusions that his business with *Graf Spee* would terminate easily. He respected the courage and tenacity of the German sailor and the unsinkable quality of German warships.

Professionally, he remembered the bitter tale of Admiral Troubridge. In World War 1 the Admiral let the German battle cruiser *Goeben* and the light cruiser *Breslau* escape his surveillance in the Mediterranean. The warships slipped into Constantinople and Turkey bought them at a fire-sale price. Turkey later entered the war on the German side and Admiral Troubridge faced a court-martial.

Commodore Harwood must ensure *Graf Spee* did not escape to Buenos Aires and allow a similar opportunity to develop in Argentina. The British Admiralty generously awarded meritorious actions but flailed the lash harshly for failure. Harwood had no intention of losing this unique chance to show his mettle.

Although confident of ultimate victory, Harwood fretted about the probable cost in material and men. 'Bobby' Harwood believed the Germans would not quit until everything they could fire was depleted. What would be the final consequence?

At 1615hrs, the Commodore sent a signal to the British cruiser squadron:

'MY OBJECT, DESTRUCTION, NECESSITATES KEEPING FORCES TOGETHER. MY APPRECIATION: RELY ON TIME

OF SAILING AND INITIAL COURSE FROM SHORE. FOR SUBSEQUENT MOVEMENTS RELY ON CUMBERLAND AIRCRAFT RECONNAISSANCE.'[3]

Commodore Harwood's dependence on shore information rested on the young American who had watched *Graf Spee's* arrival in Montevideo. Mike Fowler, with persistence and help from his Chicago employer had set up a broadcasting station on the roof of *El Edificio del Comercio*. Marconi, the radio company, shared the top floor of this building with a British Shipping Advisory group. On the floor below, the British Legation had their offices.

From his birds-eye position, Mike Fowler could see everything taking place in the harbor. Since early morning on December 16, he had relayed the exciting story, as it unfolded, to American listeners. The BBC picked up Fowler's broadcast and sent it over their international radio network. Among his enthralled listeners no one could match the interest of the cruiser crews guarding the Plate. A temporary hookup to their loudspeaker systems sent Fowler's words crackling through the ships. They would know the moment *Graf Spee* moved.

○ ○ ○

Ashore, at 5pm on December 16, Millington-Drake had delivered yet another note to Dr. Guani. The British Minister aggressively demanded the Uruguayan Government intern *Graf Spee*. He claimed skilled elevator workers from Siemens had passed one-and-one-half days aboard the ship. The Port Authority had not cleared them, hence, an obvious violation of the neutrality laws. Guani patiently warded off the tirade and promised to look into the matter. Millington-Drake then advised the Uruguayan Minister, another British freighter, *Dunster Grange* would sail out of Montevideo at 6pm. The British Minister reminded his friend of the twenty-four-hour rule in the Convention.

Dr. Guani took this news with grim demeanor. His Latin eyes were deadly cold when he growled. 'Señor Minister, no more merchant ships will sail from Montevideo after 8pm tonight. I'm tired of pressures exerted by both belligerents in this incident. I tell you, these harassments are uniting the nations of the American Continent against encroachments into our territorial waters and on our neutrality.'

Millington-Drake felt a trickle of political alarm run through his body. Great Britain did not wish to anger the American nations, specifically, the United States. President Roosevelt needed every political asset to persuade the United States to support the Allied cause. Any malodorous incident in Montevideo could backfire and have serious political import in the United States. Great Britain's opposition to a proposed 300-mile neutral zone off the Atlantic coast had already soured relations. Powerful American lobbyists, arguing that United States remain neutral in the European war were gaining points.

The lanky, thin faced Minister flashed his best smile and said 'Your Excellency, is obviously fatigued. You have just cause to complain of violations. There is no question of a legitimate grievance, assuming the international community agrees with Argentina and Uruguay's joint claim of sovereignty in the Estuary.'

Millington-Drake knew the international maritime nations had never approved the joint proposal. They still regarded a three-mile limit from each country's coast as the neutral zone. 'Anyway,' the Englishman added, 'you may remember that *Graf Spee* fired the first shots against *Achilles* in the Estuary.' Millington-Drake paused and summed up his defense in a silky tone. 'You will recall that the German warship fired her guns near English Bank. If the Government of Uruguay has a complaint it surely should be leveled at the Third Reich.'

Dr. Guani had no mood for word games. 'Captain Fuentes in command of our national cruiser, *Uruguay,* says differently. Fuentes was on the scene and in his report to General Campos says that *Achilles* fired first.' Guani pursed his lips slowly. 'We shall see' he said softly.

The Uruguayan Minister rose from his chair to suggest the discussion be over. They concluded their meeting with the usual smiles and political parlance, though a slight chill in a previously warm relationship remained.

When Millington-Drake returned to his office he found an official response from Guani to his Formal Note. Miss Shaw, his secretary, had attached a neat scribble, 'reply from Dr. Guani'. The Minister opened the letter and read it through carefully.

Date: December 16, 1939, from the Ministry of Foreign Affairs in Montevideo, to Mister Eugen Millington-Drake, Envoy Extraordinary and Minister Plenipotentiary of Great Britain:

Sir,

I beg to acknowledge receipt of Your Excellency's Note of 14th inst., No.105, referring to the presence in Montevideo harbour of the German battleship Admiral Graf Spee, relative to the neutrality ruling followed by the Government of the Republic. As Your Excellency points out, Articles 12, 14, and 18 of Ch. X111 of the Hague Convention dated 18th October, 1907, are those which have been taken into consideration in granting to the German vessel a period of time exceeding twenty-four hours in order that repairs sufficient to ensure seaworthiness may be carried out - provided always that her fighting strength is in no way increased.

Moreover, the Government of the Republic bore particularly in mind Article 18 which forbids belligerent vessels using harbours, roads or territorial waters of neutrals for renewing or increasing their military supplies, armaments or crews.

It is admitted that, within the meaning of the said Convention of the Hague, it is permitted to carry out repairs in order to ensure the seaworthiness of the ship or ships without discrimination as to whether the damage sustained be caused by bad weather, by enemy fire or any other cause. The delegation appointed by Great Britain to the Hague Conference of 1907 is responsible for Articles 15 and 19 of the said Convention, by which it was held that belligerent ships seeking refuge in neutral waters in order to evade capture, damage or destruction by enemy ships be interned, and the reparation of damage sustained in combat expressly forbidden. Although the British motion was supported by a number of other delegations, the majority view was that put forward by Russia, according to which a neutral State need not investigate the cause of the damage.

The Government of the Republic maintains, however, that in order to comply duly with Articles 17 and 18 above mentioned, all repairs likely to increase the fighting strength of the ship be forbidden, as well as the renewal of armaments, or any work affecting her military capacity. With this in view, the necessary orders were issued on 14th December for a Commission of Naval Technicians to examine, without delay, the nature and extent of the damage suffered by the German warship in order that the necessary time be allowed for carrying out, as quickly a possible, the authorised repairs.

Numerous historical precedents may be cited in support of this thesis. One of the best known occurred during the World War of 1914 when Holland allowed repairs to a submarine after damage in action, such repairs being limited to those necessary to ensure the seaworthiness of the vessel without her fighting strength being increased in any way or manner. In the same way the Brazilian Government applied this ruling, in the said war, in the case of the cruisers Glasgow and Carnarvon, enabling them to repair, in a Brazilian harbour, damage sustained in action.

The Uruguayan Government, in issuing the decrees of 14th and 15th December 1939, a copy of which I beg to enclose herewith, has adhered strictly to the rulings of the Hague Convention. Once again I assure Your Excellency of my highest esteems.[4]

Signed, A. Guani.

Millington-Drake re-read the letter several times. He found no legal flaw in the document and murmured a word of praise at the professional skill of Guani. The British Minister had another appointment with the Uruguayan Minister at 9pm. He intended to use all of his considerable charm to weld the tiny fracture that had appeared in their professional relationship. Millington-Drake also needed to know what had happened in Guani's 6pm meeting with Herr Langmann.

Promptly, at 9pm, Millington-Drake entered the office of the Minister of Foreign Affairs. Doctor Guani seemed calm though tightly controlled. This meant trouble for someone.

The British Minister apologized for his earlier indiscretions and said he would not take more than a few minutes of the Uruguayan's time. Following a short discussion, he stressed the importance of continuing good relations between Uruguay and Great Britain, and, with a few more words of personal content, took his leave.

When he returned to his office, Millington-Drake composed a long telegram to the Foreign Office in Whitehall. It was headed 'IMMEDIATE'. Telegram No. 165. Dated 11:30pm, 16 December 1939.

DR. GUANI WAS IN A CALMER AND MORE FRIENDLY MOOD. . . HE INFORMED ME THAT IN THE COURSE OF HIS INTERVIEW WITH THE GERMAN MINISTER, THE

LATTER HAD PRACTICALLY HELD HIM RESPONSIBLE FOR ANY CONSEQUENCE OF THE REFUSAL OF ANY EXTENSION OF TIME FOR REPAIRS. IN VIEW OF THE ALMOST UNARMED STATE OF URUGUAY, THE MATTER WAS A SERIOUS ONE . . . HE HAS THEREFORE MADE AN APPEAL TO THE BIGGER NATIONS OF THE AMERICAN CONTINENT AND HAD MET WITH FULL SYMPATHY AND OFFERS OF SUPPORT. HE THEREFORE ASKED THAT I WOULD PERSUADE H.M.GOVERNMENT NOT TO PRESS HIM TOO HARD, AS IT APPEARED THAT HE WAS ON THE POINT OF ALIGNING ALL OF THE AMERICAN CONTINENT AGAINST GERMANY.

LATELY I AM INFORMED FROM GOOD SOURCE THAT CAPTAIN LANGSDORFF INTENDS TO TAKE ADVANTAGE OF THE EARLY MORNING MIST AND TO SAIL TOMORROW, SUNDAY MORNING, AT SOME TIME BETWEEN 3AM AND 5AM.[5]

Mr. Eugen Millington-Drake, satisfied with his performance, decided to call it a day. There was much to take care of in the morning.

In the dark of night on Saturday 16 December, HMS*Cumberland,* HMS*Ajax* and HMNZS*Achilles* patrolled the Estuary of the River Plate. They were sailing, in company, on a north and south line, five miles east of the English Bank light buoy.

Wonderful news had arrived in late afternoon from the Admiralty. Commodore Henry Harwood was promoted to Rear-Admiral effective from December 13, 1939. In addition, His Majesty King George V1 had bestowed the K.C.B.(Knight Commander of the Order of the Bath) to Harwood and a C.B.(Commander of the Order of the Bath) to Captains Woodhouse, Parry and Bell. Newly promoted, Rear-Admiral Sir Henry Harwood, when he recovered from his pleasant surprise, sent a signal to his squadron:

I HOPE THAT EVERY ONE OF YOU WILL TAKE TO YOURSELVES THE CREDIT FOR THE HONOUR WHICH HAS BEEN BESTOWED UPON ME BY HIS MAJESTY THE KING. NO COMMANDER COULD RECEIVE BETTER SERVICE FROM HIS CAPTAINS, NOR I, NOR THEY, A

HIGHER STANDARD OF EFFICIENCY AND OF RESOLUTE ACTION THAN WAS DISPLAYED BY THE OFFICERS AND MEN CONCERNED IN THE BATTLE OF THE PLATE.[6]

Harwood's squadron maintained their patrol at action stations. Anticipation of a knockout victory permeated the British ranks. Morale had reached a crescendo.

Chapter 15
Fight Or Scuttle

Directly from his stormy, 6pm meeting with Dr. Guani, Herr Langmann rushed to the German Legation where Langsdorff and Ascher awaited his report. Time left for decision was relentlessly narrowing. What changes, if any, had the Minister managed to concoct? Herr Langmann's brisk deportment and flushed face told the story. He greeted the officers with his familiar salute and said, 'Gentlemen, by 8pm tomorrow, December 17, you must do what must be done. Foreign Affairs is unable to move the deadline.'

Captain Langsdorff accepted the news calmly. He had already arranged an 8pm meeting with Captain Niebuhr and Commander Kay to discuss military action. Langsdorff and Ascher left the legation immediately and returned to *Graf Spee*. They had no time to lose. For his part, Otto Langmann sent a telegram advising the Foreign Office in Berlin of Uruguay's tenacity. Ribbentrop's pride would suffer a serious setback: He must advise Admiral Raeder of this political failure.

Langsdorff was neither surprised nor unprepared for Langmann's failure to extend the deadline. Before leaving *Graf Spee,* to come to the Legation, he had met with Lieut-Commanders Wattenberg, Klepp and Höpfner. He had asked them, individually, for their viewpoints:

Wattenberg, a tall, slim, elegant man was a naval officer of the highest quality. Listed as First Navigating Officer, he was also considered a technical expert. Captain Langsdorff had regularly consulted Wattenberg and Ascher on tactics. A daring officer with realistic caution, Wattenberg gave Langsdorff his view of the situation:

(a) *Graf Spee* is disabled. She cannot return to Germany or continue her cruise.

(b) Shallow water in the upper Estuary denies *Spee* sea-room to defend against attack.

(c) Enemy forces waiting in the Estuary, (one 8-inch heavy cruiser and two 6-inch light cruisers) with torpedo capability, aircraft reconnaissance and tactical advantages, are superior.

(d) These three clearly identified cruisers may be supported by a battle cruiser and an aircraft carrier.

Wattenberg summed up his analysis:

'We have two choices: Sail out to certain defeat or scuttle the ship. In either case, *Spee* is lost but a final battle might achieve enemy losses. Scuttling, is our most practical choice but may bring dishonor on the ship and the Navy. We must avoid this at all cost.' Wattenberg expected to fight a final battle.

Captain Langsdorff talked next with Lieut-Commander Höpfner. Wattenberg and Höpfner had expertly navigated *Graf Spee* in the vast empty oceans during the raider cruise. In earlier years, as a merchant officer, Höpfner had sailed these waters and knew intimately the shallow vagaries of the Plate Estuary. He had navigated *Graf Spee* directly into Montevideo harbor, without a local pilot.

Höpfner was a big, gruff man with sharp intelligence. His comments paralleled Wattenberg's:

'Montevideo has three possible exit routes. None afford enough depth or sea room to engage an enemy and avoid taking hits. The maximum water depth in the immediate exit area is 25ft. *Graf Spee* draws 22ft leaving three-feet clearance under the hull. Engaged in action, *Spee* would probably run aground. After using all ammunition we could be captured in salvageable condition. It makes sound sense to destroy the ship with explosives now in hand but this is certain to draw criticism.'

Captain Höpfner believed that sidestepping a final battle would sully naval honor.

Captain Langsdorff then talked with Lieut-Commander Klepp. *Graf Spee's* Chief Engineer was a tall man who wore a professorial beard. Klepp was inclined to be conservative, sometimes overcautious. He repeated Wattenberg's main points and agreed with Höpfner that scuttling was a logical decision.

In addition, the Chief recapped *Graf Spee's* engineering problems: 'Our high pressure steam system, essential to clean the fuel, must be repaired before going to sea. After four months at sea the diesel engines need a major overhaul. A break-out toward Buenos Aires might amplify our problems; shallow water and notorious mud conditions in the Punta

Indio Channel could result in engine fouling (*Spee's* cooling system drew ocean water from the keel area into the engines). Anyway, if we broke out into open water, the ship's structural condition could present an extreme hazard on a North Atlantic voyage, even if unmolested.'[1] Klepp believed *Admiral Graf Spee* had served loyally. They should destroy her before the enemy learned her technical secrets and her flaws. Klepp also mentioned that scuttling might cause a slur on naval honor.

Captain Langsdorff had made notes as each ranking officer stated his case. All top professionals, they would follow his orders to the end. No one envied his responsibility for material and men.

° ° °

Prior to 8pm, Langsdorff and Ascher arrived aboard *Graf Spee*. Niebuhr and Kay were waiting in the captain's cabin. Diggins told them that another British ship had sailed at 6pm. Langsdorff immediately convened the tactical meeting in his cabin. Final orders had not yet arrived from the High Command in Berlin. Only a tentative decision could be taken but the atmosphere was tense.

Langsdorff sat at his desk, as usual smoking a pipe. Niebuhr, Kay and Ascher sat in front, in a half circle. Diggins, always present at such meetings, prepared to take notes. Captain Langsdorff quickly recapped the situation and finished by declaring two acceptable choices:

(a) Break out: (to open sea or Buenos Aires).

(b) Scuttle the ship.

Gunnery Officer Ascher said that until the ship cleared the dredged channel he could use only the forward turret. Lack of sea-room prohibited broadside action. Ascher reminded the meeting the optical range-finder in the foretop was defunct. Radar equipment could locate an object at fifteen miles but because of inexact side direction it offered no benefit in gun sighting. Lack of the foretop range-finder hindered automatic sighting of the main armament and restricted *Spee's* firepower.

Commander Kay, the Executive Officer, a giant with long spidery legs, straightened in his chair and asked, 'What about the short trip to Buenos Aires?'

Kay had less deep-sea experience than the other senior officers; his career had advanced mainly in training petty officers ashore and he had maintained strict discipline on board *Graf Spee*. Although Langsdorff had often quarreled with Kay during their association he appreciated his courage and dedication to duty.

Langsdorff took his pipe from his mouth, 'Buenos Aires is a possibility but it carries a heavy penalty if not totally successful.' The Captain checked notes lying on his desk. 'Chief Engineer Klepp tells me that mud in the Punta Indio Channel might multiply our problems. Besides, if we take hits, as seems almost certain, we could be grounded in the shallows, or worse, be forced to slink into Buenos Aires like a whipped dog.'

Commander Kay responded with typical bluntness, 'Klepp is an old woman,' he said. 'In this situation we have no choice but to fly the flag into *Tommy's* teeth and give him a hot handful of German spirit.'

Ascher joined in the discussion. 'I might agree with Commander Kay if there was a possibility of sinking an enemy warship. Our disadvantages make this highly unlikely. We could lose the ship in salvageable condition and many of our men in a pointless venture.'

Captain Niebuhr listened knowingly to the discourse. A veteran of World War 1, he understood the codes of honor that underpinned the German navy. 'The loss of a ship is a disaster but not dishonorable. How the ship is lost decides the issue,' he offered.

Commander Kay took this comment as a cue to elaborate his choice. 'Our men, like *Graf von Spee's* courageous men at the Falklands in 1914, will gladly give their all for the honor of the Flag and the Fatherland,' he said. 'I think we should challenge *Tommy* to do his worst.'

Langsdorff looked inquiringly at Ascher. *Graf Spee's* elfin gunnery officer was quick to respond:

> "I predict a grim prospect. British propagandists have already claimed victory in this engagement. It would compound their victory if the ship is captured or wrecked in a one-sided contest. Even if our technology somehow avoids seizure, the world will observe the sensitivity of a pocket battleship to inferior firepower."

The fiery little officer turned toward the giant Kay. 'I believe we should destroy everything with the explosives we have on hand. This removes all initiative from the enemy and makes sound tactical sense.'

Ascher faced Captain Langsdorff, 'Of course Captain, that solution gives a propaganda bonanza to the British, especially if our officers and men are interned in Uruguay.'

Langsdorff nodded, 'Yes, but a technical victory for the Fatherland,' he noted, 'And perhaps we can do better.'

The Captain looked across his desk at the Attaché. 'Captain Niebuhr,' he said, 'What help can we expect from Buenos Aires to transport our men if they become refugees from a shipwreck?'

Niebuhr understood immediately what was behind Langsdorff's question. 'Of course Captain, we have friends with access to small ships in Buenos Aires. We can surely get their support.'

Langsdorff read this as a positive answer: 'Gentlemen, our chances of inflicting significant damage to the enemy seem remote.' He picked up the cold pipe from an ashtray on his desk and examined it. 'I cannot take my men into a futile battle, solely to appease tradition. It makes no sense.' Almost musing to himself, he added, 'But, if we scuttle *Graf Spee* and get everyone to Argentina?' Langsdorff looked over his pipe toward Commander Kay. 'That would magnify our technical victory and our men might get better conditions than in Uruguay.' He smiled and added, 'Perhaps even released as refugees from a shipwreck, if the Argentine government accepts our argument.'

Commander Kay responded despondently. 'Perhaps you are right my Captain, but the world will see a refusal to fight as an act of cowardice. The honor of the Flag and the Fatherland will be smeared.'

Langsdorff tapped cold ashes from his pipe into the ashtray and said, decisively, 'So be it, Gentlemen. My conscience refuses to send one thousand brave young men to face death without just cause. We will scuttle the ship and land the men in Argentina unless Berlin orders otherwise.'

Captain Niebuhr had a final word for Langsdorff as the meeting adjourned. 'I will organize help from Buenos Aires,' he said. 'The Delfino Brothers have several tugs and lighters. We will instruct them to pick up your men in international waters.'

Langsdorff, always optimistic replied, 'Excellent, we can move *Tacoma* closer to *Graf Spee* and try to block the view from shore. We will transfer the men to her and go meet whatever rescue ships they can provide from Buenos Aires.'

As the officers were preparing to leave the Captain's cabin the sentry knocked and entered with a report from the Port Authority. At 6pm the freighter *Dunster Grange* had steamed out of Montevideo. Everyone knew the British would demand the twenty-four-hour rule upheld. *Graf Spee* could not legally sail before 6pm December 17, yet must leave Uruguayan waters by 8pm the same night – according to the Convention: *Graf Spee* had a two-hour gap in daylight to exit Montevideo.

Captain Langsdorff shrugged. 'Well Gentlemen it seems we have little choice. Our high pressure steam system will be repaired by this evening. In favorable conditions we might have gone out in the morning mist, but to confront the enemy on a summer evening would be madness.'

Soon after the meeting, Lieut-Commander Klepp reported that the high pressure steam system was finally repaired. He apologized for the delay but explained that multiple damage in the condenser and the auxiliary boiler needed painstaking work to repair. Langsdorff congratulated the Chief but advised him that he expected to blow up the ship next evening.

Klepp responded dryly that in that case outsiders would remain ignorant of the vulnerability of the ship's propulsion system: Fuel oil, pumped from the bunkers into a settling tank, moved through the cleaning system to a holding tank. High pressure steam, generated in the funnel area, was essential to the fuel cleaning function. This vital system of pipes and valves had no armored protection. Scattered shrapnel had caused crippling damage during the battle – the engines drew their fuel from the holding tank.

Langsdorff had noted this serious oversight. It was imperative to covertly relay this information to the High Command. Changes must be made to *Graf Spee's* sister ships without attracting attention and drawing political criticism on the pocket battleships.

Klepp also mentioned that he had solved the mysterious gas burns on the wounded men. Ardexin, a firefighting chemical normally stored in the engine-room, caused similar burns to mustard gas when in contact with human flesh. Surplus quantities stored on deck had burst during the battle. The injured men were all near this area. Klepp believed this answered the poison gas question. Langsdorff was happy to know that his instincts in this matter had proved correct. He could not imagine the Royal Navy shelling ships with mustard gas.

Now, he must go ashore to meet Herr Langmann and await final orders from Berlin. He had complete confidence that Admiral Raeder would leave the ultimate fate of the mission in his hands. Raeder and Langsdorff were veterans of the Imperial Navy. The ritual role of a Captain to control action at the front was sacrosanct. However, Field Marshall Hermann Göring perpetually badgered Hitler with criticism of the Navy. A slim chance remained that Hitler would overrule Raeder's authority.

Langsdorff decided, since time was running out, to act on his own initiative. In anticipation of Raeder's concurrence, before leaving the ship he ordered all secret documents destroyed. No matter, if ordered to fight or scuttle the ship, he must ensure all important papers were eliminated to avoid capture.

○ ○ ○

In Berlin, Admiral Raeder received the message from Ribbentrop: Uruguay refused to extend the deadline. He did not procrastinate. Without delay he sent a radiogram to update the *Graf Spee* Commander's orders.

> *AS ENVOY REPORTED IMPOSSIBILITY OF EXTENDING TIME LIMIT, INSTRUCTION ACCORDING TO RADIOGRAM 1347/16, NOS. 2 AND 3 REMAIN IN FORCE*[2]

Captain Langsdorff must fight his way out or scuttle the ship. As Captain of *Graf Spee*, and in the best position to assess the correct action, the decision lay on his shoulders.

On December 16, at 8.40pm, Raeder's instructions arrived at the German Legation. Captain Langsdorff shared the text with Herr Langmann and Captain Niebuhr. Langmann's secretary, Dr. Franz Rademacher was present to take notes. Also, in the room was a Party associate and close friend of Otto Langmann. An executive of the Delfino Brothers Shipping Line, Sanstede could help transport *Graf Spee's* crew to Argentina.

Langmann had exhausted any chance to improve the political situation. It was now the responsibility of the military to take action. 'So, Captain Langsdorff, you must choose. Fight a final battle and gain glory and everlasting honor. Or destroy your ship without a fight and risk dishonor, derision and loss of your career.'

Captain Langsdorff detected a genuine note of sympathy in the Minister's voice. Langmann was not relishing the Captain's problem. Langsdorff replied easily. 'Excellency, I have no wish for high honor at the cost of innocent life. My ship and my career are the same. I am happy to sacrifice both in the cause of common sense.'

Captain Niebuhr shook Langsdorff's hand. 'I wish you good luck, Captain,' he said. Now we must act swiftly and initiate the plans we discussed.'

Niebuhr ran quickly through a list of items that Langsdorff had previously requested: 'We will arrange for tugs to pick up your men at the edge of the territorial limit. Our Legation will shelter Diggins and the other men you wish left in Montevideo to apply for attaché status. The Military Hospital will accept the wounded crewmen who are in the ship's hospital.' He paused, 'Is there anything more?'

Langsdorff thought for a moment, 'No thanks, Captain,' he said, 'I have a few words to write before I return to the ship.'

When the others had gone about their business, Langsdorff sat at a desk in the Legation and wrote a letter. Addressed to Herr Langmann but intended for general publication, it was a strong political protest. Langsdorff blamed prominent Ministers of the Uruguayan government for political overtones that prompted the destruction of his ship.

The Captain needed much more time to pen another important letter. A note of farewell to his wife required careful thought. He pictured Ruth and the children visiting his mother to celebrate Christmas in Düsseldorf. How could he explain the terrible duty he could not refuse? Langsdorff's credo coincided with tradition. The honor of *Graf Spee* and the Navy must be maintained at all cost.

Chapter 16

Protest!

Captain Langsdorff had decided to scuttle his ship and risk defamation. His conscience drove him to overrule tradition and avoid spilling courageous blood in useless action. Three days of political pummeling in Montevideo had left a sense of sadness in his heart. The Hague Conventions, designed to instill humanity into the horrors of war, were extremely malleable – perhaps unattainable.

In his previous experience in Berlin, Langsdorff had developed political savvy. He knew the misty world of political maneuvering. A political protest must expose the partisan politics that led to *Graf Spee's* premature expulsion from Montevideo. Langsdorff addressed his letter of protest to the German Minister in Montevideo. Otto Langmann promised to give it to the Uruguayan Government when *Graf Spee* left the harbor.

Montevideo, 17 December 1939:
Your Excellency,
Before leaving the port I wish to express through your intermediary my deepest gratitude for the innumerable demonstrations of sympathy and for the chivalrous sentiments shown by the people of Uruguay toward my valiant dead and wounded, demonstrations and sentiments which continue to be shown. I shall never forget these manifestations of the Uruguayan people. At the same time, I desire to express my deep gratitude to the authorities, both for the prompt measures of help taken from the moment of the unexpected arrival of the Graf Spee and for the very effective assistance given to my wounded and the honors rendered to my dead.

It was to my great regret that amid these demonstrations of true human sentiments a jarring note was struck. By reason of what you have told me, regarding your interview with the Foreign Minister of the Republic of Uruguay, I am forced to regard as final and binding the time limit fixed as 20.00hrs 17 December 1939 – before which time the Admiral Graf Spee must put to sea, even if the repairs vitally necessary to make the vessel seaworthy cannot be completed by then. I hereby register a formal protest against the decision of the Government of Uruguay. I base my decision upon the following points:

1) In accordance with Article 17, Chapter X111 of the Hague Convention, permission for warships of belligerent powers to remain in a neutral port may be granted for a period sufficient to carry out repairs as are essential for the safe navigation of such vessels. As far back as the year 1914 there was a precedent for this in South America. For 'several weeks' [sic] (one week) the British cruiser Glasgow lay in port carrying out repairs.

After an expert survey of the damage, I requested a period of fourteen days to carry out repairs in respect of the damage which compromised the sea-worthiness of my ship.

2) The commission of experts sent by the Uruguayan Government was in a position while on board my ship to ascertain that the fighting capacity of my vessel (by which I mean her engines and armament) had suffered to such a small extent that there was no need for me to utilize the period of time I originally requested in order to increase her fighting capacity. The said commission was able to ascertain that the hull of my ship gave evidence of damage, the repair of which was essential to the sea-worthiness of the vessel.

In addition, it was patently obvious to this commission that the cooking installations and bakery on board were in damaged condition – and that it is essential (considering the large crew borne) that these installations be in good working order before a long period on the high seas could be contemplated. Article seventeen, Chapter X111 of the Hague Convention, is concerned with damage such as that which I have described.

On the basis of the communication made to you by His Excellency the Foreign Minister, the commission of experts appointed by the Minister of Defense declared that a period of seventy-two hours would suffice to make good the damage. The decision of the Uruguayan Cabinet was based on this.

3) In spite of strenuous efforts, it was not possible within the time allotted to repair the damage to my ship with the means at our disposal in Uruguay. This could have been ascertained beyond any doubt at any time, if a further investigation had been carried out on board.

I hereby make formal declaration that the contractor entrusted with repairing the damage to my ship was obstructed by the port authorities of Montevideo. On December 16, for a space of some hours after 18.00hrs, none of the men engaged for the work were permitted to come aboard. Permission for this was finally granted only after an official from the German Legation had intervened.

I hereby declare that the decision of the Government of Uruguay compels me to leave the harbor of Montevideo with a ship which could not be sufficiently repaired to ensure the maximum safety of navigation. To put to sea in such a vessel would be to bring danger upon my crew (over one-thousand men) by negligence. When I say "danger" I do not mean such danger as would be involved in action with the enemy. I am referring exclusively to the danger that would inevitably menace a ship at sea in such a condition.

4) The decision taken by the Government of Uruguay is therefore a flagrant violation of the efforts to humanize warfare, which led to the signing of the International Convention of the Hague.

5) I cannot explain to myself the evident difference between the attitude of the people of Uruguay (except in the case mentioned in part 3 above) and that of its authorities, and the decision of the Uruguayan Cabinet. This suggests that pressure had been exerted by the aforementioned Cabinet Ministers.

I, for my part, although it would have been within my technical possibilities, abstained carefully from such pressure.

Early in the morning of December 13, I engaged the British cruiser Exeter on the high seas. The British cruisers Ajax and Achilles took part in this action. After Exeter had been put out of action I decided to make for the port of Montevideo to repair my vessel. I was aware that the British Government recognizes only the three-mile zone (even in the waters of the River Plate). As soon as my ship had reached the zone over which the countries contiguous to the Plate claim condominium (and in spite of the British interpretation of this claim as it was known to me), out of respect for the feelings of the two peace-loving nations I abstained from further part in the action.

I stress particularly the point that in spite of a favorable tactical position and in spite of good visibility I did not open fire on the British cruiser standing off the Isla de Lobos until the enemy had fired on my ship and the shot had fallen close.

6) I do not recognize the grounds for the decision of the Government of Uruguay – nevertheless I shall respect the time limit imposed. Inasmuch as the Government of Uruguay refused to grant me time to make my ship seaworthy as laid down in the Hague Convention, I am not minded to place my ship (which has suffered no diminution of its fighting power during the action) under the control of that Government.

Under these circumstances I have no alternative but to sink my ship. I shall blow her up close inshore and disembark my crew if this may be possible.[1]

Signed, Kapitän-zur-See, Hans Langsdorff (Admiral Graf Spee)

Captain Langsdorff did not return aboard *Graf Spee* until 2am December 17. Lieut-Commanders Ascher, Wattenberg and Klepp anxiously awaited his return.

A preamble was unnecessary. When everyone was seated in his cabin, Langsdorff simply said, 'We will blow up the ship.'

Lack of sleep and constant pressure showed in Langsdorff's deportment. His handsome, straight-nosed face was haggard. Large black circles shadowed the sharp blue eyes. 'I intend to go down with my ship, as we have often discussed' he said softly.

Stunned, the three senior officers exchanged glances. Ascher spoke for all of them 'How will you manage this, my Captain?' he asked.

Langsdorff and his officers had occasionally debated the tradition, inherited from earlier times that a captain and his ship were joined in fate. Langsdorff had always maintained a preference to stay with his ship until the end.

Now, he answered Ascher's question truly to form. 'We will rig the ship with explosives to eliminate everything of interest to the enemy and sail her into international waters. I will personally trigger the charge while on board.' Langsdorff spoke in a flat toneless voice.

Wattenberg picked up the argument. 'But Captain, surely it would be wiser to lead the men safely into Argentina rather than give the enemy further satisfaction.' There was little conviction in his plea. Wattenberg understood Langsdorff's intention.

Captain Langsdorff pulled a briar pipe from a drawer and filled it with tobacco. 'Gentlemen,' he said. 'Every military agency in Germany and the rest of the world will examine our actions in this matter.' He lit the pipe and a cloud of smoke puffed into the air; Langsdorff was always informal in close company with his men. 'The honor of the *Graf Spee* and the Navy must not be tainted in any way,' he explained. 'My commitment to my ship will underpin our traditions of honor if we are criticized for evading a final battle.'

Ascher made another plea, 'Sir, if my observation of large warships in the Plate was faulty, perhaps we could fight our way out and reach deep water.' He knew before he finished speaking that Langsdorff would not accept this argument. They had earlier agreed that *Cumberland,* a powerful heavy cruiser with eight 8-inch guns, in company with two light cruisers held an overpowering advantage in the Estuary. *Graf Spee* had shown unexpected sensitivity to 8-inch shelling in the previous action. To verify his support Ascher added, 'Sir, I will be proud to sail out with you to finish the fight, whatever the outcome.'

Langsdorff put the pipe, which was still lit, into the glass ashtray on his desk. 'We have clearly seen and identified the *Cumberland* Saturday morning,' he said. '*Cumberland,* with her 8-inch guns and the cruisers that followed us have an indisputable advantage in the Estuary. Numerical superiority, shallower draft and greater speed gives them dominance. Spotting aircraft will help them place shot and torpedoes while we have insufficient sea-room to maneuver and avoid them.'

Lieut-Commander Klepp entered the discussion with a droll comment. 'As you know Sir, our steam system is now repaired. However, any shell bursts in the funnel area will repeat the problem.' Klepp loathed criticizing *Graf Spee's* design but continued for the benefit of the others. 'This essential component of our fuel system is located above the armored deck, without adequate protection.'

Langsdorff struggled to remain alert. Exhaustion was creeping through his body like a slow poison. He stretched his arms down each side of his chair, clenched his fists and tensed the muscles, trying to focus on the argument. 'All of this is elementary,' he said. 'We will blow up the ship tonight outside territorial waters. Tugs coming from Argentina will trans-load our crew from *Tacoma.*' He straightened in his chair and resumed his command voice. 'Take immediate steps to destroy all important technical equipment and papers.'

Turning toward Ascher, Langsdorff said 'Please ask Commander Kay to arrange a full assembly of the ship's crew as soon as possible.'

Early in the morning, December 17, Captain Langsdorff addressed the full crew. Various units had met irregularly on deck with Petty Officers the previous afternoon to receive repair instructions. Some repairs were still advancing at top speed in preparation for a break out. Now, the full complement stood in front of the Captain on the after-deck. Langsdorff told them the ship would not attempt to break out. All hands must prepare for trans-shipment to Buenos Aires in makeshift vessels.

The crew received the news with mixed emotions. Some felt a retreat was an act of cowardice and would prefer to fight to the end. Others believed it would be idiotic to sail out against overwhelming odds without any hope of success. Everyone trusted the Captain to make the best decision possible and prepared to comply implicitly with his orders.

After his speech to the crew, Langsdorff returned to his cabin. Seated at his desk he selected a legal size sheet of paper and began writing a letter to his wife, Ruth. She would be visiting his mother in Düsseldorf with their two children.

Hans Langsdorff had experienced many crises in his life. He had known delirious happiness and desperate sorrow. Never had he encountered such emotions that filled his being as he wrote this letter of farewell. The date, December 17, was significant. Jochen, their son, had turned fifteen just three days ago. A cruel coincidence of timing compounded a terrible plight. This farewell letter, would arrive in Düsseldorf at Christmas, traditionally a joyous time in the Langsdorff family. He began to write the letter to explain, as clearly as possible, his lack of choice: How can one excuse an obligatory suicide?

Langsdorff labored and filled one side of the large page. He reversed the sheet to finish the letter with loving words that flowed from his heart when a sharp tap on the cabin door diverted his attention. 'Enter!' he called, wondering who would be visiting at this time.

Lieutenant Rasenack, the artificer responsible for maintaining the ship's gun systems, entered the cabin. 'Please excuse me, my Captain,' he said, 'I have received orders, by phone line, to destroy all electronic and technical instruments.'

Rasenack was a small man with a huge responsibility. The gun-sight system was top flight electronic technology that demanded expert attention. 'Sir, because of the confusion these last two days I wished to be certain of my duty before destroying the equipment,' he explained.

Captain Langsdorff knew that Rasenack was dedicated to his highly specialized equipment. He waved to a chair at the side of his desk. 'Please take a seat, Lieutenant,' he ordered.

The Captain's briar, removed from the ash tray, was soon scenting the cabin with a fragrant aroma. 'It is essential we destroy as much as possible before the ship is blown up,' he began. 'You must know that the English would pay a king's ransom to examine our secret gunsight controls. We cannot risk the *krängungsgerät, seitenvorzündwerk* or other vital technology to fall into enemy hands,' he explained.

Rasenack was a non-smoker but the pleasant smell of the Captain's tobacco helped calm his anxieties. 'Yes Sir, I understand' he said. 'So, we will blow up the ship?' he asked.

'Yes Lieutenant, unfortunately we have no other sensible choice.' Langsdorff took a long draw on the pipe. 'Perhaps you can work with Gunnery Officer Ascher and Chief Engineer Klepp to design an explosive device to ensure the ship is unsalvageable. We do not expect she will sink deep enough to avoid looting after the blast.'

Lieutenant Rasenack rose from his chair. 'Yes Sir,' he said, 'I shall contact Lieut-Commander Ascher immediately.'

Rasenack had joined *Graf Spee* on her maiden voyage in 1936. Since then he had served under two admirals and three captains. Captain Langsdorff was significantly different from the others. He carried a blend of authority and compassion that endeared him to his men. Langsdorff had commanded *Graf Spee* in keeping with the legendary record of the World War I raider *Emden.* He had paralleled Captain von Müller's tradition of honor and chivalry, but faced with disaster, had decided to scuttle his ship. This decision, though humane, was a heartfelt tragedy. Rasenack and his group, if directed, would boldly follow their Captain into the jaws of hell. The dapper Lieutenant noticed black puffy circles under Langsdorff's eyes and the limp weariness that enwrapped the Captain. Rising to his feet, Rasenack saluted and left the cabin.

Deep in thought, Lieutenant Rasenack reported immediately to gunnery officer Ascher. They discussed a system to effectively blow up the ship. Rasenack was shocked when Ascher said the Captain wished to trigger the blast personally. Langsdorff had proposed long lead wires, running from several explosive charges, to a common contact switch. Rasenack argued that a jumble of wires running through doorways could easily disconnect and abort the explosion. Ascher gratefully accepted this theory; the gunnery officer welcomed a tangible argument to dissuade Langsdorff from suicide. Finally, they agreed that Rasenack would work with Lieut-Captain Albert Müller, a skilled electrical engineer. Together they must design a more efficient method to destroy the ship.

When Rasenack left his cabin, Langsdorff gazed thoughtfully at the blank white sheet on his desk. As he rehearsed in his mind the final words to his wife he drew slowly on his pipe. When the comforting smoke billowed around his head, he resumed his painful task.

Chapter 17

Auf Wiedersehen, Admiral Graf Spee

On Sunday December 17, excitement mounted in Montevideo. *Graf Spee* must leave Uruguayan waters by 8pm or face internment. Three British cruisers guarded the River Plate, eager to finish the fight. HMS*Cumberland* had reinforced *Ajax* and *Achilles* on December 14. She was the kingpin in the British force:

A three funneled, County-class heavy cruiser, *Cumberland* was a powerful warship. About 192m long, she carried eight 8-inch and eight 4-inch guns, plus two quadruple anti-aircraft pom-poms. Heavy steel sides(5-inch) and decks(4-inch) gave her adequate protection in her class. Her main guns, an improved caliber, gave her lethal firepower. Eight 21-inch torpedo tubes and a spotter aircraft brought her standard weight(9,800-tons) closer to 13,000-tons when fully loaded. *Cumberland* could maintain 32-knots, even in an aggressive sea.

Graf Spee had longer reach with 11-inch guns but only the armor on her main turrets and control tower came close to *Cumberland's*. In the shallow Estuary, the Royal Navy could count on the heavy cruiser, backed by two light cruisers, winning the day. Only the cost, in loss of blood, remained in doubt.

In Montevideo, hundreds of thousands of spectators, in a festive mood, filled every possible vantage point to see the coming action. People, primed with curiosity, peered from every high building that faced the sea front. Thousands more jostled against each other, twenty persons deep in a line winding five miles east along the waterfront. What would Captain Langsdorff do with his pocket battleship? Would he fight his way out or die in the attempt?

People in their homes listened to a radio broadcast coming live from Montevideo. Mike Fowler, on the roof of *El Edificio del Comercio*, had an excellent view of *Graf Spee.* For two days his excited voice had entertained listeners in every corner of the globe. All hands on the British cruisers in the Estuary listened alertly to every word. Fowler was their best source to mark any German move.

In the British Legation Millington-Drake finished a telegraph addressed to the Foreign Office in Whitehall. The political pot was starting to boil. The Minister knew that Dr. Guani had requested an all-American conference to discuss the *Graf Spee* incident. Representatives of the nations of continental America would meet in the *Cabildo* this afternoon.

The Minister's telegraph read, in part:

> *. . . OF THE UTMOST IMPORTANCE THAT OUR CRUISERS DO NOT FIRE THE FIRST SHOT WITHIN THE ESTUARY, CLAIMED BY URUGUAY AND ARGENTINA AS JOINT TERRITORIAL WATERS.*[1]

Millington-Drake worried that the British cruisers, in their exuberance to finish *Graf Spee,* would make a political *faux-pas*. He believed many American countries supported Argentina and Uruguay's joint claim of territorial rights within the entire Estuary. This exceeded by far the three-mile limit recognized by Great Britain and other European nations. Dr. Guani's efforts to unite the American countries against Germany might backfire to Britain's disadvantage if Uruguayan and Argentinean claims were blatantly ignored.

In Whitehall, the First Lord of the Admiralty, Winston Churchill, followed closely the drama in the River Plate. Naval architects, at Churchill's request, had reviewed the design of the German pocket battleships. They knew the ships weighed about 12,000-tons. British experts analyzed *Graf Spee's* dimensions, huge armaments and essential auxiliary equipment. They figured that *Graf Spee* could not possibly carry adequate armor protection. Unusually heavy damage to the warship, sustained in the action, supported their calculations. *Ajax* and *Achilles* would seriously punish her if they could land their six-inch shells. *Cumberland* with eight-inch guns could definitely destroy the pocket battleship if she landed her shots.

Churchill, a canny political veteran with vast naval experience, believed that the cruisers already in place could overwhelm *Graf Spee,* should she choose to fight. The First Lord of the Admiralty had higher ambitions. He knew that the German battle cruisers *Gneisenau* and *Scharnhorst* were operating in the North Atlantic. If these powerful units tried to help *Graf Spee* in any way, he wished to match their efforts with HMS*Ark Royal* and HMS*Renown*, now oiling at Rio de Janeiro. Churchill was reluctant to race these potent units helter-skelter into Montevideo and perhaps miss a larger catch.

In strange coincidence, the present case was opposite to the situation he faced in World War 1. In December 1914, Churchill had conspired with First Sea Lord Admiral Fisher to rush HMS*Invincible* and HMS*Inflexible* at top speed to the Falklands. These new battle cruisers were reinforcements for the British squadron so badly depleted in the Battle of Coronel. Fortunately, *Invincible and Inflexible* arrived at the Falklands one day ahead of Graf von Spee's cruisers; in the Battle of the Falklands they wiped out von Spee's Cruiser Squadron.

On December 17, 1939, Churchill wrote to Prime Minister, Neville Chamberlain, then visiting troops in France:

> *If the Spee breaks out as she may do tonight we hope to renew the action of the 13th with the Cumberland, an 8-gun ship, in place of the 6-gun Exeter. The Spee knows now that Renown and Ark Royal are oiling at Rio, so this is her best chance. The Dorsetshire and Shropshire who are coming across from the Cape are still three or four days away respectively. It is fortunate that the Cumberland was handy at the Falklands, as Exeter was heavily damaged. She was hit over a hundred times, one turret smashed, three guns knocked out, and sixty officers and men killed and twenty wounded. Indeed the Exeter fought one of the finest and most resolute actions against superior range and metal on record.*
>
> *Every conceivable precaution has been taken to prevent the Spee slipping out unobserved, and I have told Harwood (who is now an Admiral and a K.C.B) that he is free to attack her anywhere outside the three-mile limit. We should prefer however that she should be interned, as this will be less creditable to the German Navy than being sunk in action. Moreover a battle of this kind is full of hazard, and needless bloodshed must never be sought.*[2]

Meanwhile, unaware of Churchill's orders to apply the three-mile limit within the Estuary, Millington-Drake pursued his business. Captain Daniel had reported renewed activity aboard *Graf Spee*.

Provisions, taken from *Tacoma,* were carried back to the German freighter. Occasional meetings, observed between *Spee's* crew and petty officers, suggested a change of plan. Some crew members and their gear had boarded *Tacoma,* now lying closer to the warship. The British Minister updated Whitehall with frequent telegraphs. He relished his pivotal position in the flow of information between local and offshore agencies.

In the Estuary, the captains of the British cruisers, waiting Langsdorff's next move, monitored Mike Fowler's broadcast with tense interest. Squadron Commander (Rear-Admiral Sir Henry) Harwood knew the deadly power of the German's 11-inch guns. In the first encounter with *Graf Spee,* his heavy cruiser *Exeter* was crippled and seventy-two British sailors lost their lives.

Confident of victory but unsure of the cost Harwood was ready to risk his squadron again to finish the damaged raider. Henry Harwood hoped his losses would be small but he must end the threat of this deadly pillager whatever the cost. He had advantages over *Graf Spee* in the mouth of the River Plate:

The pocket battleship must exit from the harbor in a dredged channel. Six-miles long, the narrow channel led into a huge area with a maximum water depth of 25-feet. At least twenty-miles of these conditions remained before *Graf Spee* could reach slightly deeper water(maximum 30-feet). Notorious shifting sandbanks made these shallow waters unpredictable. Waging a sea battle in this hazardous space promised incalculable problems. The cruisers drew 17ft, much less water than *Graf Spee.* Intelligence reports of *Spee's* damage advised that she was vulnerable to 8-inch and 6-inch shells. With his three cruisers, aided by a spotter aircraft, Harwood would risk the power of *Spee's* 11-inch guns to deliver a maiming blow with shells or torpedoes.

○ ○ ○

Tension mounted in Montevideo. At 6.45pm a black cloud of smoke puffed out of *Graf Spee's* funnel. Slowly, amid the rattle of heavy chains, the forward anchor rose out of black, sucking mud. Idling diesels revved into powerful life. *Graf Spee* swung round and moved slowly into the exit channel. Two flags waved lazily from their halyards high on the ships masts. A makeshift steel patch on the port bow covered a large hole suffered in the previous battle. Nonetheless, the damaged warship presented a powerful, beautiful picture as she moved gracefully toward her fate. Swathed in crimson rays from the setting sun, the stately vessel coasted to the territorial limit. About four miles from the shoreline, off Montevideo, she hove to and set anchor. Hundreds of thousands of spectators watched every move and the world listened in.

○ ○ ○

When *Graf Spee* entered the exit channel, with four sea launches trailing in her wake, *Tacoma* also drew anchor. The Hamburg-America Liner was named in honor of Tacoma, a Washington State City; she carried a painting received from the city to commemorate her maiden voyage in her stateroom. At the declaration of war in September, the owners had ordered Captain Hans Konow to enter a neutral port and await instructions. Konow discharged his passengers then made his way to Chile where he caught the attention of British agents. His onward voyage to Uruguay was monitored and reported to the Admiralty. On December 14, *Graf Spee's* first day in Montevideo, *Tacoma* had won a bitter argument to load a large cargo of diesel fuel. The Port Authority had argued that she wanted more fuel than needed for a homeward voyage to Hamburg. As both German ships lay in harbor, Captain Konow supplied grapefruit and other materials to *Graf Spee. Tacoma* now made rapid progress and drew little attention as she turned in the direction of Buenos Aires. All eyes were watching *Graf Spee*.

Captain Patrick Dove was viewing the scene from a high building. The British merchant captain felt mixed emotions as he watched the German warship sail out. For eleven days Dove had been the sole prisoner aboard the German raider. He became friendly with the ship's captain. Langsdorff's chivalry and integrity had impressed Dove. As a patriotic Briton, Dove wanted *Graf Spee's* mission ended. But he prayed that Langsdorff would safely and honorably extricate himself from his terrible predicament.

Meanwhile, on board *Graf Spee*, an explosive torpedo head and demolition charges lay in the four engine rooms and both main turrets. Six petty officers carefully connected individual timing devices to the six torpedo heads. They coupled chronometers with insulated hands to

Final Moments on Graf Spee*: Lt-Cmdr.Wattenberg,Capt.Langsdorff, Lt-Cmdr. Ascher & signalman.* – Diego M. Lascano

batteries and hand grenades, as makeshift timers to prime the explosion. Then they meticulously set the timers to explode precisely at 7:54pm. Everyone worked in silence. Any error could pre-empt an explosion that would abort the mission and end their lives. When each petty officer completed his task, he joined a small group assembled on the after-deck.

At zero hour minus twenty minutes an alarm bell rang throughout the ship. Captain Langsdorff and Lieut-Commanders Ascher and Wattenberg, in company with a signalman, left the bridge and joined the group on the after-deck. All were immaculately dressed. Virgin-white shirts and cap-covers contrasted starkly with the blue-black serge of their uniforms. In reverent stillness they held a final salute as the battle flag of *Admiral Graf Spee* came down for the last time. Heavy-hearted, they folded the flag then boarded a launch tied alongside the ship. Langsdorff personally counted the men onto the launch to ensure everyone was present. Finally he jumped into the boat and ordered a course toward *Tacoma*. Smartly, the launch made distance from the abandoned warship and eased speed.

In melancholy silence the Germans awaited the inevitable. After several tense minutes a horrendous explosion erupted from *Graf Spee*. Roaring flames swept the stricken warship as additional explosions broke her in half and sent thick clouds of greasy black smoke wafting into the air. Like an earthquake, the force of the blast shook the city of Montevideo. As thousands of stunned spectators watched *Admiral Graf Spee* writhing in her death throes, the dying sun lit the scene with an unreal hellish glow.

Launch with Lt-Cmdr. Ascher, Capt. Langsdorff and others leaves Graf Spee *minutes before explosion.*
– Diego M. Lascano

Captain Langsdorff in a soft voice ordered Wattenberg to make an entry into the ship's log. '*Admiral Graf Spee* was put out of service at 8pm December 17, 1939.' The launch quickly moved away from the burning ship and headed toward *Tacoma.*

○ ○ ○

Despite the sharp eyes of British watchers in Montevideo, more than one-thousand men had unobtrusively transferred from *Graf Spee* to *Tacoma.* Beginning Sunday morning, small groups of sailors had stowed aboard the German freighter while pretending to take on supplies. Packed like fish in a can, the German seamen stuffed the holds and passageways of the cargo ship.

Now, less than a mile from the blazing pocket battleship, three small vessels, flying Argentinean flags, were tied up alongside *Tacoma.* Two tugs and a lighter, chartered from Buenos Aires in a secret move, had arrived exactly as planned at the rendezvous. In the gloaming light the *Graf Spee* crew transferred from *Tacoma* to the Argentinean tugs. The stop-gap fleet hoped to land the men in Buenos Aires. Everything was going perfectly, according to a well-laid plan:

At 3am on Sunday morning, Captain Rodolfo Hepe, superintendent of Delfino Brother's tugs, had received a phone call at his home in Buenos Aires. Hepe's sleepy response quickly enlivened. He was asked to come immediately to the German Embassy.

On arrival at the embassy, Hepe received instructions to take at least two tugs to a rendezvous point near Montevideo. There must be space to pick up one-thousand seamen and bring them to Buenos Aires. The rendezvous would take place at 7.30pm that very day, December 17. Secrecy was essential to cover his exit from Buenos Aires.

Hepe was aware of *Graf Spee's* predicament and wished to help the ship in any way possible. How could he stage the rendezvous without the British getting knowledge of the mission? They had eyes and ears in every corner. Normal telephone and wireless communications could be intercepted and might alert the enemy. Personally, in his car, Hepe rounded up a few trusted seamen to man the tugs.

In the early hours of December 17, two tugs, one towing a lighter, slipped moorings and crept out of Buenos Aires harbor. On this quiet Sunday morning nothing stirred. The tugs entered the exit channel without being challenged and headed for the estuary. Waiting vessels, anchored in the roads, might explain their activities.

At precisely 7.30pm, the tug *Coloso,* with Captain Hepe in command, approached the starboard side of *Graf Spee*. The pocket battleship lay about four miles from the Uruguayan shoreline. As Hepe neared the warship a launch sped toward his tug. A German naval officer directed him toward the steamer *Tacoma,* lying three kilometers to the south west. The officer told Hepe to hurry as *Graf Spee* would soon explode. Hepe's other tug, *Gigante,* towing the barge *Chiriguano,* was diverted from the port side of the warship toward *Tacoma.*

A few minutes before 8pm, as *Coloso, Gigante* and *Chiriguano* reached *Tacoma,* Hepe heard a mind-splitting, crunching explosion erupt from *Graf Spee.* Great flashes of flame, mixed with mushrooming billows of smoke, rose high into the air. Greasy black clouds poured from the innards of the stricken warship. Explosion followed explosion, in sequence, and turned *Graf Spee* into a blazing funeral pyre. Her after-deck was broken across the width of the ship and the control tower, burning like a torch slowly toppled to starboard. All hands on the tugs and on *Tacoma* stopped in stunned silence. Unashamed tears ran down the cheeks of the German sailors. Their proud ship, now in her death throes, was part of their lives. Progressively, *Graf Spee* burned and disintegrated as additional blasts tore her apart. Orders rang out for the men to board the tugs and broke a time-warp that had frozen them in place. Immediately the tugs made fast on each side of *Tacoma,* Jacobs

Graf Spee scuttled in shallow (25ft) water 4-miles off Montevideo.
– Gilbey Collection

ladders were tossed over the sides. Seamen swarmed down the ropes onto the tugs like well-drilled assault troops. Swiftly, confidently they scrambled down the swaying ladders and found space in the farthest corners of the tugs.

Trans-loading was barely completed when a group of Uruguayan tugs steamed into sight. Leading the Uruguayans, the tug *Enriqueta* ordered the Argentinean tugs to halt their operation and go into Montevideo. *Spee's* navigator Höpfner, in command of the tug *Gigante* uttered an expletive and called for full speed ahead. The tug immediately churned the waters into foam and surged away from the challengers. *Gigante's* lighter *Chiriguano,* weaving crazily on her tow-line, soon settled and trailed smoothly. Uruguayan crews tried to snag the fast-moving vessels with boarding lines but the German sailors repelled their attempt. As the space from the Uruguayan tugs widened, Höpfner called for lights out and escaped in the growing darkness.

All Uruguayan tugs now concentrated their efforts on *Coloso.* They bumped and jostled Hepe's vessel until finally they had her penned. *Enriqueta,* directing the Uruguayan operation, ordered *Coloso* to go to Montevideo.

Sea launches that had carried the demolition crew from *Graf Spee* were sailing nearby. Captain Langsdorff ordered his wheel-man to approach Enriqueta and asked permission to go aboard the Uruguayan tug. In company with Lieut-Commander Ascher, he climbed aboard *Enriqueta* to talk with her Commander, Mr. Albert Jack.

The German officers could not know that *Enriqueta* was under British orders. She had been chartered by the Marine department of the Consulate, and placed under Jack's command. Mr. Jack had no authority to interfere with the Germans although he had a Uruguayan port official aboard his vessel. Still, the discussion between Jack and Captain Langsdorff was amicable. They talked in English and Langsdorff argued that he and his men were shipwrecked. They hoped to land in Argentina from Argentinean vessels. While the talks went on, a Uruguayan corvette, *Zapican,* came close to investigate the action. Langsdorff agreed to go on board the corvette and explain his position.

Commander Alberto Sghirla welcomed Langsdorff and Ascher aboard his ship. They talked at length in French, a language barely comprehensible to Langsdorff, and shared a comradely glass of whisky. Langsdorff argued that the Uruguayan government had ordered *Graf Spee* to leave Montevideo. He had destroyed his ship, in international waters, and intended evacuating his men to Argentina. Langsdorff claimed his legal right to act in this manner. At one point he offered to go, under custody of Sghirla, to Montevideo. In the final word, Sghirla could see no objection to Langsdorff's move to Argentina and allowed the Germans to continue. Langsdorff had achieved a remarkable retreat but further duty to his men and his flag still lay ahead.

Graf Spee *scuttled off Montevideo.*

Chapter 18

They Also Serve

Circa 1936:
Elizabeth Langsdorff.
– Langsdorff Family

In Düsseldorff, Thursday December 14, Elizabeth Langsdorff was busy. Seventy years old, bristling with energy, she checked her list of essentials for this special day. It was her grandson's birthday: Jochen turned fifteen years old today.

Tonight, the family would have a special dinner with Jochen as guest of honor. In the past, the large dining room in Langsdorff's three story townhouse at 31 *Gartenstrasse* had held many memorable gatherings. None surpassed the excited anticipation of tonight's dinner. Wartime rationing would be ignored and a meal served reminiscent of the old days.

In the harsh realities of war, the Good Lord alone knew when the Langsdorff family would be together again. Elizabeth held a deep Christian faith inherited from her father, a Lutheran pastor.

Jochen, with his mother Ruth, and baby sister Inge were visiting their grandmother and aunt Anneliese in Düsseldorf. Their grandfather, Judge Ludwig Langsdorff, had died five years earlier. The small family would commemorate Jochen's birthday and stay to celebrate Christmas with Elizabeth and Anneliese. Jochen's father, Hans, was serving

1937: Hans Langsdorff with baby Inge and son Jochen. – Langsdorff Family

somewhere on the high seas with his ship *Admiral Graf Spee.* They had not heard from him since August. Hans' brother, Uncle Reinhard, called to serve in the Army as a reservist officer, was also absent on war duty.

Jochen's mother had almost regained her full vitality after a depression suffered in 1936 when her younger son died. Seven-year-old Kläuschen suffered a diabetic complication. Death came suddenly. Within a few days the little boy was gone. An angelic, golden-haired child, Kläuschen's loss struck grief into the hearts of the family, especially Ruth.

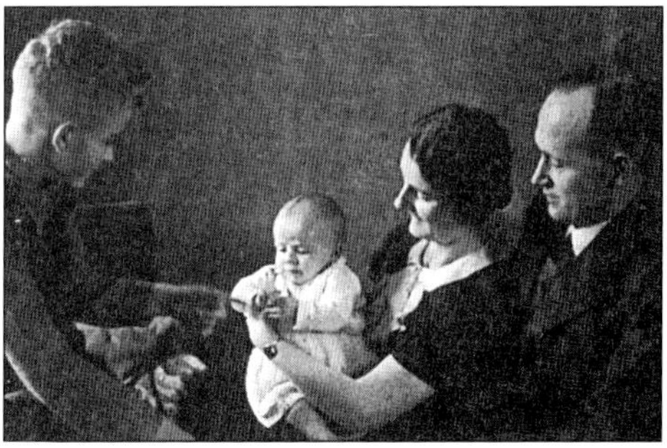

1937: Jochen, Inge, Ruth and Hans. – Langsdorff Family

In July 1937 Ruth gave birth to her third child, a perfect baby girl. Inge brought joy to the family and helped dim the pain of Kläuchen's death. Slowly Ruth progressed to a level of acceptance. But as the year 1939 ended, the anxieties of a mushrooming war played heavily on her mind. Ruth's parents lived in Dresden and remained unaffected by the burgeoning conflict. However her husband Hans, in command of the pocket battleship *Graf Spee,* was on active service. Ruth drew solace and strength from mother-in-law Elizabeth's effervescent, optimistic attitude and the freewheeling style of her sister-in-law, Anneliese.

Delicious smells of cooking filtered into the dining room from the ground floor kitchen. Elizabeth and Anneliese carefully placed the crystal and dinner settings on the crisp white tablecloth that covered the long oblong table. Ruth busily prepared a smaller table in the adjoining living room to lay out a birthday cake and a few wrapped gifts for Jochen.

Customarily, when the family had gathered, the guest of honor would make a formal entrance into the living room Candles would burn on the birthday cake, with gifts strewn around it, on a small antique table. Everything was prearranged but the celebrant would fane surprise when he entered the room. Perhaps it was a silly custom but always lots of fun. Jochen was now upstairs keeping watch on his baby sister.

Finally, as the December daylight faded to darkness, the family waited expectantly in the dimly lit living room to receive the guest of honor. Jochen knocked shyly on the solid wooden door and Elizabeth called, 'Please come in.' Jochen stood momentarily framed in the doorway then stepped forward to kisses, and congratulations from his Grandmother, his Mother and Aunt Anneliese. Tiny Inge ran forward and hugged her big brother round his knees. Laughing, the little group gathered round the small table. Fifteen candles flickered on an ornate cake covered with white icing. Shadows, reflecting from the candlelight, danced on the ceiling and walls of the living room. Jochen took a deep breath and blew out all the candles in one long puff. The three women sang 'happy birthday' while the delighted boy beamed happily.

Elizabeth noticed a fleeting similarity between Jochen and his father. The boy's frame was taller and broader than Hans, and his hair darker, but when Jochen smiled, his handsome face beamed in the same way as his father. Jochen was a happy-go-lucky lad who made friends easily although the memory of Kläuschen still lived in a private corner of his heart.

In the dining room, with plates of steaming food before them, Elizabeth said 'Grace' and added a prayer to guide and protect Hans and Reinhard, wherever they may be. During dinner she reminded Jochen that he was the oldest male Langsdorff at home this Christmas. So, he must recite the story of the Nativity. This recitation of the birth of Christ was a family tradition on Christmas Eve. Anneliese suggested that the old tradition be suspended because of the war. Thirty-nine years old, she always sought to break the norms. Jochen assured her that he would enjoy learning the recitation.

When the splendid dinner was finished and coffee served, Anneliese switched on the radio to listen to the news broadcast. She had developed this routine since the outbreak of war. The broadcast opened with a lead story that chilled the whole family:

Admiral Graf Spee has fought a victorious sea battle in the South Atlantic, off Uruguay.

Very few details followed the announcement except to say the pocket battleship had tackled three British cruisers. *Graf Spee* had knocked the largest cruiser, *Exeter,* out of action and damaged the other two. The German warship had scored a great success – according to the report.

Other items on the broadcast went unheeded as the Langsdorffs absorbed the impact of the news. All were relieved that at last they had news of Hans. Elizabeth led them in a spontaneous prayer asking that God keep him safe and well.

Anneliese, with typical optimism accepted the news as a first indicator of heroic action by her brother and his ship. She loved and admired her oldest brother with unqualified fervor. Hans would certainly emerge victorious, whatever the circumstances.

Elizabeth and Ruth were more somber in their thoughts. Radio news rarely revealed the facts in these days of propaganda inspired information. But at least they knew where Hans was serving and hoped for the best prognosis in the coming hours.

Fifteen-year-old Jochen was totally overwhelmed by the news. Pride swelled within his breast that his father was a national hero. This was surely Jochen's best birthday ever.

Next morning, Jochen, rushed to meet the newspaper delivery boy at the door. *The Düsseldorfer Nachrichten* carried a comprehensive story of the *Graf Spee* action. Despite uplifting reports of the pocket battleship's heroic fight the downside news allowed that the ship was now in Montevideo harbor. Apparently the damage she had received was more serious than first reported. Although every vantage point was pressed into the reports the propaganda slant could not conceal a tone of caution.

The Langsdorffs read further reports in the evening edition and nourished positive thoughts that all was well with *Graf Spee* and her heroic captain. Elizabeth, tried to convey confidence and courage to Ruth, behaving as cheerfully and optimistically as possible but a dull pain of anxiety weighted her heart.

On Saturday December 16, Düsseldorf newspapers proudly proclaimed Captain Langsdorff a hometown hero. They reported a complete list of nine British freighters sunk by *Graf Spee* for a total of

50,000 tons. Also, British prisoners held on board *Graf Spee* had words of praise for Captain Langsdorff and his crew. Thirty-six valiant *Graf Spee* crew-members who lost their lives in the battle had received a ceremonious burial on December 15 in Montevideo. The paper reported the Royal Navy had assembled powerful ships in the Estuary of the River Plate to prevent *Graf Spee's* escape: Germany awaited further heroic action.

Ruth and the Langsdorff family now knew the perilous task facing Hans in Montevideo. The propaganda made every effort to focus positive points for the German public but obvious questions arose. Why was *Graf Spee* in Montevideo in light of a successful sea-battle? Could she expect help in an attempt to break out? What was being done in Montevideo to aid the cause? Lack of specific information in the Düsseldorf press could not divert the inherent questions left for the Langsdorffs.

Unknown to them, neutral international newspapers had already published a more comprehensive story including the deadline imposed on *Graf Spee* to leave Montevideo. An ominous pall fell over the family as they waited for additional news. What could they do? Elizabeth led them in prayer.

Sunday, December 17, began as usual with the Langsdorff family walking to church service. It was a cold overcast morning in Düsseldorf. Church bells calling the people to prayer seemed to resound with unusual clarity. Elizabeth, Ruth, Anneliese and Jochen, with baby Inge holding onto his hand, made their way toward the *Johanniskirche*, about two city blocks from *Gartenstrasse*.

Morning newspapers reported that Hans had received some minor wounds. Also, an eye specialist in Montevideo, Dr. Meerhoff, had found signs of poison gas burns on some wounded crewmen. The Langsdorff family walked in silence, dwelling in their thoughts on the developments taking place in far-off Montevideo.

During the church service the pastor offered prayers for the dead who had fallen in the South American sea-battle. He brought attention to the men facing deadly peril in Montevideo and included their families who were wracked with anxiety for the safety of their loved ones. Parents, wives, children and sweethearts lived the hazards of war at home. Their participation was surely as real as the men at the front. Fear of the unknown took a toll as terrible as any cruel fact. The Parson called for the Lord to give the families courage and strength in their trial. Many members of the congregation knew that the family of Captain Langsdorff was present in the church.

In the foyer of the church after the service, a few friends chatted with the Langsdorffs. All offered their help and expressed hope that Hans would emerge safely from the ongoing problem. Doctor Grüters, an old friend of the family, asked if Elizabeth or Ruth knew about a deadline imposed on *Graf Spee* to leave Montevideo. Grüters was usually well informed. He mentioned a rumor, purported to originate from the neutral press, that *Graf Spee* must leave Uruguayan waters tonight or face internment. Grüters assured the Langsdorffs that Hans would extricate himself and his men from Montevideo with valor and honor.

Nothing significant appeared in the Sunday newspapers to enlighten the family. Anneliese and Jochen believed Captain Hans Langsdorff would not submit *Graf Spee* to internment but would fight his way out. What other honorable choice was possible?

The daily newspaper *Düsseldorfer Nachrichten,* on Monday morning December 18, carried a large picture of Captain Langsdorff on the front page. Printed above the picture was a startling headline,

> *ADMIRAL GRAF SPEE SCUTTLED IN THE ESTUARY OF THE RIVER PLATE.*

According to the story line, *Graf Spee* was forced to sail out of Montevideo in unseaworthy condition. The Führer had ordered the ship blown up to avoid internment and save lives. Captain Langsdorff had registered a strong political protest against the Government of Uruguay. The ship's complement had escaped from Uruguay and was safe in Buenos Aires, Argentina.

The deceitful comment that Hitler had ordered the destruction of the ship confused the Langsdorffs. If the report was correct, Hans was safe in Argentina but initial success had apparently turned into disaster. *Graf Spee* must have sustained heavy damage if she was not seaworthy. If Hitler had really ordered the ship destroyed, thank the Lord. Hans had often stated he would choose to perish with his ship if faced with calamity.

Thirsting for further information the family listened to every radio news broadcast and read intensely every daily newspaper. By Tuesday, December 19, the ministry of propaganda had given their slanted version of the Battle of the River Plate and the aftermath to the German people:

The British heavy cruiser *Exeter* had been severely damaged with a loss of sixty lives and many others wounded. The Uruguayan Government had insisted *Graf Spee* must observe a 72-hour deadline. Forced to leave neutral waters to escape internment, *Graf Spee* must face a powerful group of British warships waiting in the Estuary. The Führer had ordered *Graf Spee* blown up to save her secrets and to avoid any needless bloodshed.

According to this report, which was incorrect, Hitler had taken the responsibility for destroying the ship. Ruth could not understand why Hitler had taken the initiative away from Hans. Ancient tradition in the Navy normally let the front-line Captain control his ship's action. She knew Hans would be glad the men were safe but wondered if his pride had suffered.

Elizabeth, his mother, felt relieved that Hans had emerged safely although it appeared Hitler had placed him in less than honorable light. She knew her son would have defended the honor of the flag to the end. Anneliese and Jochen expressed outrage that Hitler had assumed the Captain's traditional responsibility.

Every-one in the family believed that Hans would have found an honorable resolve to the problem. Surely there must be more to this strange story. Anyway, thank God Hans and his crew had escaped safely.

Chapter 19

Requiem

Inside the Arsenal in Buenos Aires, in the early hours of Wednesday, December 20, Captain Langsdorff prepared to end his life. On the desk in his tiny bedroom, he neatly arranged his last letter to Ruth alongside the letter to the German Ambassador. A smile flitted across his face as he completed this final official act in a long and enjoyable career. There had been moments of danger but all of it had enriched his sense of existence. Langsdorff did not fear death. Near the end of World War 1 his minesweeper had struck a mine and sank. Rescuers fished him out of the North Sea more dead than alive. It was a time when many of his friends lost their lives and he felt privileged to survive.

However, an emotional conflict now engaged his thoughts. Professional integrity left him no choice. He must satisfy traditional mores. But his high level of compassion prompted a gnawing regard for his family. Hans Langsdorff loved his family and basked in the warmth of their love. Death in this manner would hurt them deeply. Surely they would understand that he preferred to die than to live in any shadow of dishonor.

As always his mother would recognize his need to fulfill his duty and her great religious strength would soften her grief. His siblings Anneliese and Reinhard would understand that his commitment to duty was larger than life. Most of all, his son Jochen must know that his father had lived in honor, fought in honor and died in honor.

Only Ruth, may feel abandoned. As the product of a military family (her father was a career army officer) martial death was no stranger. But knowing he gave his life when the action had ceased could be a bitter blow. Ruth must understand his irrevocable duty to commit this final act. In his last letter he had opened up his heart and strived to explain his duties and emotions. Langsdorff prayed his wife would understand and accept his need to die.

Thoughts of achievements in the past that seemed difficult to surmount flitted through his mind. Langsdorff remembered the thrill when they had received an invitation to attend a party in 1928, hosted by President Hindenburg. They endured a tough time learning to tango for the occasion. Amazingly, with patience and persistence they could dance quite well. It had been a wonderful evening.

Smiling at the memory Langsdorff rose, closed the window above his desk and drew the thin curtain into place. With his hands he brushed minute specks from the blue-black serge of his uniform then straightened his jacket and tie. Satisfied with his appearance, he walked slowly across the room to the little table by his bed.

Carefully, he picked up the folded battle flag and reverently opened it to its full size on the floor. The vivid red flag was quartered by a black cross, with a large white circle in the center backgrounding a black swastika. A black Imperial cross dominated the top left-hand quarter of the flag. The *kriegsmarineflagge* filled most of the space between a single bed and two cupboards installed along the opposite wall.

Langsdorff took a moment to smooth some creases on the flag that did not meet with his inspection. Calmly, he went back to the bedside table and removed a Mauser six-shot pistol from the drawer. A quick check proved the pistol loaded and ready to fire.

Captain Langsdorff stepped unhurriedly toward the battle flag. If anyone heard the single shot ring out in the early hours, no-one stirred. Only the whir of an electric generator vibrated the still air.

○ ○ ○

In the morning of December 20, *Graf Spee's* staff officers were gathered in the Arsenal for the pre-breakfast meeting. Time moved on and Captain Langsdorff did not appear. The officers were surprised. Langsdorff valued punctuality in his meetings – he was seldom late. Still, they waited for the Captain without concern. No doubt he would have a good explanation and apology.

Finally, as the hour advanced and the Captain did not show, Lieutenant Dietrich volunteered to check his room. (Dietrich had become adjutant when Diggins stayed in Montevideo). He walked to Langsdorff's room – next door to the meeting-room – and knocked softly on the door. Smiling, he assumed the Captain had overslept.

Receiving no answer to a third knock, he cautiously opened the door. Dietrich immediately saw the Captain's figure lying prostrate on

December 20, 1939: Guard of Honor for Captain Langsdorff in Buenos Aires. – Gilbey Collection

the flag. Sensing the worst scenario, he quietly reported to Lieut-Commander Ascher. Together, they returned to the scene. Captain Langsdorff lay on the floor, spread-eagled on his beloved ship's flag. A pistol had slipped from his right hand. Gently, they closed the door and reported their finding to Commander Kay.

The Executive Officer immediately roused *Spee's* surgeon, Dr. Friedrich Körting, to accompany him to the Captain's room. They found Langsdorff with a single bullet wound in his right temple. Dr. Körting examined Langsdorff and declared him dead. Two letters lay on Langsdorff's desk. One addressed to Baron Thermann the other to the Captain's wife, Ruth. Commander Kay took the letters and reported the tragedy to the Argentine authorities while Körting stood watch at the Captain's door.

Police and military authorities soon arrived on the scene to investigate the incident. A medical report stated bluntly that Captain Hans Langsdorff had died following a self inflicted gunshot into his right temple. Langsdorff's letter to the Ambassador had explained everything.

Word quickly spread to *Graf Spee's* incredulous crew that their beloved captain was dead. Sadly, events soon confirmed the awful news. In the early evening, December 20, in a shady cordoned area of the Arsenal, Captain Langsdorff's remains lay in state. Langsdorff's cap and

December 21, 1939: Captain Langsdorff's funeral in Buenos Aires.
– Gilbey Collection

medals rested on top of a closed casket surrounded by bouquets of flowers. Two officers and two crewmen stood mournfully at attention as guards of honor.

Next day, an assembly of *Graf Spee's* complement heard Lieut-Commander Ascher deliver a moving eulogy. Ascher, a tough little veteran, read from his prepared speech in an emotional voice. Blinking away tears he praised Captain Langsdorff for his valor, integrity and compassion. Nothing stirred the becalmed air as Ascher finished his address. Even the muted voices of the men singing their final hymn seemed to hang sympathetically in the stillness.

In the afternoon, December 21, 1939, Captain Hans Wilhelm Langsdorff was buried in the *Cementerio de la Chacarita,* Buenos Aires. Huge crowds jammed the streets as the funeral procession progressed through the city center. At the burial ground, in the German section of the cemetery, Commander Kay addressed a large international crowd, come to pay respect to Captain Langsdorff. Friends and enemies in the current war presented wreaths. Captain Pottinger, one of the British merchant officers captured by *Graf Spee,* personally placed a bouquet subscribed by his comrades. Military and civilian dignitaries from diverse states expressed their sympathies. Captain Hans Langsdorff, the epitome of human decency, had earned his place in their hearts.

Chapter 20

No Other Way

Düsseldorf morning newspapers on Wednesday December 20, carried no news at all about *Graf Spee.* With Christmas less than a week away, Elizabeth resolved to celebrate the birth of the Christ-child in the customary way. She considered it essential they continue a normal life despite their anxieties.

On the first floor of the Langsdorff house, a beautiful *Tannenbaum* sat in the living-room awaiting decoration. The family had agreed that Jochen would recite the story of the Nativity on Christmas Eve. After the recitation, they would sing carols and open their gifts as usual. Then they would enjoy a festive dinner served in the traditional way. Next morning, Christmas Day, the family would attend church service.

Ruth was bearing up very well and seemed happy to accept the positive news that Hans was safe in Argentina. Jochen spent time reading and memorizing the story of the Nativity and presented his normal cheerful attitude. The lad reasoned it useless to worry about unknown factors. One day his father would explain everything and it would make sound sense. Anneliese busied herself in her social work. She liked to help people in poverty or temporary distress. Serenely confident that Hans would prevail in his own way, she felt thankful he had survived the ordeal in Montevideo: The family were totally unaware of the tragic events in Buenos Aires.

In late afternoon, Wednesday, December 20, Elizabeth was talking with Gertrude, the Langsdorff's cook and housekeeper. They were discussing the Christmas menu in the kitchen, on the ground floor. Three sharp knocks on the door echoed through the hallway leading to the kitchen. Elizabeth responded and felt faint when she saw the elderly mail carrier with his special delivery. Thoughts of dreadful news, delivered in this way during World War 1 rushed through her mind. Reinhard? This was her first reaction.

'Good morning, madam.' The messenger's soft sympathetic voice forced Elizabeth to gather herself. 'I have a telegram for Frau

Langsdorff' he said, and presented his documents for a signature.

Elizabeth read the address on the face of the envelope, Frau H.W. Langsdorff c/o Frau E. Langsdorff 31 Gartenstrasse, Düsseldorf. She realized that the telegram was meant for Ruth. Dull foreboding numbed her mind as she invited the mail carrier into the kitchen and sent Gertrude upstairs to bring Ruth.

Ruth soon appeared in the kitchen. Her face turned ashen as she signed the messenger's receipt: Intuition pre-empted the message. Gertrude led the mail carrier to the door as Ruth opened the envelope.

It was a standard memo, pre-printed in readiness for the occasion, only the specific name and rank needed to be added.

Ruth read the message, gave a sharp intake of breath and let the telegram fall to the floor. Elizabeth recovered the sheet and scanned the content:

> *IT IS WITH GREAT REGRET THAT WE MUST INFORM YOU THAT YOUR HUSBAND KAPITÄN ZUR SEE HANS WILHELM LANGSDORFF HAS LOST HIS LIFE IN PERFORMANCE OF HIS DUTY. THE FÜHRER, THE NAVY AND THE GOVERNMENT WISH TO EXPRESS DEEPEST SYMPATHIES AND CONDOLENCES.*

The cruel words leapt from the page and impaled the womens' hearts. 'Dear God,' gasped Elizabeth, putting her arms around Ruth.

The two stricken women clung together as tears dripped slowly down Elizabeth's cheeks. Ruth conversely, gazed abstractedly into space. Elizabeth could feel her trembling grief. She asked Gertrude to prepare a sedative and led Ruth upstairs to her bedroom.

When Ruth was attended and warm in bed Elizabeth went upstairs to the top floor to advise Jochen. She knocked on the bedroom door and entered. Jochen lay on the floor, his back leaning against two large cushions that rested against the warm radiator on the wall. A copy of the bible lay open on the floor at Luke 2. The lad wished to recite a flawless rendition of the Nativity story to please his grandmother. Elizabeth sat beside her grandson on the floor. She had never done this before. Something unusual was going on.

Jochen saw the traces of tears on her face. 'What's wrong Grandmother?' he asked.

Fighting back her tears, Elizabeth pulled the boy to her breast and said softly, 'We have received very bad news about your father.'

Jochen put his hands on her shoulders and stretched back to look into her eyes. 'Father is wounded?' he asked.

Elizabeth mustered all her strength. Controlling her emotions, she replied, 'No, Jochen. I'm sorry to say your father is dead.'

'But how can that be?' asked the boy in disbelief.

'We don't have any information except a telegram from the Navy,' she said. 'Perhaps we'll learn more when the radio news is broadcast.'

○ ○ ○

Elizabeth was calm when Anneliese arrived home in the early evening. She gave her daughter the news and prepared for the rush of tears that followed. She held the sobbing young women for a few moments. 'We must be brave, my dear,' she said. 'Hans would wish us to be strong.'

> A curt announcement on the late news gave a crucial extra detail: *'Captain Hans Langsdorff wished to follow the fate of his ship. In the ancient traditions of the Navy a captain and his ship are inseparable. In taking his own life, Captain Langsdorff ensured the honor of the flag and the Third Reich is preserved.'*

Elizabeth, Anneliese and Jochen heard the broadcast while drinking a bedtime beverage in the living room. The cruel news stunned them all. Ruth was still sleeping from the effects of her medication. 'In taking his own life?' whispered Elizabeth. 'Suicide? What on earth has happened?'

'If this is true there must be a very good reason,' said Anneliese. 'Hans has never lacked courage or honor. It's unthinkable he would need to prove either.'

'Of course you're right, aunt Mück,' added Jochen, using Anneliese's family nickname. 'I can't understand what's happened in Montevideo.'

'None of us understand, my child,' said Elizabeth. 'We must ask the Lord for strength, understanding and most of all, patience. The full story will come out in due time.' In a firm voice she led them in prayer before retiring to bed.

First thing in the morning Elizabeth visited Ruth in her bedroom. It was an uneasy meeting. Ruth seemed calm but still groggy from the sedative. How would she react to the latest news? Elizabeth explained that apparently Hans had committed suicide.

Ruth remained dry-eyed. 'Hans is dead,' she said in a flat voice. 'No matter how or why, he is gone. Nothing can change this fact.'

'Would you like to stay in bed a little longer?' asked Elizabeth. 'I can bring you another small sedative and look after the baby.'

'Yes, please,' answered Ruth. 'You are so good.'

In the morning newspaper of December 21, a small obituary appeared for Captain Langsdorff. Brief in words and tone it gave the same information that had been broadcast the previous evening.

Only four days remained until Christmas. Elizabeth and Anneliese rehashed the festive plans they had made earlier. Christmas, a time of great joy and celebration in the Langsdorff home, would be a difficult burden this year. Finally, they agreed that the feast should go on as planned. Hans would wish it this way for the sake of the children.

Time ran rapidly toward Christmas. No further information about *Graf Spee* appeared in the news. Other major happenings took place in various war zones and claimed the headlines of the day. All the Langsdorff women busied themselves, preparing for the coming feast.

Slowly, even in this early stage Elizabeth and Anneliese were absorbing their sorrow. Jochen, the only 'man' in the house was showing a staunch example to the women. Ruth busied herself with little Inge and helped decorate the tree. She remained stoic but rather vacant. Elizabeth often tried to engage her in conversation, without success.

Mail arrived every morning with greetings of the season from family and friends. On Saturday December 23, a telegram from Reinhard expressed his grief in the death of his brother and asked if the family had any details. A censor's black pen had obliterated many of his words. It was impossible to discern where Reinhard was stationed yet comforting to know he remained well.

Later in the morning a special delivery brought a package consigned to Ruth. It carried the official stamp of the Foreign Office. The package contained an envelope addressed to Ruth in Hans' handwriting. Ruth opened the envelope and with quivering lips read the letter, written in old German script.

Admiral Graf Spee,
Montevideo, 17 December 1939:
My Beloved Ruth,

I am writing this letter on the last day as Commandant of this proud ship. The English have managed to entrap us in such a way that a battle against a superior force to break out would mean our downfall and the danger of the ship going into enemy hands, because, it cannot sink completely in the shallow waters; meanwhile, we have little chance of significantly damaging the enemy. So, my decision was not easy but two fixed guidelines have led me since the beginning of our operations:

In the first place, I assume total responsibility, even though I have the absolute resolve of my faithful crew, when there is little chance of damaging the enemy and advancing our cause.

Second, My men are denied a choice to risk death but the honor of the ship and the flag must be maintained until the very end.[1]

Ruth read the long page and turned it over to read the continuation, written on the reverse side. In mid-page her tears began to flow. Not hysterical angry tears, but slow viscous drops that trickled down her cheeks, releasing her pent-up grief. She finished the letter and handed it to Elizabeth.

The older woman slowly read the letter. When she reached the second page, she felt a sense of encroaching on Ruth's privacy. Hans expressed his love and appreciation of their life together. He asserted his confidence that the children would prosper under Ruth's care. Hans asked that the children remember their father and finally closed the letter saying, '*I go to my God in peace*'.

Somehow, strangely, the letter dispensed a calming influence. Like a magical balm, Hans' words soothed and comforted their anguish. Elizabeth had noted the words, 'I assume total responsibility'. Instinctively she knew that Hans had made the decision to scuttle the ship. It made complete sense. He had done this to prevent senseless risk to his men and explained why he gave his own life.

Ruth was sitting in the living room quietly sobbing into a handkerchief. Elizabeth walked over to her and placed a hand gently on her shoulder. She said nothing. Nothing needed to be said. Elizabeth knew that Ruth would now begin to heal.

Next day, Sunday December 24, the family went to church as usual. The Pastor asked the congregation to pray for Hans Langsdorff and to give his family strength in their time of need. After the service, friends gave their condolences. It all seemed so unreal.

In the early evening Elizabeth, as she had done on Christmas Eve for countless years, rang a tiny hand-bell in the living room. The urgent high-pitched tone reached every corner of the large house and called the family together to begin the Christmas festivities.

Elizabeth, Anneliese and Ruth, with Inge on her knee, seated themselves comfortably in the living room. Jochen stood in the center of the floor, ready to deliver his recitation of the Nativity. Yellow candles, silver balls and sparkling tinsel shrouded the *Tannenbaum.* Brightly packaged gifts lay on small side tables around the room. Elizabeth rose to her feet, said the appropriate prayers for the season and asked Jochen to tell the story of the Nativity.

Jochen smiled nervously and began the monologue:

'Now it came to pass in those days that a decree went forth from Caesar Augustus that a census of the whole world . . . '

There was scant conviction in the lad's voice as he recalled the story. Ruth, seated directly in front of Jochen, looked pale-faced and solemn. Baby Inge toyed busily with the single string of pearls around her mother's neck. Elizabeth nodded encouragingly to the boy and glanced at Anneliese for support as the young man progressed through the tale.

'. . . to register together with Mary . . . and she brought forth her first born son . . . '

Jochen seemed to grow and gather strength as he spoke.

'. . . shepherds living in the fields and keeping watch over their flock . . . '

There was an air of confidence now rising in Jochen's tone. His shoulders were straight and his eyes flashed as he continued the story. Elizabeth remembered the times when Hans stood at that spot to make a presentation. Animated yet elegant, cool and precise, these were his assets and Jochen had inherited his father's traits.

'. . . the Angel said, 'Behold, I bring you good news of great joy . . . '

Everyone was now listening to the narration. Even the baby stared with rapt attention at her brother. Jochen finished the monologue perfectly. The family applauded and the boy blushed with embarrassment. Anneliese then led the little group in singing several traditional Christmas songs.

Normally happy and vivacious, the songs this year softly filled the room with a melodious beauty that helped expatriate the family's sorrow. Each member of the family then opened their 'surprise' gifts, while the others expressed congratulations.

Later, in the dining room, a steaming meal lay in large serving dishes on the long oblong table. Silver tableware and crystal glasses further adorned the white damask covering. The sparkling settings enhanced and reflected light that added to the festive scene. Muted Christmas music issued from the radio, turned low to allow conversation. Small talk between the family was sparse and unnaturally stilted.

When the meal was served, a discussion broke out concerning the journey of the Holy Family and the birth of Christ. Everyone joined in the conversation.

Suddenly Jochen asked a question that stopped the exchange abruptly. 'Grandmother, do you think father behaved correctly in Montevideo?'

Elizabeth, momentarily stunned by the bluntness of the question answered. 'But, of course My Dear,' she said. 'Why would you raise a doubt?'

Jochen, assured by Elizabeth's certainty pursued the question. 'There will always be accusations that he should have faced the British ships. How will the people understand his reasoning?'

Anneliese picked up the discussion. 'Jochen, your Father sank his ship then gave his life to shield his men and the flag from any charge of dishonor. How can this be wrong?'

Elizabeth rose from her seat, 'I believe we can find something in the Gospel of Saint John which might help us.'

She went to the bookshelf and returned to the table with a well-worn bible. Thumbing through the pages, she stopped when the right chapter appeared. 'Here we are,' she said. 'Saint John Chapter 10. *"I am the good shepherd; and I know mine and mine know me, as the Father knoweth me and I know the Father; and I lay down my life for my sheep".'*

Elizabeth could easily have recited this passage from memory but now it gave added authority coming directly from the book. 'You see,

Jochen, the Lord is talking about total unselfish commitment.' She closed the book decisively and tapped it with her palm. 'Your Father gave his life unselfishly. You can be certain he is resting at peace with his God, just like he said in his last letter. In time, people will understand, that for a compassionate honorable man, there was no other way.'

Christmas 1939 struck the Langsdorff family with a combination of devastation and rebirth. An intensified pool of family unity counter-balanced the crushing grief of a tragic loss. All members of the family drew strength from each other and life went on.

Chapter 21

Conclusion

During the final three months of 1939, international political fencing stalled the land war in Europe. Since the devastation of Poland in September, only the war at sea had played a major role. At this time, called the phoney war, the Hague Conventions cast a spirit of human decency over the war at sea.

At the beginning of the war, Germany depended heavily on iron ore supplies from Sweden. Admiral Raeder had often suggested German occupation of Norway to protect the routing of this vital war material. Raeder, a strong proponent of surface warships, hoped an invasion of Norway would mollify criticism of his strike-and-hide naval strategy. Surface warships would play a major role in his invasion plan.

Although German submarines had experienced some technical troubles they were scoring encouraging successes against merchant shipping. Tactical experts, in Germany's military planning, had long advocated a fundamental shift from capital ships toward U-boats. They argued that the evolution of aircraft and bomber technology signaled an end to surface warship dominance. A full scale program toward U-boat warfare was essential in the national interest: Submarines were more effective and cheaper to build and operate.

Graf Spee's experience in action had shown how poorly the pocket battleships reacted to bombardment. Raeder's staff had recognized this failing. Standing orders – to avoid conflict with warships, even if inferior – reflected the problem. The ships were designed as commerce raiders and in this respect they were brilliant. However, the pocket battleships' compromise between armament and speed had failed to deliver a viable warship. Too slow to evade a cruiser and too poorly protected to absorb moderate gunfire, they were never intended to fight battles.

Langsdorff had also found many technical problems in his ship. *Graf Spee's* prototype engines, after four months without major overhaul, were a shambles. Additional operational problems with the steam system, aircraft, powder magazine coolant etc., would take the glitter away from the ship's aura if exposed. The prestigious pocket battleships would lose face and Raeder's shaky political position could become untenable. Consequently, the navy kept 'in-house' serious operational problems that emerged during *Graf Spee's* cruise and battle action.

Langsdorff's controversial actions in Montevideo had caused Admiral Raeder political embarrassment: Göring poured scorn on the navy for lack of fighting spirit. Ribbentrop angrily scolded Raeder for Langsdorff's intrusion into foreign politics. Goebbels, who had trumpeted *Graf Spee's* supposed victory to the world, kept quiet about the action in Montevideo; his propaganda department had more positive war news to dispense. Despite Langsdorff's well-intentioned courageous actions, he was *persona non grata* in the top levels of power in Nazi Germany.

Lieut-Commander Ascher escaped from Buenos Aires January 4, 1940 and carried a report of *Graf Spee's* woes to Berlin. Unobtrusively, the Navy modified *Admiral Scheer* and *Deutschland*. To avoid any future embarrassment, Hitler had ordered the latter renamed *Lutzow*. Any political fallout from Montevideo was quickly and quietly cleaned up. Important details about the incident never became public knowledge in Germany.[1]

Politically, Admiral Raeder abandoned Captain Langsdorff. Raeder claimed that Langsdorff had lost *Graf Spee* when he ignored standing orders 'not to seek battle with warships'.[2] Privately, he sent a letter to Elizabeth Langsdorff, praising her son as an excellent officer and remarking favorably on his noble character. Uninformed conversationalists in official circles muttered that Langsdorff had disobeyed standing orders and thereby lost his ship. Furthermore, he declined a valorous battle to break out of Montevideo.

The Captain's name, with his reputation, was swept under the carpet. Pension rights, awarded to his family, emphasized this disfavor. Personal suicide did not equate with 'lost in action', therefore, benefit payments were reduced by roughly fifty-percent. Langsdorff's son, Jochen, suffered derision from his peers. Without facts to present as defense he could only fall back on his firm belief in his father's integrity.

o o o

In 1940, the slumbering land-war jumped to violent life. Norway, the low countries and France soon joined crumpled Poland in the arms of the Third Reich. The German juggernaut swept through Europe and The Second World War quickly ballooned into the most vicious conflict ever known. Air-force strategy accelerated as new technology advanced the use of bombers. Like a blazing forest fire, the war roared out of control, consuming everything in its path. Human losses soon surpassed the death toll of World War 1. Hague Conventions became mere bookmarks in the war plans of belligerents. Non-combatant civilians, previously protected, became strategic assets or war targets. Uncountable human and material losses soared daily. The noble soul of man became irreversibly stained.

Sorrow and tragedy visited and ravaged millions of people in the Second World War – the Langsdorffs shared the pain. In 1943, the Langsdorff home in Düsseldorf fell in ruins under Allied bombing. In 1944, Jochen, a 20-year-old naval Lieutenant, lost his life in a high risk midget submarine attack; he was reported missing in action on 20 December. A Christmas greeting, broadcast from a prisoner-of-war camp, quoting young Langsdorff's name, raised hopes that Jochen had survived. But, in 1945 his identity tags washed ashore and he was presumed dead. Captain Langsdorff's brother Reinhard came home, seriously wounded, from the Russian front. He survived to work as a constitutional lawyer on the post-war German Constitution. Later, he helped form the Constitution for the new State of Israel.

Elizabeth Langsdorff lived through her trials and passed away peacefully in 1954, aged eighty-five. Langsdorff's wife Ruth and her daughter Inge visited Hans' grave-site in Buenos Aires in 1955. The German Ambassador, Dr. Hermann Terdenge, presented the Captain's ceremonial sword and dagger to the ladies in a moving ceremony.

Sir Eugen Millington-Drake, the British Envoy in Montevideo in 1939, compiled an anthology in 1965. [*The Drama of Graf Spee and the Battle of the River Plate.]* It presented reports, unpublished letters and statements from prestigeous British and German sources. Sir Eugen examined both sides of the South American drama in an objective way. Later he organized meetings between the former enemies in postwar London and Germany. In 1979, after his death, many British veterans of the Battle visited Buenos Aires and Montevideo as guests of the German veterans. Hatreds that prevail when men take up arms are put to rest when they associate as professional equals. This magnanimity was unusual in the aftermath of the Second World War. Captain Langsdorff

Montevideo 1940: Rear-Admiral Sir Henry Harwood visits Mr. Eugen Millington-Drake. – DiegoM.Lascano

would have appreciated and enjoyed the ambience generated at these reunions.

No one could ever deny Langsdorff's compassionate character or his chivalrous, gentlemanly ways. These traits were self-evident to everyone he met. However, the impression now embedded in history brands Langsdorff as a mediocre warrior who lacked initiative. This assessment is totally unfair. The facts show that Langsdorff fulfilled every requirement of a front line officer. Moreover, he preserved his own high standards of decency and imprinted them into his operations. Captain Langsdorff believed in the principles set out in the Hague Conventions and followed them to the letter.

Iron Crosses, First and Second class, awarded to Langsdorff during *Graf Spee's* cruise, contradict any charge of inefficiency. Only extreme bad luck can account for his engagement against three cruisers. The Arado spotter plane, had she lasted two days longer would have warned *Spee* of the cruisers' presence. Langsdorff would surely have taken steps to avoid them. Unlucky timing also played a part in the action. A tiny time-lag on December 13 would have seen *Spee* change course and miss the initial contact with the cruisers.

Most military commanders will agree that luck, positive or negative, will decide many actions. Langsdorff's good luck ran out on that fateful morning. This in no way detracts from the splendid action fought by the British. Langsdorff himself was first to congratulate them.

When faced with a military conundrum in Montevideo, did Langsdorff fall short? Any objective answer to this question requires a look into the standards of the era. Many senior officers in the world's military in 1939 retained a 'thin red line' attitude. No one appreciated any kind of voluntary withdrawal. Taking a backward step in a conflict invited defeat. Charges of cowardly action and peer contempt would definitely accrue. Flags and standards, bravely carried through generations of blood-soaked battlefields must remain untarnished. Honor and pride demanded no less.

Langsdorff grew up in this era and accepted his duty to honor the flag and the old traditions. However, he regarded human life as a precious pawn in the deadly game of war. His own men came first in this equation but the enemy was also human. Langsdorff, a well trained highly intelligent naval officer, was a free thinker who liked to march to his own beat. He would never blindly follow any well-worn path, regardless of precedent. Modern statistics show clearly that Langsdorff's assessment of his plight in Montevideo was accurate: The enemy held the upper hand. *Cumberland, Ajax* and *Achilles* would have won a bloody victory in the shallow Estuary. Moreover, *Graf Spee* would likely have fallen into enemy hands in salvageable condition. The Captain's orders forbade such eventuality.

He destroyed *Graf Spee* in the shallow water and evacuated his men to Buenos Aires – no mean accomplishment. British experts picked over the cooled hulk in Montevideo but recovered little of strategic value. Most of *Graf Spee's* officers escaped from Buenos Aires and returned to Germany to pursue their careers: Wattenberg and Diggins became submarine commanders. They sank many ships before being sunk and captured. Both were held as honorable prisoners-of-war and repatriated after the war.

Langsdorff's actions in Montevideo fully satisfied his orders and his personal concern for human life. In effect, he achieved a reasonable withdrawal. Still, he faced a final choicc, to protect the honor of the flag or satisfy his personal obligations. In Langdorff's code-book the flag's honor must prevail – there was no other way. Captain Langsdorff filled every requirement of his trade and closed his life with a clear conscience. His final letter to his wife concluded *'I go to my God in peace.'* These simple words summarize perfectly the philosophy of Captain Hans Langsdorff.

o o o

Notes

Chapter 1:
1. Millington-Drake, *The Drama of Graf Spee and the Battle of the River Plate,* p. 368
2. Ibid., p. 249
3. Ibid., p.241

Chapter 2:
1. Langsdorff, Reinhard *Mein Bruder Hans,*(unpublished diary) p. 84
2. *Jane's Fighting Ships of WW2,* p.41

Chapter 3:
1. Donat, Rudolf *Kriegstagebuch,* p. 23

Chapter 4:
1. Millington-Drake, p. 109
2. Donat, *Kriegstagebuch,* p. 88
3. Rasenack, *La Batalla del Rio de La Plata,* p. 69

Chapter 5:
1. Donat, *Kriegstagebuch,* pp. 169-172
2. Ibid., pp. 173-174

Chapter 6:
1. Ibid., p. 197
2. Ibid., p. 201
3. Millington-Drake, p. 147

Chapter 7:
1. Ibid., p. 165

Chapter 8:
1Ibid., p. 240

Chapter 9:
1. Pope, *The Battle of the River Plate,* p.172

Chapter 10:
1. Millington-Drake, p. 290 (footnote)

Chapter 11:
1. Ibid., p. 296

Chapter 13:
1. Pope, p. 174
2. Ibid., p. 175
3. Ibid., p. 177
4. Ibid.,p. 176
5. Donat, *Kriegstagebuch,* p. 219

Chapter 14:
1. Millington-Drake, p. 306
2. Ibid., p. 313
3. Ibid., p. 313
4. Ibid., pp. 317-318
5. Ibid., p. 319
6. Ibid., p. 332 (footnote)

Chapter 15:
1. Ibid., p. 307 (footnote)
2. Pope, p. 178

Chapter 16:
1. Donat, *Kriegstagebuch,* p. 222

Chapter 17:
1. Millington-Drake, p. 335
2. Ibid., p. 335

Chapter 20:
1. Langsdorff Family

Chapter 21:
1. Donat, *Kriegstagebuch,* p. 210
2. Langsdorff Family

Bibliography

Buchan, John, *Naval Episodes of the Great War,* Thomas Nelson & Sons Ltd. London (1938).

Campbell, Commander A.B., *The Battle of the Plate,* Jenkins, London (1940).

Churchill, W.S., *The Gathering Storm,* Houghton Mifflin, Boston (1948).

Dove,Captain Patrick, *I was Graf Spee's Prisoner,* Withy Grove Press, London (1940).

Gray, Edwin, *Hitler's Battleships,* Leo Cooper, London (1995).

Hanfstaengl, Ernst, *Hitler: The Missing Years,* Arcade, New York (1994).

Hitler, Adolf, *Mein Kampf,* Houghton Mifflin, Boston (1971).

Hoyt, Edwin P., *The Phantom Raider:(Moewe),*Cromwell New York (1969).

Hoyt, Edwin P., *The Last cruise of the Emden,* McMillan, New York (1966).

Hoyt, Edwin P., *Count von Luckner-Knight of the Sea,* McKay,New York (1969).

Irving, David, *Memoirs of Field Marshall Keitel,* Kimber, London (1965) .

Irving, David, *Hitler's War,* Viking, New York (1977).

Killen, John, *The Luftwaffe*: A History, Muller, London (1967).

Lascano, Diego M., *Admiral Graf Spee, Historia en imágines del acorazado alemán,* Lascano, Argentina (1998).

Jane's,Warships of World War 11, Harper Collins, Glasgow (1996).

Lascano, Diego M., *Historias de los marinos del Graf Spee,* Lascano, Argentina (1998).

Laurence, Ricardo E., *Desde Wilhelmshaven a Montevideo,* Laurence, Argentina (1992).

Laurence, Ricardo E., *Operativo Graf Spee,* Laurence, Argentina (1996).

Manchester, Wm., *The Last Lion, (W.S. Churchill),* Little Brown, Boston (1988).

Mann, Thomas, *This War, Secker & Warburg,* London (1940).

Millington-Drake, Sir Eugen, KCMG, MA, (OXON.), *The Drama of Graf Spee & The Battle of the River Plate,* Peter Davis, London(1964).

Neave, Airey , *Nuremberg,* Hodder & Stoughton , London (1978).

Pope, Dudley, *The Battle of the River Plate,* Ramage, London (1974).

Potter, John Deane, *Fiasco,* Book Club Associates, London (1970).

Rasenack, Captain F.W., *La Batalla del Rio de La Plata,* Beutelspacher, Buenos Aires, (1989).

Roskill, Captain S.W., *White Ensign, The British Navy at War 1939-1945,* U.S. Naval Institute, Annapolis (1960).

Shaw, Captain Frank H., *Epic Naval Fights,* Werner Laurie, London (1955).

Shirer, Wm. L., *The Rise And Fall of the Third Reich,* Ballantyne, New York (1983).

Simpson, Wm., *Hitler & Germany*, Cambridge University, New York (1991).
Speer, Albert, *Inside the Third Reich*, Collier, New York (1981).
Taffrail, *The Navy In Action*, Hodder & Stoughton, London (1940).
Taylor, Fred, *Goebbel's Diaries 1939-41*, Hamilton, London (1982).
Tusa, Ann & John, *The Nuremberg Trial*, McMillan, London (1983).
Westwood, J.N., *Fighting Ships of W.W. 2*, Sidwick & Jackson, London (1975).

PAMPHLETS:

Bludau, Dietrich, *Der Kommandant Panzerschiff Admiral Graf Spee*, E.S. Mittler & Sohn, Bonn (1990).

Ropers, Frank D., *Die Selbstversenkung des Panzerschiffes Admiral Graf Spee*, E.S. Mittler & Sohn, Bonn (1982).

NEWSPAPERS:

Düsseldorfer Nachrichten: Thursday December 14 - Friday December 22, 1939.

La Union (Santiago de Chile) Thursday December 14 - Friday December 22, 1939.

The Evening Citizen (Glasgow, Scotland) Thursday December 14 - Thursday December 21, 1939.

UNPUBLISHED MATERIALS:

Donat, Rudolf, *Kriegstagebuch - Panzerschiff Admiral Graf Spee*(Captain Langsdorff's log-book, printed and distributed in Germany 1993).

Langsdorff, Reinhard, *Mein Bruder Hans*, (unpublished diaries by Captain Langsdorff's brother).

Admiral Raeder/ Elizabeth Langsdorff, 30 December, 1939 (personal letter).

Captain Rodolfo Hepe/ Captain Gerhard Ulpts. 9 February, 1940 (personal letter).

Dr. Franz Kertzendorff/ Sir Eugen Millington-Drake, 20 October, 1963 (personal letter).

Captain Langsdorff's College Record, Düsseldorf Gymnasium (27 February, 1912).

Captain Langsdorff's naval passbook (1912 - 1939).

Index

About the Author

Joseph Gilbey is a freelance writer. Born in Scotland, he immigrated to Canada in 1957. After a 30-year career in the aircraft, mining and automotive industries he retired in 1987. Since retirement, Gilbey has traveled extensively throughout Europe, Mexico, Central and South America. On a visit to Montevideo in 1994 he became captivated with the unique story of Captain Hans Langsdorff. A search for information led from Uruguay to Argentina and Germany. Gilbey held conversations with prominent officers and crewmen who had served with Captain Langsdorff aboard *Graf Spee* and interviewed Captain Langsdorff's daughter. Correspondence with surviving veterans in the Ajax Association in England aided the project. Five years of research and analysis have clarified many obscure details that had clouded the true story of Captain Langsdorff.